AMERICAN HISTORY
After 1865

By Ray Allen Billington

Patricia M. Lynn

About the Author

1. Present position: William Smith Mason Professor of History, Northwestern University. Formerly taught at Clark University and Smith College. Held summer school positions at Western Reserve University, Ohio State University, and Harvard University.

2. Publications: *The Protestant Crusade* (Macmillan, 1938); *Westward Expansion: A History of the American Frontier* (Macmillan, 1949). Co-author: *The United States. American Democracy in World Perspective* (Rinehart, 1947), and *The Making of American Democracy* (Rinehart, 1950). In press and to be published in the spring of 1951: *The Journals of Charlotte L. Forten* (Dryden Press, 1951). Has written articles and reviews for many historical journals.

About the Book

1. Material has been systematically arranged in outline form with important topics printed in bold type.

2. Basic facts, names, and dates have been underlined in color so that all important information can be seen at a glance.

3. Interpretative sections in each chapter relate the past to present day America.

4. A list of eight or ten of the most useful books on special subjects are added to each chapter with brief comments.

5. A tabulated table of references to the major textbooks directs the reader to more detailed discussions of the subject matter contained in each chapter of the outline.

6. Includes a complete section of questions and answers with helpful hints on how to prepare for examinations.

LITTLEFIELD COLLEGE OUTLINES

A. W. LITTLEFIELD, General Editor

ACCOUNTING, COST
ACCOUNTING (CPA EXAMS)
ACCOUNTING, ELEMENTARY
ADMINISTRATION, BASIC
ADMINISTRATION, PUBLIC
ADVERTISING, Principles
ALGEBRA, COLLEGE
ANATOMY, HUMAN, ATLAS
ANTHROPOLOGY, DICTIONARY
BENTHAM'S FICTIONS, THEORY†
BIOLOGY, General
BUSINESS ORGANIZATION
CALCULUS
CHEMISTRY, Elementary
CHEMISTRY, General*
CHILD, JUDGMENT, REASONING†
CITIZENSHIP, Tools for Good
CONSTITUTION, ANALYZED
CONSTITUTION, LEADING CASES
CONSTITUTIONS, MODERN
CORPORATE FINANCE
CREDITS AND COLLECTIONS
DOCUMENTS, BASIC AMERICAN
ECONOMIC HISTORY OF U. S.*
ECONOMICS, Principles
ECONOMICS, DICTIONARY
EDUCATION, PHILOSOPHY OF*
EDUCATORS, SOCIAL IDEAS*
ENGLISH ESSENTIALS
ETHICAL THEORY, FIVE TYPES†
FICTION, MODERN WORLD
FOREIGN POLICY, AMER.*
GOVERNMENT, AMERICAN
GOVERNMENT, AMER., DICT.*
GOVERNMENT, COMPARATIVE*
GOVERNMENT, U. S. (Visual)*
GRAMMAR, AMER., DICT.*
HISTORY, AMER., DICT.*
HISTORY, AMER., to 1865*
HISTORY, AMER., Since 1865*
HISTORY, AMERICAN, Before 1877
HISTORY, AMERICAN, After 1865
HISTORY, ANCIENT*
HISTORY OF ENGLAND
HISTORY, EUROPE, 1500-1848
HISTORY, EUROPE, After 1815
HISTORY, FAR EAST
HISTORY, MEDIEVAL*

INSURANCE, DICTIONARY
INSURANCE, General Principles
LANGUAGE, LOGICAL SYNTAX†
LITERATURE, AMERICAN
LITERATURE, AMERICAN, DICT.*
LITERATURE, ENGLISH, Vol. I
LITERATURE, ENGLISH, Vol. II
LITERATURE, RUSSIAN, DICTIONARY*
LITERATURE, SPANISH, HISTORY
LITERATURE, WORLD, DICTIONARY*
LITERATURE, WORLD, TREAS.*
MARKETING
MATHEMATICS, NATURE OF†
MATHEMATICS TABLES
MIND, GROWTH OF THE†
MONEY AND BANKING
PHILOSOPHICAL STUDIES†
PHILOSOPHICAL SYSTEMS*
PHILOSOPHY*
PHILOSOPHY, DICTIONARY OF*
PHILOSOPHY, LIVING SCHOOLS*
PHILOSOPHY, WORLD TREASURY*
PLATO'S WORKS, ABRIDGED*
POLITICAL SCIENCE
PSYCHOLOGICAL TERMS, HANDBOOK
PSYCHOLOGY, ABNORMAL*
PSYCHOLOGY, ABNORMAL, R'D'GS
PSYCHOLOGY, EDUC.
PSYCHOLOGY, EDUC., R'D'GS
PSYCHOLOGY, GENERAL
PSYCHOLOGY, INDIVIDUAL†
PSYCHOLOGY, MODERN
READING, RAPID
RELIGION, ENCYCLOPEDIA*
RELIGIONS, LIVING SCHOOLS*
SALESMANSHIP
SAVAGE SOCIETY, CRIME CUSTOM†
SHAKESPEARE'S PLAYS, SYNOPSES
SOCIOLOGY, An Introduction
SOCIOLOGY, DICTIONARY OF*
SPELLING ESSENTIALS
STATISTICAL PRESENTATION
SYNONYMS, AMERICAN, DICT.*
THERMODYNAMICS, ENGINEERING
THESES, TYPED MSS., PREP.
THESIS WRITING
THOUGHT, SCIENTIFIC†
WESTERN CIVILIZATION, READINGS
WORD ORIGINS, DICTIONARY OF*

* Asterisk indicates titles in the new Students Outline Series.
† Dagger indicates titles in the International Library of Psychology, Philosophy and Scientific Method.

AMERICAN
HISTORY
After 1865

By Ray Allen Billington
WILLIAM SMITH MASON PROFESSOR OF HISTORY
NORTHWESTERN UNIVERSITY

1960

LITTLEFIELD, ADAMS & CO.
PATERSON, NEW JERSEY

Printed in the United States of America

How to Use This Outline

Every student of history should have two objectives in mind: to *understand* man's past, and to *interpret* that past in the light of present-day experience. *Understanding* is possible only when the record of man's multitudinous activities is first freed of unimportant details, then arranged in an orderly pattern. When this has been done the student does not have to memorize a mass of unrelated facts; instead he can follow the course of history as he would a proposition in logic, reasoning from related event to related event. *Interpretation* is possible only when the student is sufficiently well versed in both past history and present-day problems to recognize the relationship between the two.

The purpose of this history in outline is to make easier the understanding and interpretation of America's past between the Civil War and the present. With this in view, several unique features have been introduced:

1. All factual details have been eliminated save those considered essential by most teachers. In addition, the most important information has been emphasized by *underlining in color* basic facts, names, and dates.

2. Material has been systematically arranged in outline form, with headings and subheadings printed in **bold type.** By following the phrases in **bold type** through a section or a chapter, the student can construct a brief and easily memorized outline of any subject.

3. Each chapter concludes with a section interpreting the material, and showing the connection between events discussed there and modern America.

The careful student who wishes to benefit most from these features should follow a standard procedure in studying for any examination. First, he should read thoroughly and carefully the text and collateral material assigned in the course he is taking, making notes on the outside reading. Then he should study this outline, noting that certain facts and interpretations are in both the text and the outline, while others are in the text alone. These latter are less essential than the former, but should be remembered if possible.

Next, the student should prepare an outline of this outline by copying out the topics in bold type in the chapter or chapters he is studying. This is recommended because most of us have visual memories; by writing something down we store that information in our minds. Moreover, that skeleton outline, which will fill less than a sheet of paper, will be easy to remember. Having learned that outline thoroughly, the usual student in an examination will be able to recall the more detailed treatment of the subject in this fuller outline, and from that most of the subject matter in the text. He should also pay attention to the names and events underlined in color, remembering that those are of such importance that they appear commonly on examinations.

Finally, having learned the factual story, the student should study the interpretative sections carefully, seeking to supplement them from his own knowledge of the past and present. By thinking about the material in this way he will not only achieve better understanding, but will be equipped to apply his knowledge in his own life.

Two other features of this history in outline are designed to help the student. At the end of each chapter is a section entitled "Additional Reading" which lists eight or ten of the most useful books on the subjects considered, together with brief comments indicating their nature and point of view. These bibliographies should help the student select, from the longer lists given in most texts, the few books that are essential if he wishes to do further reading. Finally, the volume ends with a section in which various types of examination questions are discussed and a number of sample questions given. The student should study carefully those questions pertaining to the section of the subject on which he is to be examined, and if possible should write out answers to several of them. By comparing his answers with the corresponding sections of this outline, he will be able to realize and correct his own defects before taking an actual examination.

R. A. B.

Contents

CONTENTS

CONTENTS

Standard Textbooks in American History

Listed below are the most widely used textbooks that deal with American history after 1865. The table that follows indicates the exact pages in these texts that are summarized in this OUTLINE.

Bailey, Thomas A., *The American Pageant: A History of the Republic* (Boston: D. C. Heath & Co., 1956).

Baldwin, Leland D., *The Stream of American History*. Vol. II (New York: American Book Co., 1952).

Baldwin, Leland D., *Survey of American History* (New York: American Book Co., 1955).

Barck, Oscar T., W. L. Wakefield, and H. T. Lefler, *The United States: A Survey of National Development* (New York: Ronald Press, 1950).

Billington, Ray A., B. J. Loewenberg, and S. H. Brockunier, *The United States. American Democracy in World Perspective* (New York: Rinehart & Co., 1947).

Carman, Harry J., and H. S. Syrett, *A History of the American People*. Vol. II New York: Alfred A. Knopf, 1952).

Chitwood, Oliver P., F. L. Owsley, and H. C. Nixon, *The United States: From Colony to World Power* (New York: D. Van Nostrand Co., 1954).

Chitwood, Oliver P., and F. L. Owsley, *Short History of the American People*. Vol. II (New York: D. Van Nostrand Co., 1955).

Craven, Avery, and Walter Johnson, *The United States. Experiment in Democracy* (Boston: Ginn & Co., 1952).

Curti, Merle, R. H. Shryock, T. S. Cochran, and F. H. Harrington, *An American History*. Vol. II (New York: Harper & Brothers, 1950).

Faulkner, Harold U., *American Political and Social History* (7th ed., New York: Appleton-Century-Crofts, Inc., 1957).

Harlow, Ralph V., *The Growth of the United States*. Vol. II (New York: Henry Holt & Co., 1951).

Harlow, Ralph V., and N. S. Blake, *The United States: From Wilderness to World Power* (New York: Henry Holt & Co., 1957).

Hicks, John D., *The American Nation* (3rd ed., Boston: Houghton Mifflin Co., 1955).

Hicks, John D., and G. E. Mowry, *A Short History of American Democracy* (2nd ed., Boston: Houghton Mifflin Co., 1956).

Hofstadter, Richard H., William Miller, and Daniel Aaron, *The United States: The History of a Republic* (New York: Prentice-Hall Co., 1957).

Morison, Samuel E., and H. S. Commager, *Growth of the American Republic*. Vol. II (New York: Oxford University Press, 1950).

Parkes, Henry B., *The United States of America: A History* (New York: Alfred A. Knopf, 1953).

Riegel, Robert E., and D. F. Long, *The American Story*. Vol. II (New York, McGraw-Hill Co., 1955).

VALUABLE READING GUIDE TO IMPORTANT TEXTBOOKS

Find the chapter in the outline and read down for textbook references to more extensive readings. Follow your textbook by correlating chapters indicated on the top line with those listed opposite the authors' names in extreme left hand column. Other important books are listed in bibliography.

CHAPTER IN THIS OUTLINE	1	2	3	4	5	6	7	8	9	10	11	12	13	14	15
Bailey	459-482	519-541	565-585	438-518		542-564	586-605	606-628	650-705	629-649	706-765	766-830	831-856	857-879	880-950
Baldwin, *Stream*	891-933	103-179	35-102	5-34	180-242	243-282	283-306	307-350	351-417	418-463	464-546	547-638	639-675	676-714	715-912
Baldwin, *Survey*	327-345	390-427	358-389	345-351		429-453	351-357	486-501	454-485	501-519	520-552	553-587	588-621	622-654	655-781
Barck, Wakefield and Lefler	480-494	532-557	617-634	459-531	557-578	593-616	635-657	579-592 658-675	676-695 715-725	696-714 725-730	731-785	786-860	861-892	893-923	924-1001
Billington, Loewenberg and Brockunier	259-285	286-307 386-409	341-365	308-340 461-464	434-444	366-385 410-433	444-456	457-487	487-587	588-604	605-623	623-655	655-696	697-718	719-758
Carmen and Syrett	3-45	75-149	46-74	248-280	150-183	209-247	184-208	281-306	338-389	307-337	390-442	443-510	511-606	607-639	640-680
Chitwood, Owsley and Nixon, *United States*	460-495	532-540	570-580	496-511	540-548 584-592		593-611	613-630	651-688	631-649	690-737	738-769	770-792	793-818	819-893
Chitwood and Owsley, *Short History*	3-107	111-161	178-199	203-264	162-177	123-139	265-309	313-389	393-477	376-389 457-466	469-544	514-615	616-655	655-666	667-720
Craven and Johnson	417-440	441-454 461-465	466-485	486-500	454-461		500-513	563-576	514-562	576-594	595-655	656-708	709-758	759-802	803-886
Curti, Shryock, Cochran and Harrington	573-597	3-70	128-139	153-180	139-147 181-210	71-127 211-269	141-152	306-328	270-305	328-346	347-378	381-431 498-520	521-547	548-581	582-620

CHAPTER IN THIS OUTLINE	1	2	3	4	5	6	7	8	9	10	11	12	13	14	15
Faulkner	396-413	415-446	447-465	466-498	525-530	503-524	498-502 530-542	543-577	597-662	578-596	663-685	686-751	752-778	779-794	795-857
Harlow, *Growth*	1-40	88-95 104-114	69-81	41-68 182-211	81-87 95-103 115-133	134-181	212-225	226-254	280-361	255-279 362-378	370-448	**448-531**	532-565	566-597	598-666
Harlow and Blake, *United States*	372-394	424-435	412-420	395-411 484-502	420-423 435-452	453-483	503-511 535-540	512-534	540-564 575-592	564-574 593-605	606-653	654-710	711-729	730-749	750-848
Hicks, *American Nation*	1-34	127-169	54-76	35-53 105-126	170-204	77-104 245-263	205-244	267-286	332-401	287-331	403-479	480-548	549-611	612-632	633-776
Hicks and Mowry, *Short History*	376-407	409-456	479-496	497-514	457-478	534-551	515-533	555-574	595-629	575-594 630-650	651-674	675-720	721-766	767-785	786-862
Hofstadter, Miller and Aaron	386-410	411-425 456-472	434-455	426-433 481-485	473-479	509-549	495-508	550-562	574-601	562-573	602-627	628-649	650-675	676-690	690-757
Morison and Commager	1-55	105-113 123-141 174-188	79-104	56-78 214-235	113-122 141-173 189-213	266-313	236-265	314-335	354-444	336-353	445-496	497-579	580-631	632-697	698-827
Parkes	375-387	387-421	422-442	443-456	457-460	464-517	460-463	518-529	543-564	529-542	565-584	588-607	610-645	645-647	648-733
Riegel and Long	1 420-453	23-42	1-22	77-97	43-49	50-76	98-110	110-129	130-185	186-209	210-246	247-287	288-327	328-369	370-476

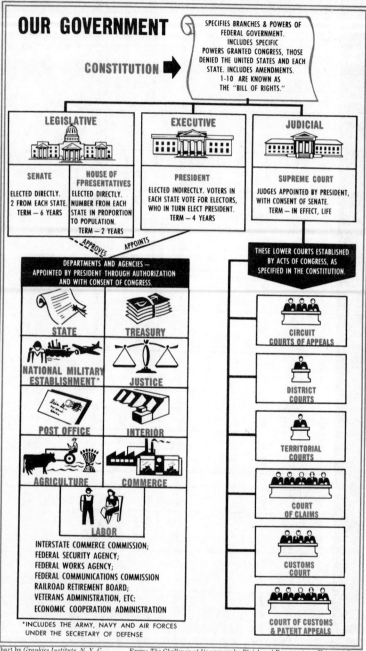

OUR GOVERNMENT

CONSTITUTION ➡

SPECIFIES BRANCHES & POWERS OF FEDERAL GOVERNMENT. INCLUDES SPECIFIC POWERS GRANTED CONGRESS, THOSE DENIED THE UNITED STATES AND EACH STATE. INCLUDES AMENDMENTS. 1-10 ARE KNOWN AS THE "BILL OF RIGHTS."

LEGISLATIVE

SENATE
ELECTED DIRECTLY. 2 FROM EACH STATE. TERM — 6 YEARS

HOUSE OF FPRESENTATIVES
ELECTED DIRECTLY. NUMBER FROM EACH STATE IN PROPORTION TO POPULATION. TERM — 2 YEARS

EXECUTIVE

PRESIDENT
ELECTED INDIRECTLY. VOTERS IN EACH STATE VOTE FOR ELECTORS, WHO IN TURN ELECT PRESIDENT. TERM — 4 YEARS

JUDICIAL

SUPREME COURT
JUDGES APPOINTED BY PRESIDENT, WITH CONSENT OF SENATE. TERM — IN EFFECT, LIFE

APPROVES — APPOINTS

DEPARTMENTS AND AGENCIES — APPOINTED BY PRESIDENT THROUGH AUTHORIZATION AND WITH CONSENT OF CONGRESS.

THESE LOWER COURTS ESTABLISHED BY ACTS OF CONGRESS, AS SPECIFIED IN THE CONSTITUTION.

STATE

TREASURY

NATIONAL MILITARY ESTABLISHMENT*

JUSTICE

POST OFFICE

INTERIOR

AGRICULTURE

COMMERCE

LABOR

INTERSTATE COMMERCE COMMISSION;
FEDERAL SECURITY AGENCY;
FEDERAL WORKS AGENCY;
FEDERAL COMMUNICATIONS COMMISSION
RAILROAD RETIREMENT BOARD;
VETERANS ADMINISTRATION, ETC;
ECONOMIC COOPERATION ADMINISTRATION

*INCLUDES THE ARMY, NAVY AND AIR FORCES UNDER THE SECRETARY OF DEFENSE

CIRCUIT COURTS OF APPEALS

DISTRICT COURTS

TERRITORIAL COURTS

COURT OF CLAIMS

CUSTOMS COURT

COURT OF CUSTOMS & PATENT APPEALS

Chart by *Graphics Institute*, N. Y. C.   From: *The Challenge of Democracy* by Blaich and Baumgartner, Harper & Bros.

Chapter I
The Reconstruction Period
1865-1877

⟪ THE RECONSTRUCTION PROBLEM

A twofold problem faced the United States when General Robert E. Lee's surrender (April 9, 1865) ended the Civil War: 1) how could the eleven Confederate states be restored to their former position in the Union; and 2) how could the economically prostrate South be rehabilitated? Northern politicians were largely responsible for attempts made to solve the first problem, while Southerners were primarily concerned with the second. Hence the story of Reconstruction must be divided into two parts, one dealing with political events, the other with social and economic progress.

I. POLITICAL RECONSTRUCTION. The triumphant North was called upon to decide whether the defeated southern states should be kept perpetually subservient, restored to their full rights in the Union, or readmitted with limited self-government. Divergent opinions among the victors made the solution difficult.

A. Factors Influencing the Formulation of a Reconstruction Policy. The task of restoring the Confederate states to statehood was complicated by several factors:

1. The Constitutional Factor. Northerners before and during the war had held that secession was illegal and that the rebellious states were still in the Union; Southerners had maintained their legal right to secede. With the war over,

1

Southerners were anxious to return to the United States as soon as possible, yet to do so they must adopt the Northern view. Northerners, on the other hand, wishing to inflict penalties on the Confederates, were forced to accept the South's contention and argue that secession was legal. Both sides found this transition difficult.

2. The Economic Factor. This influenced opinion in two ways: 1) The war had cost the North heavily. The Union war debt amounted to almost $3,000,000,000, and casualties to 360,000 persons. Many Northerners were determined to make the Confederates pay for these losses, while Southerners, convinced that their cause was both legal and just, refused to do so. 2) Northern industrialists, irked by the South's prewar record of aiding agriculture at the expense of manufacturing, were determined to keep the section politically subservient. Only in this way, they felt, could they secure the tariffs, sound-money laws, easy credit, and government bounties needed for business expansion.

3. The Social Factor. Humanitarians in the North viewed political reconstruction as a means of forcing the South to accept the principle of racial equality. Like the industrialists, they favored a program that would allow the federal government to dominate the Confederacy until that section granted political and social equality to the freed slaves and economic privileges to the poor of both races. They also wished to punish the plantation owners for keeping Negroes in bondage.

4. The Psychological Factor. The hatred bred of war did not die easily. Northerners insisted that Southerners be punished; Southerners were in no mood to accept the olive branch from their victorious enemies. Some Confederates fled to Mexico, England, or Canada, while those who remained were suspicious and distrustful. Cooperation under these circumstances was difficult.

5. The Political Factor. The Republican Party viewed the northern victory as its personal triumph. Its leaders felt that their party should be rewarded by perpetual political dominance; the future of America would be threatened, they believed, if the secession-minded Democrats ever regained supremacy. Hence they weighed the political as well as the social effect of each Reconstruction law before Congress, favoring only those that promised to weaken the Democrats and strengthen the Republicans. This narrow policy led to a division within the party, for most Northerners were more concerned with the restoration of the Union than with political quarrels. One faction, the *Moderate Republicans* under the leadership of Presidents *Abraham Lincoln* and *Andrew Johnson,* favored a mild policy toward the South. The other, the *Radical Republicans,* wished to adopt a harsh policy aimed at perpetual political subservience for the section. Its leaders were Charles Sumner, Benjamin Wade, and *Thaddeus Stevens.* The battles between these factions complicated the legislative process throughout the period.

B. The Stages of Political Reconstruction. The story of political Reconstruction falls into four stages: 1) the period before Lincoln's assassination on April 4, 1865; 2) the years between 1865 and 1866 when President Andrew Johnson tried to carry out his own policy; 3) the period from 1866 to 1868 when the Congressional Reconstruction policy was formulated; and 4) the period after 1868 when southern opposition gradually negated the Congressional measures.

1. The Lincoln Reconstruction Plan.

a. FEATURES OF THE PLAN. Abraham Lincoln, whose love of Union transcended sectional hatred, held throughout the war that the southern states could not legally secede, nor did he deviate from this stand as peace approached. Using his power as commander in chief, he issued a proclamation on *December 8, 1863* which established a procedure for political Reconstruction. This provided: 1) that all Confederates except prominent military and political leaders could regain citizenship by taking oath to support the Constitution and the *Thirteenth Amendment* abolishing slavery; 2) that when 10 per cent of the number of people in each state who had voted in the election of 1860 met these requirements they could set up a government which would be recognized by the President. This was the *Presidential Reconstruction Plan,* or *Ten-per-cent Plan.* During 1864 Lincoln used it to set up state governments in Tennessee, Louisiana, and Arkansas.

b. CONGRESSIONAL REACTION. Congress refused to accept the President's moderate program, for the radicals feared that it would not secure equality for the Negroes, punishment for Confederate leaders, or continued victories for the Republicans in southern states. Their reply to Lincoln was the _Wade-Davis Bill_ (July 8, 1864), which provided: 1) Congress rather than the President would administer the Reconstruction program; 2) a majority of the population of each southern state, rather than 10 per cent, must take an oath of allegiance before a government could be established; 3) high Confederate officials and military leaders were disenfranchised; 4) slavery was abolished; and 5) Confederate debts were repudiated. Lincoln disposed of the Wade-Davis Bill by a pocket veto, but Congress answered with the _Wade-Davis Manifesto_ (August 5, 1864), which castigated the President for usurping congressional authority. Lincoln's political skill might have averted the growing conflict, but his assassination on April 14, 1865, ended hope of compromise.

2. The Johnson Reconstruction Plan.

a. CHARACTER OF JOHNSON. Andrew Johnson, a War Democrat who had been Lincoln's running mate in the election of 1864, had neither the political acumen nor the popular backing to battle the congressional radicals. Moreover, the President's murder convinced even moderate Northerners that the South must be punished severely.

b. THE JOHNSON PLAN. Despite these handicaps, the _Johnson Reconstruction Plan_ was based largely on Lincoln's policy. Announced during his first weeks in office, it: 1) proclaimed a general amnesty for all Southerners except Confederate leaders and those whose wealth exceeded $20,000; 2) recognized the governments of Virginia, Tennessee, Arkansas, and Louisiana as constituted under Lincoln's Reconstruction Plan; and 3) informed the remaining southern states that they could re-enter the Union when they had repudiated their war debts, abolished slavery, disavowed their ordinances of secession, and ratified the Thirteenth Amendment. By December 4, 1865, when Congress met, all the southern states save Texas had fulfilled these terms and were ready to be readmitted.

3. Congressional Reconstruction Policy. When Congress convened it refused to seat representatives from the reconstructed states, holding that the southern commonwealths had reverted to territorial status by seceding, and were now under complete congressional control. Instead, a radical Republican _Committee of Fifteen,_ made up of members of both houses and dominated by Representative Thaddeus Stevens of Pennsylvania, began formulating its own reconstruction policy.

a. EARLY CONGRESSIONAL STEPS.

I. _Freedman's Bureau._ A bill (February, 1866) extended the life of the _Freedman's Bureau,_ a wartime agency that had cared for freed slaves. The measure was vetoed by Johnson, but a later bill embodying the same features was passed over his veto on July 16, 1866.

II. _Civil Rights Act._ This measure (April, 1866) forbade the states to discriminate against Negroes, guaranteed persons of color the equal protection of the laws, and decreed that cases rising under the act be tried in the federal courts. It was passed over Johnson's veto.

III. _Fourteenth Amendment._ Fearful lest the Civil Rights Act be declared unconstitutional, radical Republicans

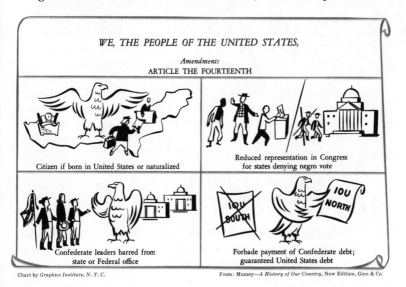

WE, THE PEOPLE OF THE UNITED STATES,

Amendments
ARTICLE THE FOURTEENTH

Citizen if born in United States or naturalized

Reduced representation in Congress for states denying negro vote

Confederate leaders barred from state or Federal office

Forbade payment of Confederate debt; guaranteed United States debt

Chart by *Graphics Institute, N. Y. C.*   From: Muzzey—*A History of Our Country,* New Edition, Ginn & Co.

formulated the *Fourteenth Amendment*. This provided that: 1) all persons born or naturalized in the United States were citizens with full rights; 2) southern states must grant Negroes the vote or suffer the loss of a portion of their congressional representation; 3) former Confederates could not hold office until pardoned by Congress; 4) the Confederate war debt was repudiated; and 5) the measure be enforced by Congress rather than the President or the courts.

b. Congressional Elections of 1866. These elections allowed the people to choose between the *Presidential Reconstruction Policy*, which allowed the southern people to shape their own institutions, and the *Congressional Reconstruction Policy*, which gave control over the South to Congress.

I. *The Presidential Campaign.* The presidential cause was handicapped by two things: 1) In most districts the choice was between a radical Republican and a copperhead Democrat, forcing even moderate Republicans to vote the radical ticket; 2) Johnson conducted an inept campaign for his candidates, making immoderate speeches and sinking to vituperation rather than stressing issues.

II. *The Congressional Campaign.* The radicals campaigned astutely, appealing to patriotic instincts and hushing basic questions. Moreover, they were aided by three developments in the South: 1) A bloody *race riot* in New Orleans (July, 1866) convinced northerners that the ex-slaves must be protected. 2) *Black Codes* adopted in most southern states indicated that Southerners intended to reduce the Negroes to a status resembling slavery. These codes regulated the social and economic status of freedmen, even providing that "vagrants" could be fined $50 and, if unable to pay, apprenticed for six months. 3) The persistence with which southern states elected former Confederate leaders to office demonstrated that the people had not learned the lessons of war.

III. *Results of Elections.* The radical Republicans won a sweeping victory, which they interpreted as a mandate for their program.

c. Congressional Reconstruction Plan (March 2, 1867). This measure, adopted after the elections: 1) ruled that no lawful governments existed in any of the southern states save Tennessee; 2) divided the South into five military districts under commanders who were instructed to protect life and property; and 3) decreed that no state could return to civilian rule until its voters, both white and colored, framed a constitution that guaranteed Negro suffrage and was acceptable to both Congress and the people. Each must also ratify the Fourteenth Amendment.

d. ENFORCEMENT OF CONGRESSIONAL RECONSTRUCTION. Recognizing the doubtful legality of their plan, radical Republicans took steps to insure its administration by Congress rather than the courts or the President.

I. *Denial of Court Authority.* An act of March 7, 1868, denied the Supreme Court jurisdiction over the Reconstruction acts. The radicals believed this necessary as the Court had, in two cases, threatened the constitutionality of the measures: 1) in *Ex Parte Milligan* (1866) it had ruled that military trials were illegal in areas where civil courts were functioning; and 2) in *Ex Parte McCardle* (1868) it had accepted jurisdiction in the case of a Mississippi editor who had been convicted by a military tribunal.

II. *Denial of Presidential Authority.* Two acts of March 2, 1867, removed administration of the Reconstruction Act from the President: 1) The *Army Appropriations Act* decreed that military orders could be issued only by the general of the army; 2) The *Tenure of Office Act* prohibited the President from removing any federal officials without Senate consent. Together these laws vested control of the military districts in *Edwin M. Stanton,* a radical Republican who was Secretary of War, and prevented Johnson from dismissing Stanton.

III. *Impeachment of Johnson.* Still fearful of the President, the radicals laid plans to impeach him. Their opportunity came on February 21, 1868, when Johnson dismissed Stanton. Three days later the House voted to impeach Johnson for violating the Tenure of Office Act and for other "high crimes and misdemeanors." He was tried before the Senate, and escaped conviction by only one vote. Although vindicated, Johnson's power was so weakened that he accomplished nothing in his remaining months in office.

e. ELECTION OF 1868. Calling themselves the National

Union Republican Party, the *radical Republicans* nominated General *Ulysses S. Grant* for the presidency, before adopting a platform that lauded congressional reconstruction and promised payment of the national debt in gold. The *Democrats,* seeking a *"New Departure"* to win votes, nominated Governor *Horatio Seymour* of New York, and endorsed the *Ohio Idea.* This promised repayment of federal bonds in "greenbacks," or paper money, rather than in gold, a proposal designed to appeal to debtor elements among eastern workers and western farmers suffering in the postwar deflation that began in 1867. Grant was victorious by an electoral vote of 214 to 80, although his popular majority was only 300,000 votes. The votes of 700,000 Negroes elected him. The result was no mandate for radical policy.

4. Failure of Congressional Reconstruction.

a. ENFORCEMENT OF CONGRESSIONAL POLICY. Even before Grant's election, Johnson faithfully, if unwillingly, carried out the Congressional Reconstruction Act. By the spring of 1868 all states but Texas and Virginia had adopted constitutions. The Mississippi constitution was rejected by the voters, but the other seven states set up governments which ratified the Fourteenth Amendment, and in June, 1868, were readmitted to the Union by Congress. The *Fourteenth Amendment* became effective in *July, 1868.* Thus only three states—Mississippi, Texas, and Virginia—were under military rule when Grant took office. Radicals decided that these states should not be admitted until they had ratified the *Fifteenth Amendment,* which forbade the states to deny the vote to any citizen because of "race, color, or previous condition of servitude." All three did so by 1870.

b. SOUTHERN OPPOSITION TO CONGRESSIONAL RECONSTRUCTION. Between 1870 and 1877 the center of the conflict over Reconstruction shifted to the South. There two factions contested for control of each state: 1) Democrats seeking to re-establish white supremacy, and 2) radical Republicans determined to secure equal rights for Negroes. In this group were Negroes, northern *carpetbaggers* who had come south to lead the freedmen, and southern *Scalawags,* or whites who had deserted to the Republican camp.

This faction was backed by radicals in Congress who were always ready to pass laws for its support.

I. *Reasons for Republican Defeat.* The white Democrats were eventually triumphant in this contest. This was because: 1) The Reconstruction legislatures lost support by accumulating huge debts and by increasing taxes from fourfold to fourteenfold. Many of their expenditures were legitimate, for the cost of physical reconstruction was heavy, interest rates high, and the dollar inflated. Yet tax increases are never popular. 2) Many carpetbaggers and scalawags were corrupt. They, rather than the Negroes they led, were responsible for most of the dishonesty that discredited the Reconstruction legislatures. 3) The traditions of white rule and local rule were too strong in the South to be broken easily. 4) A rising conservative class, made up of landholders and businessmen, was soon powerful enough to spearhead an attack on radical policies. These *Bourbons* wanted to keep the Negro subjugated in order to assure a cheap labor supply as well as white supremacy. Moreover, knowing they were in the minority, they sought to secure political supremacy for their class by driving a racial wedge between the lower classes.

II. *Form of Southern Opposition.* Opposition to radical rule in the South took two forms: 1) In states where whites were in a clear majority—as Tennessee and North Carolina—Democrats regained control of the state government by legal means; 2) In others, where federal troops remained to enforce racial equality, extralegal devices were employed. Most effective were secret societies—such as the *Ku Klux Klan* and the *Knights of the White Camelia*—to intimidate the Negroes. Their program of terrorism kept Republicans from the polls, allowing the Democrats to recapture the legislatures. Congressional radicals attempted to suppress these societies by passing the *Force Act* (1870) and the *Ku Klux Klan Act* (1871). These gave the President power to: 1) suspend the writ of habeas corpus; 2) supervise congressional elections; and 3) employ troops to assure Negroes civil and political rights. Their enforcement led to the suppression of the secret societies by the end of 1872.

c. END OF CONGRESSIONAL RECONSTRUCTION. By 1872 the United States was tired of radical Reconstruction policies. In the election of that year the Republicans divided, with one faction advocating the end of congressional control of the South. Although the radicals re-elected Grant by a narrow majority, they realized that they must change their program. This was done in 1872 when an *Amnesty Act* restored the franchise to almost all Confederates. As a result, white Democrats gradually regained control of the southern states. By 1877, when *Rutherford B. Hayes* was inaugurated as President, only South Carolina and Louisiana remained in radical hands. In both these states two governments existed, one representing a minority group of carpetbaggers, scalawags, and Negroes backed by federal troops, the other based on white supremacy and supported by nearly all whites. President Hayes, convinced that the radical governments did not represent the majority will, withdrew the troops in *April, 1877*. Democrats immediately seized control. Political Reconstruction was ended, with the radical program completely rejected.

II. SOCIAL RECONSTRUCTION. The economic and social rehabilitation of the South was as much a part of Reconstruction as the political revival of the area. That significant progress was made was less the result of the ill-directed efforts of radical Republicans than of the labors of Southerners themselves, principally the freed slaves and small farmers.

A. The Plight of the South.

1. The Economic Problem. The South was in a desperate situation when the Civil War ended. Livestock had been slaughtered. Fields were left barren by marauding troops, or neglected because farmers had no seed to plant. Plantations and homes were destroyed, or were decaying away. Many principal cities had been bombarded into rubble. Railroads were torn up, bridges destroyed, and the entire transportation system was in confusion. With the collapse of Confederate money, finances were chaotic. Not a bank or insurance company was solvent, while the securities in which thousands had invested their savings were worthless. All goods had to be imported from the North on credit, at exhorbitant interest rates.

2. The Social Problem. Schools and churches were closed everywhere. Four million freed slaves, suddenly endowed with legal and social privileges for which they had not been trained, must adjust themselves to freedom. Many, intoxicated by release from bondage, wandered about the countryside. Others waited for the government to give them the "forty acres and a mule" that rumor told them would be theirs. For a time all work was at a standstill as Southerners wrestled with the problem of devising a new labor system and an economy suited to freedom.

B. The Economic Revival.

1. Agricultural Readjustment. The first need was to revive agriculture. At first landowners tried to operate plantations with gangs of hired Negro workers, but this was contrary to the whole spirit of emancipation. Gradually, *share cropping* and *tenant farming* were introduced. These methods were necessary in a region where workers lacked means to buy their own farms, but the Negro share croppers were little better off than under slavery. Living in shacks, and working long hours in cotton fields, they were always in debt to landowners and storekeepers.

2. Breakup of Plantations. Gradually, however, the more energetic climbed upward economically as they accumulated capital needed to buy land. Their opportunity came when heavy taxes levied by Reconstruction governments forced plantation owners to throw their holdings on the market. Between 1860 and 1880 the number of farms in the South doubled, while the size of the average farm decreased from 335 acres to 153 acres. This land redistribution benefited the Negro less than the small farmers and former poor whites. During the Reconstruction period this group laid the economic basis for its later political supremacy.

3. Results of Agricultural Changes. The whole South benefited from the displacement of plantation agriculture by small-scale farming. By 1870 the yield per acre was greater than at any time before the war. By 1879 the cotton crop was greater than in 1860, while the value of minor crops now surpassed that of cotton.

C. The Social Revolution. The democratizing influence of land redistribution was paralleled by social gains for the hitherto underprivileged classes in the South, both white and colored. The Reconstruction legislatures were responsible for this improvement. Their Negro members, thirsting for means of self-improvement and conscious of the needs of the lower class, passed dozens of progressive laws. In many states roads were built, public buildings improved, taxation systems modernized, poor relief inaugurated, and land distributed to the needy. More important were their educational innovations. Nearly all "carpetbag" legislatures established compulsory free schools for the children of both races. The program for human betterment outlined during these years has not yet been fully achieved in the South.

III. THE BALANCE SHEET OF RECONSTRUCTION. An assessment of the results of the Reconstruction policies adopted between 1865 and 1877 indicates that the era's legacy to the future contained both harmful and beneficial features:

A. Harmful Results.

1. Less Intelligent Leadership Was Provided for the South. The disenfranchisement of the Confederate military and civil leaders forced members of this well-educated group into oblivion. Their eclipse elevated the former small farmers and poor whites to positions of political and economic supremacy. The vision of these men was cramped by a background of poverty and ignorance, while their hatred of Negroes accentuated the race problem.

2. The Racial Issue Was Sharpened. Southern whites thereafter associated Negroes with carpetbaggers and scalawags whose reign had produced corruption and fraud. Hence they concluded that Negro participation in politics was dangerous, and systematically restricted voting to whites.

3. The South Became Unnecessarily Economy-Minded. Shocked by the expenditures of radical Republican legislatures, Southerners concluded that good government and economy were synonymous, even though social gains must be sacrificed.

4. One-Party Government Was Fastened on the South.
The Reconstruction legislatures convinced southern whites
that the Republican Party was the party of "niggers" and
corruption; thereafter no self-respecting white man would
vote anything but the straight Democratic ticket. From 1876
to 1916 that party was completely supreme below the Mason-
Dixon Line; not until 1928 was there any serious deflection
in the *"Solid South."* The harmful results were noticeable
both locally and nationally:

a. LOCAL RESULTS. One-party rule stifled democracy
in the South. Two competing parties would have bid for
support by broadening the voting lists, promising social legislation, and campaigning for progressive measures dear to
the people. With only one party in control, voting lists were
contracted by depriving Negroes of the franchise, while the
South lagged behind other sections in social legislation, education, and other measures to benefit the masses.

b. NATIONAL RESULTS. These were of two sorts: 1)
One-party rule prevented an alliance of lower-class elements
in the South and West. Hence northeastern industrialists,
with their opposition divided, were able to control the government through the late nineteenth century. 2) The Democratic Party was burdened with a conservative wing which
blocked much progressive legislation, particularly during the
twentieth century when the remaining members of that party
followed a liberal course. This was the case especially as
conservative Southerners, elected time and again without
opposition, gained control of many congressional committees
through seniority, then used their powerful positions to
frustrate the majority will.

5. Sectional Hatred Was Increased. Southerners hated
the North for its radical policies and Negro rule; Northerners hated the South for its insistence on white supremacy.
The wartime wounds would have healed much sooner had
they not been inflamed during the Reconstruction period.

B. Beneficial Results.

1. The Redistribution of Property forced on the South
by the Reconstruction legislatures ultimately benefited the
entire section. Wealth was more equitably spread, crops
diversified, and agriculture placed on a sounder basis.

2. The Educational System and Social Legislation
proposed by the radical governments, although not achieved
at the time, laid a basis for many of the gains made since.

*3. Reconstruction Was Less Brutal Than It Might
Have Been.* No Confederate leader was executed, almost
no land confiscated, and few Southerners punished. Although the radical policies seemed harsh to Southerners,
they were far milder than those adopted in other countries
following civil wars. As the South awakened to this fact,
its resentment was slowly forgotten, allowing the two sections to merge into one during the late nineteenth century.
By 1898, when Congress removed the last political disabilities from ex-Confederates, the animosities of the Civil War
were all but forgotten.

ADDITIONAL READING

A brief survey, factual and fairly impartial, is found in
James G. Randall, *The Civil War and Reconstruction*
(1937). More extended studies, all of which paint the traditional picture of corrupt carpetbaggers and blameless
southern whites, are: Claude G. Bowers, *The Tragic Era*
(1929); R. S. Henry, *The Story of Reconstruction* (1938),
and E. M. Coulter, *The South During Reconstruction*
(1947). More modern studies, emphasizing the social rather
than the political, show the beneficial results of the radical
program. A pioneer work stressing this viewpoint is Howard K. Beale, *The Critical Year* (1930), which deals with a
broader period than the year 1866. Even more important is
W. E. B. DuBois, *Black Reconstruction* (1935), which,
although biased, gives a full account of the valuable legislation passed by the Reconstruction legislatures. Paul Buck,
The Road to Reunion (1937), deals delightfully with the
forces reuniting North and South after the war. Social and
economic developments during the era are the theme of Allan
Nevins, *The Emergence of Modern America* (1927).

Chapter II

The Economic Revolution
1865-1890

❨ THE INDUSTRIALIZATION OF THE UNITED STATES

The most important force reshaping American politics, diplomacy, life, and thought in the late nineteenth century was industrialization. Between 1865 and 1890 the United States changed from an agricultural country to an industrialized nation, fully adjusted to a machine civilization. This transformation can best be shown statistically:[1]

	1860	1890	% of Increase
Population	31,450,000	62,600,000	99
Number of farms	2,000,000	4,500,000	120
Number of factories	140,500	355,400	153
Value of farms	7,980,500,000	16,100,000,000	101
Value of factories	1,000,000,000	6,500,000,000	555
Value of farm products		2,500,000,000	
Value of manufactures	1,900,000,000	9,400,000,000	394
Industrial workers	1,300,000	4,200,000	223

These figures spelled out a revolution in every phase of life. The history of the period, outlined in the following chapters, is largely a history of the changes wrought by the mechanization of American society.

---

[1] All figures are in round numbers to facilitate memorizing.

15

I. CAUSES OF THE ECONOMIC REVOLUTION.

Many factors were responsible for this rapid transition from an agricultural to a machine civilization.

A. Plentiful Raw Materials. The rich natural resources of the East had scarcely been tapped by the pre-Civil War generation, while still greater riches waited exploitation in the West. _Lumber_ could be obtained from the virgin forests that covered the Great Lakes country, the Rocky Mountains, the Pacific Northwest, and parts of the South. The United States contained about half the world's _coal_ reserves, concentrated in a belt running west from Pennsylvania. _Iron ore_ was found in Pennsylvania and Alabama, but especially in Minnesota and Upper Michigan. The _Mesabi Range_ of Minnesota by 1900 furnished one-third of all ore used in the United States, and one-sixth of the world's supply. Lake steamers, carrying the ore to the coal fields of Pennsylvania, Ohio, and Illinois, produced such steel cities as Detroit, Toledo, Cleveland, and Gary. _Oil_ was found beneath Pennsylvania and later in the Southwest. _Copper_ from Michigan supplied industry until the 1880's when the mines of Montana and Arizona assumed supremacy. _Silver_ from Colorado and Nevada, and _gold_ from California and South Dakota were also used by industry. _Lead_ was plentiful in Colorado, Missouri, and Illinois.

B. Available Capital. This came from two sources:

1) _Foreign capital,_ especially from England, Holland, and Germany, financed many industries. Investors there were eager to finance American industries partly because higher interest rates were paid, and partly because the United States bought more abroad than it sold there. The difference, which was owed foreign capitalists, was reinvested in this country. Foreigners owned $3,300,000,000 in American securities in 1900. 2) _Domestic capital_ was made available with the decline of commercial activities. High insurance rates on American vessels during the Civil War allowed England to capture much of the carrying trade of the Atlantic basin, while the steam-driven steel vessels perfected by British shippers after the war proved more economical than the wooden sailing vessels of the United States. American ships, which carried 66 per cent of American commerce in 1860,

carried only 9 per cent in 1900. Hence money formerly invested in commerce flowed into industry. As factories expanded, more and more capital was created for reinvestment.

C. Available Labor. This came from two sources:

1. From Within the United States. The millions of Civil War soldiers seeking jobs were soon supplanted by workers released from the farms. Improved agricultural machinery allowed the nation to produce all food necessary with constantly fewer men. To give one example: In 1830, 183 minutes of labor was needed to produce a bushel of wheat, in 1900 only 10 minutes. Between 1870 and 1890 better farm machines freed 4,430,000 men from agriculture for work in industry.

2. From Abroad. Between 1860 and 1900 almost 14,-000,000 immigrants reached the United States. This influx was caused by overcrowding at home, a desire to escape military service, religious or racial persecution, and the liberalization of European laws forbidding emigration. Equally important were the attracting forces: the demand for cheap labor in the United States, and the activities of shipping and railroad companies who advertised for immigrants.

a. THE OLD IMMIGRATION. At first, immigrants came from northern and western Europe, especially Great Britain, Germany, and the Scandinavian countries. Most of these, with the exception of the Irish, migrated to the West, where many settled in Chicago, Cincinnati, St. Louis, Milwaukee, and other cities. There they were available as factory workers, as were the Irish who concentrated in the eastern cities.

b. THE NEW IMMIGRATION. Beginning in the 1880's the bulk of the immigrants came from southern and eastern Europe. The Italians, Poles, Russians, Austrians, and Jews who made up this "new immigration" had no money for farms; instead they sought jobs as unskilled workers in steel mills, mines, manufacturing plants, and railroads. Accustomed to low living standards, they were willing to work for poor pay amidst intolerable working conditions. About one-third were *birds of passage* who intended to return to the Old Country with their savings.

c. MINOR IMMIGRANT GROUPS also contributed to the labor supply. French-Canadians from Quebec flocked into New England's textile mills, while Mexicans filled the cities of California and the Southwest. Peasants from China and Japan helped build the western railroads before forming colorful "Chinatowns" in cities everywhere. As all sought jobs, factory owners could bid the price of labor down to a point, in real wages, never known in the United States.

D. American Ingenuity. Mechanical and managerial skill allowed industrialists to offset their greatest handicap: competition with cheap-labor areas abroad where living standards were lower. This was done by:

1. Mass Production Techniques were employed so successfully to meet the artificial demands created by the Civil War that they spread to most industries in the postwar era. By using the *principle of interchangeable parts* (standardized units that could be fitted together interchangeably), American manufacturers could produce more cheaply than European, despite higher labor costs. These same devices were not adopted abroad, where tradition hindered innovation.

2. Inventions to improve manufacturing processes or supply more items for production were patented in large numbers; between 1865 and 1900 the number issued was 638,000, while in the whole period between 1790 and 1865 only 62,000 inventions were patented. Included in these were: the *typewriter* (1867) by Christopher Sholes; the *linotype* (1886) by Otto Mergenthaler; the *incandescent lamp* (1880) by *Thomas Alva Edison;* the *telephone* (1876) by *Alexander Graham Bell;* the *Bessemer Process* for making steel (1864) by Henry Bessemer and William Kelly; the steam turbine (1882); the *dynamo* (1880) by Thomas A. Edison; the Westinghouse air brake (1872); the railroad "parlor car" (1864) by George Pullman; the automatic coupler (1871); the refrigerator car (1875); the electric railroad (1870-1880) by Thomas A. Edison and Stephen Field; and wireless telegraphy (1896).

E. Broadening Markets. Within the United States was the largest area in the world over which goods could flow without encountering barriers in the form of differing currencies, customs barriers, or trade regulations. This _domestic market_ expanded steadily during these years because of : 1) _Improved living standards_ which accompanied industrialization. Realizing that wealth could be acquired by bold plunging rather than careful saving, Americans generally lived above their immediate means, thus consuming more goods than Europeans. 2) _Railroad building_, which increased the mileage of American lines from 30,626 in 1860 to 163,597 in 1890. Each mile of track laid expanded manufacturers' markets. At the same time _foreign markets_ were opened by the steam-driven, iron ships that came into general use after 1860.

F. Encouragement from the Government. The prevailing political theory of _laissez faire_ held that the government should not interfere in industry. This allowed businessmen to pay low wages, charge high prices, employ corrupt practices, and enter into monopolistic combines without interference by state or national governments. At the same time federal laws were passed to aid industry. These included high protective tariffs, land grants and loans to railroads, and acts requiring shipbuilders and railroads to use American-made materials.

G. Leadership Was Attracted. The ablest men of the generation were attracted into industry rather than politics. _Andrew Carnegie, John D. Rockefeller_, and _Charles Schwab_ were industrial geniuses who in an earlier generation might have become outstanding statesmen. In this period their thirst for power could be better satisfied in business than in government.

II. THE DUAL REVOLUTIONS. The two fields most affected by the revolution in economics were production and distribution.

A. Production. In the field of manufacturing three significant developments occurred after the Civil War :

1. Growth of Heavy Industry. The so-called heavy industries (iron, steel, machinery) developed more rapidly than the light industries (textiles, food processing) that had dominated the nation's economy before the Civil War. Of these the _steel industry_ was most important. Its rapid growth began in the 1880's when the _Mesabi Range_ of Minnesota was opened to provide cheap iron ore. At the same time the perfection of the _Bessemer_ and _open-hearth_ processes for converting iron into steel reduced the price of steel from $300 to $35 a ton. The industry centered about Pittsburgh, where the coal and limestone needed for smelting were plentiful. Lake steamers brought ore from Minnesota to this point. By 1900 two-thirds of the nation's steel was produced there, with lesser centers at the lower end of Lake Michigan (near the coal beds of Illinois) and in the Rocky Mountain area. The leading steel producer was _Andrew Carnegie,_ a Scottish immigrant who formed the Carnegie Steel Company in 1892. This produced one-fourth of the nation's steel. In 1901 Carnegie sold out his interests to a group of financiers headed by _Elbert H. Gary_ of Chicago and _J. P. Morgan_ of New York, in the merger that resulted in the _United States Steel Corporation,_ capitalized at $1,400,000,000. By this time the United States was the world's leading steel producer, with a capacity double that of England.

2. Geographic Dispersion of Industry. Before the Civil War, manufacturing was concentrated in the Northeast. While that section still retained its industrial supremacy, industrialization spread to the West and South:

a. THE WEST. The industries centered there were related to the agriculture that was the section's principal interest. They included firms producing farm machinery, furniture, building supplies, flour, meat, and steel. Production was centered about Chicago, with lesser centers at St. Louis, Cincinnati, Minneapolis, and other cities.

b. THE SOUTH. Before the Civil War the South produced only 8 per cent of the nation's manufactured goods. Ingredients for manufacturing were plentiful, however: 1) _Raw materials_ existed in the form of cotton for textiles; iron ore and coal in northern Alabama, where Birmingham was founded as a steel city; tobacco in North Carolina; and lumber in the lower South to supply the nation when the forests of the Great Lakes were exhausted. 2) _Labor_ could be recruited from the ranks of former slaves and poor whites at lower wages than in the North. 3) _Capital_ was provided by many small investors who believed that the South was defeated in the Civil War by its lack of industries. Determined to change this situation, and influenced by such slogans as "Bring the mills to the cotton," they scraped their savings together to purchase stock on the installment plan. The result was the gradual creation of the _New South_ which by 1900 produced half the nation's cotton textiles and boasted an industrial investment of $1,000,000,000. Industrialists, or Southern Bourbons, controlled the section as had great planters a generation before. The lot of the common people was not greatly improved, for living conditions in "mill villages" were no better than on barren fields, yet industrialization helped heal the breach between North and South by giving the two sections common problems and objectives.

3. Growth of Monopoly. Before the Civil War most factories were owned privately, by partners, or by small corporations. Combination began when the _Panic of 1873_ inaugurated a period of fierce competition between the many small businesses. To escape price cutting, owners first used the device of _pooling_, through which the several manufacturers of a product entered into a "gentleman's agreement" on the price to be charged or the geographic area in which each would sell his goods. In the 1880's pools gave way to _trusts_, formed when previously competing firms handed over their stock to a board of trustees. The first important trust was the _Standard Oil Company_ as it was reorganized in 1882 by John D. Rockefeller. This not only monopolized most of the nation's oil distribution, but was in a position to demand _rebates_ from railroads in return for its business. When competitors were bankrupted by this or similar tactics they were absorbed by the Standard Oil Company. The success of Rockefeller's trust inspired many imitators; before the close of the century 5,000 competing firms were merged into 300 trusts, each enjoying a virtual monopoly. Among these were: the United States Steel Corporation, the American Sugar Refining Company, the United States Rubber Company, the American Tobacco Company, the Amalgamated Copper Company, the Pullman Palace Car Company, and the International Harvester Company. While they allowed industrialists to enjoy the economies of large-scale production and distribution, their monopolistic character tempted manufacturers to charge excessive prices.

B. Distribution. A revolution in both internal and external transportation occurred between 1865 and 1890, as railroads and steamship lines opened new markets to manufacturers.

1. Internal Transportation. Railroad mileage in the United States increased from 35,000 in 1865 to 200,000 in 1900.

a. EASTERN RAILROADS. Although the eastern railroad network was marked out before the Civil War, two significant developments occurred:

I. *Improved Facilities* transformed the eastern railroads from unreliable carriers into today's efficient systems. This was accomplished by laying thousands of miles of track reaching to every hamlet, as well as by adopting a uniform gauge which allowed cars from one road to be used on others. Equally important were such inventions as George Pullman's "palace car" (1864), George Westinghouse's automatic air brake (1872), the refrigerator car (1875), the block signal system, and automatic coupling. Faster and heavier locomotives steadily increased the speed and comfort of travel.

II. *Railroad Consolidation* united the many competing lines into a few giant systems. The pioneer was *Cornelius Vanderbilt,* who employed a fortune made in commerce to create the *New York Central System.* By 1900 this road extended from New York to Boston, Cleveland, Detroit, Chicago, St. Louis, Cincinnati, and Indianapolis. The *Pennsylvania Railroad* in the meantime expanded west and south to Chicago, Baltimore, and Washington. A third eastern railroad, the *New York and Erie,* was the victim of two unscrupulous financiers, Daniel Drew and *Jay Gould,* whose stock manipulations drove the line into bankruptcy in 1875. Its period of expansion did not begin until 1894 when it was reorganized by J. P. Morgan. Similar combinations consolidated most of the eastern railroads by 1900.

b. WESTERN RAILROADS. At the close of the Civil War

the Far West was without transportation. During the next thirty years a number of transcontinental lines united the Pacific and Atlantic.

I. *Problems of Western Railroad Building.* In the Far West the lack of population to provide way traffic discouraged private railroad builders until the federal government came to their aid with land grants and loans. *Land grants* consisted of outright gifts of land along the right-of-way, varying from ten to twenty square miles (sections) for each mile of track laid. Between 1850 and 1871 Congress gave railroads 131,350,000 acres, while western states added 49,000,000 acres to this amount, a total area more than the size of the state of Texas. The railroads sold this land during the next few years, at an average price of $5 an acre, sometimes realizing enough to pay total construction costs.

II. *The First Transcontinentals.* Demands for a Pacific railroad mounted after the Gold Rush of 1849 peopled California. Sectional jealousies halted construction until the secession of the southern states, when lines were begun utilizing the four best routes:

1) **The Central Route** from Chicago to San Francisco through South Pass was used first. Two lines were chartered in 1862, the *Union Pacific Railroad* to build westward from Omaha, and the *Central Pacific Railroad* to build eastward from the Pacific. Each was given twenty sections (square miles) of land for each mile of track laid, as well as substantial loans. Both employed construction companies to do the actual building, the *Crédit Mobilier* for the Union Pacific, the Crocker Corporation for the Central Pacific. As these were owned by the same men who owned the railroads, the profits from the excessive sums they charged for building found their way into the pockets of the promoters. Thus the Union Pacific cost $50,000,000 to build, but the Crédit Mobilier charged the company $94,000,000, with the difference going to the men who controlled both companies. Despite this graft, the railroads were pushed to completion rapidly after the close of the Civil War released men and materials for their use. The Central Pacific used Chinese labor to build eastward over the Sierra Nevada Mountains and across Utah. The Union Pacific, employing Irish workers, winged

across the plains and through South Pass. On May 10, 1869, the two met at *Promontory*, Utah.

2) The Northern Route from Lake Superior to Portland, Oregon, was followed by the *Northern Pacific Railroad,* which was chartered in 1864 and reached Bismarck, North Dakota, before the Panic of 1873 halted construction. The road was reorganized in 1881 by *Henry Villard* and completed in 1883.

3) The Thirty-Fifth Parallel Route was used by the *Atchison, Topeka and Santa Fe Railroad,* which received a land grant from Congress in 1863. Guided by *Cyrus K. Holliday,* it reached California in 1883 over a route that crossed Kansas, passed through Santa Fe, New Mexico, and bridged the Colorado River at Needles, California.

4) The Southern Route along the thirty-second parallel was granted the Texas and Pacific Railroad, organized in 1871 to build to California, where it would meet the tracks of *Southern Pacific Railroad,* a line operated by the same promoters who controlled the Central Pacific. When the Texas and Pacific went bankrupt, the Southern Pacific built eastward to El Paso, Texas, where it joined eastern lines in 1882.

III. *Later Railroads.* After 1883, when the first four transcontinental lines were completed, numerous other roads were built into the Far West. These included the Chicago, Burlington and Quincy Railroad, the Kansas Pacific Railroad, and the *Great Northern Railroad*. The latter, built by *James J. Hill* along the northern border of the United States, was forced to create way traffic as it went to offset the lack of a land grant. By 1893, when its tracks reached the Pacific at Tacoma, Washington, Hill had scattered farms, towns, and ranches over its entire route, bringing prosperity to the Northwest as well as to the Great Northern Railroad.

2. External Transportation. The tonnage of the American merchant marine shrank from 2,500,000 in 1860 to 800,000 in 1900, due largely to the failure of shipbuilders to shift from wooden sailing to steel steam-driven vessels. During this period the carrying trade passed into the hands of British, German, and Dutch companies, which offered cheap transportation on fast steam-driven steel ships. These superior carriers brought markets in Europe, Africa, and Asia nearer to manufacturers than domestic markets had been a generation before.

III. IMPACT OF THE ECONOMIC REVOLUTION ON AMERICAN LIFE. When the Civil War began, the Americans were an agricultural people, provincial in viewpoint, unaware of the world around them, distrustful of strong government, and culturally immature. Before the close of the century they had become an industrial people, international in viewpoint, imperialistically minded, and culturally awakened. The following chapters show the way in which these changes were brought about by industrialization. The principal results of the revolution in economics, however, may be briefly summarized:

A. Social and Intellectual Readjustments.

1. The Decline of Individualism. The most important social effect of the mechanization of American life was the increased interdependence of the people. Several factors were responsible:

a. ECONOMIC FACTORS. Industrialization welded the United States into a compact economic unit, with each person dependent on many others for his livelihood. No longer could men be self-sufficient farmers or craftsmen; instead they became closely meshed cogs in the industrial machine. This tended to lessen sectional antagonisms created by the Civil War.

b. SOCIAL FACTORS. Life became more impersonal in the machine civilization. Instead of laboring lovingly to create a finished product, workers in mass-production industries were responsible for one small operation and never had the satisfaction of seeing the final fruit of their labors. At the same time, the gap between employer and employee was widened by the spread of corporate ownership. Employers were now managers responsible to boards of directors or stockholders who were too far distant from the workers to be bothered by a social conscience. Nor could individualistic workers bargain collectively with a corporation. The rapid growth of labor unions followed this realization.

c. URBAN FACTORS. As men concentrated about machines, cities became dominant units in American life. Long a rural people, Americans were forced to adjust themselves to an urban existence. This created problems that remained unsolved at the end of the century: of low living standards, of slums, and of poverty. The concentration of people in cities, however, stimulated cultural development.

2. The Decline of Laissez Faire. The decline of individualism was accompanied by an important shift in political thought. Traditionally wedded to a laissez-faire philosophy which held that the function of government was to protect life and property without interfering in economic affairs, Americans gradually became aware that this negative policy allowed industrial monopolies to overcharge consumers and stifle smaller competitors. Reasoning that only a return to free competition would end these evils, they called upon the government to force monopolies to break down into competing units. Thus they accepted a new political philosophy; government, they believed, should act positively to assure fuller lives for its people.

B. Economic Changes. Industrialization forced various segments of the population to reassess their roles in society:

1. The Farmers, long accustomed to dominating the nation, were forced into a subsidiary role as industrialists gained control. Their rebellion launched the agrarian uprisings of the last quarter of the century.

2. Workers, powerless to bargain individually with corporations, formed labor unions to press for more pay, shorter hours of work, and better working conditions. A smaller number, losing faith in an economic system that rewarded them so poorly, joined radical parties to express their discontent.

3. Humanitarians were not only concerned with the plight of the poor, but were fearful lest the decline in economic democracy would lead to a decline in political democracy. Their attack on the "gospel of wealth" underlay the political changes of the twentieth century.

C. Political Changes. A transformation in the nature of both politics and diplomacy resulted from industrialization:

1. The Degradation of Politics. As America's ablest men were drawn into industry, political offices in cities, states, and the nation were filled with second-raters, many of them corrupt. The resulting wave of fraud shocked the world.

2. Rise of Imperialism. As the United States became the world's leading producer of manufactured goods the people demanded colonial possessions such as those owned by European powers. The wave of imperialism that swept the nation at the close of the century was traceable to this attitude.

ADDITIONAL READING

An excellent interpretation of the economic revolution is found in Thomas C. Cochran and William Miller, *The Age of Enterprise* (1942), while briefer accounts which combine factual information with interpretation are found in E. C. Kirkland, *History of American Economic Life* (1939), and Broadus and L. P. Mitchell, *American Economic History* (1947). More extended is Ida M. Tarbell, *The Nationalizing of Business* (1936). Among the best of the biographies of leading businessmen are Burton J. Hendrick, *Life of Andrew Carnegie* (1932), and Allan Nevins, *John D. Rockefeller* (1940). Matthew Josephson, *The Robber Barons* (1934), is pleasant reading but unashamedly hostile to big business. The industrialization of the South is treated readably in Holland Thompson, *The New South* (1919). The role of the immigrant in the new industrial order is brilliantly treated in a series of interpretative essays by Marcus L. Hansen, *The Immigrant in American History* (1940), while the story of immigration is told in Carl Wittke, *We Who Built America* (1939). Robert R. Riegel, *The Story of the Western Railroads* (1926), describes the building of the transcontinentals.

CHAPTER III

Closing the Frontier
1865-1890

℘ THE SETTLEMENT OF THE TRANS-MISSISSIPPI WEST

At the beginning of the Civil War the settled areas of the United States extended through the first tier of states west of the Mississippi. Beyond lay an unoccupied domain of plains, mountains, and deserts, broken only by islands of settlement in California, Oregon, Utah, Texas, and a few other spots. This whole region was peopled before 1890, when the director of the census announced that an unbroken frontier no longer existed. So rapid was the westward movement of people that between 1870 and 1900 more land was settled than in all the previous history of the United States. This affected every phase of life during these years and into the twentieth century. The frontier advanced in a series of well-defined waves.

I. THE MINING FRONTIER. The California gold rush of 1849 lured 100,000 men to that state. For the next decade they sought wealth in the streams flowing westward from the Sierra Nevada Mountains, but after 1858, when all possible mining sites were appropriated, they fanned out to seek gold elsewhere. The result was a series of "strikes" throughout the West, each followed by a "rush" to that section of the country.

A. Advance of the Frontier.

1. The Colorado Rush

a. THE RUSH OF THE '59ERS. Gold was discovered near present-day Denver in 1858 by a party of prospectors under W. Green Russell. News of the strike, carried east in exaggerated form, led to the *Pike's Peak Gold Rush* of 1859. Most of the 100,000 men who reached Colorado soon returned east after failing to "strike it rich," but those staying on discovered "pay dirt" in a number of streams. Gradually a stable population was built up.

b. EVOLUTION OF GOVERNMENT. As the number of settlers increased, the Pike's Peak country underwent a transformation typical of all mining areas:

I. *Mining Camps.* The first stage began when law-abiding elements in each mining camp held a mass meeting that adopted laws concerning the size of claims that could be staked out, the punishment of criminals, and the like. Usually a committee of judges was elected to enforce the laws in these primitive democracies.

II. *Vigilance Committees.* When these crude legal systems proved incapable of curbing the gamblers, gunmen, and desperadoes attracted by the easy money, a group of the more substantial miners usually formed a *vigilance committee* to cope with the lawbreakers. Working in secrecy, they singled out the principal offenders for a quick trial that usually ended with an execution. A few examples of this sort were enough to restore order to the community.

III. *Permanent Government.* The miners were never satisfied with these extralegal governments, and as soon as possible attempted to establish relations with the United States. In Colorado the prospectors met in November, 1858, to demand admission as the *Territory of Jefferson.* Congress was unable to act on the petition until the secession of the southern states, when the Territory of Colorado was created. Colorado was admitted to statehood in 1876 after further discoveries of gold and silver at Leadville and Cripple Creek increased the population.

2. The Nevada Rush. Prospectors on the eastern slopes of the Sierra Nevada Mountains discovered gold near the Carson River valley in 1858. That autumn the fabulously rich *Comstock Lode* was found; during the next twenty years this vein yielded up gold and silver worth

$300,000,000, while the principal mining camp at *Virginia City* was transformed into a thriving metropolis. Nevada was admitted to statehood in 1864.

3. The Northern Rockies. Prospectors working north-ward from California discovered gold in the *Fraser River* district of British Columbia, then worked their way east-ward making strike after strike. The rush into *Idaho* began in 1860 with discoveries on the Clearwater River, followed by others on the Salmon and Boise rivers. Idaho could be admitted as a territory in 1863. In the meantime, gold was discovered in *Montana* during 1862. The principal rushes to that region occurred in 1863 and 1864 when towns such as Bozeman and Helena were established as mining camps. Montana became a territory in 1864.

4. The Black Hills Gold Rush. The last great rush was to the Black Hills of South Dakota, where gold was reported by a military expedition in 1874. During the fol-lowing year 15,000 miners invaded the region, most of them living about Custer City and Deadwood. In those mining camps the "wild west" had its last stand; there Billy the Kid earned his fame as a gunman while Calamity Jane gained nation-wide notoriety. Order was gradually restored, par-ticularly after the *Homestead Mining Company* took over control of the region.

B. Results of the Advancing Mining Frontier.

1. Settlement of the Far West. Although few of the prospectors participating in each rush stayed on, a stable population gradually formed about each mining camp. This was composed of miners, workers in rock-crushing mills, and farmers attracted by the prospect of high food prices. Hence many of the least attractive regions of the West, from the agricultural point of view, were settled and ob-tained territorial organization.

2. Improvements in Transportation. The peopling of isolated areas in the Far West aroused a demand for better transportation. This was first met by stage coaches operated over regular routes by government-subsidized private com-panies. Most famous of these was the *Butterfield Overland Express*, which used the southern route between the Missis-sippi Valley and California from 1857 to 1861, then moved northward to the South Pass route. The same pass was employed briefly in 1860-1861 by the _Pony Express,_ which carried mails to California in ten days. Although the completion of the California telegraph in 1861 doomed the Pony Express, stagecoaching remained profitable for several years. Between 1862 and 1866 this phase of transportation was dominated by _Ben Holladay,_ who controlled 5000 miles of express routes. Overland freighting, another profitable enterprise, was monopolized by the firm of _Russell, Majors and Waddell,_ which at one time owned 3500 wagons and employed 4000 men. The coming of the railroads in 1869 doomed both the express and freight businesses.

II. **THE INDIAN PROBLEM.** The advance of the mining frontier alarmed the Indians of plains and mountains, who felt that they must fight to retain their hunting grounds. The result was a series of wars that ended only with the red men herded onto a number of small reservations.

A. **The Early Wars, 1861-1868.** Two wars followed the Colorado Gold Rush:

1. _The Cheyenne-Arapaho War_ began in 1861 when the tribes' Colorado lands were overrun by miners. For the next three years the Indians raided stagecoaches, mining camps, and immigrant parties. The climax came in 1864 when the red men, having sued for peace, returned to their camp on Sand Creek in eastern Colorado. There they were attacked by territorial militiamen under Colonel J. M. Chivington. Almost 500 were killed in the _Chivington Massacre._ This brutal act aroused many more Indians to opposition.

2. _The Sioux War,_ which began in 1865, was caused by: 1) resentment over the Chivington Massacre; 2) anger at the defeat of the Minnesota Sioux in a minor war just fought in that territory; and 3) an attempt by the federal government to build the _Powder River Road,_ or _Bozeman Trail,_ from Ft. Laramie, Wyoming, to Bozeman, Montana. This highway, which ran through the Indians' favorite hunting grounds, was designed to connect the Montana mines with the East. Rather than surrender this spot, the Sioux took to the warpath. Between 1865 and 1867 war raged along the whole western plains area.

3. The Congressional Peace Commission. The commission was appointed in 1867 to end the war and introduce a new Indian policy. This policy was based on the belief that war was inevitable as long as Indians occupied lands wanted by whites; peace could be maintained, the commissioners believed, only by settling the red men on reservations where they could learn farming and prepare for eventual assimilation. Two reservations were created:

a. OKLAHOMA RESERVATION was set aside for the southern plains tribes as well as for the _Five Civilized Tribes_ who had been moved to the area from the Southeast before the Civil War. Eventually 75,000 Indians from twenty-two tribes were settled there.

b. BLACK HILLS RESERVATION, in western Dakota, was assigned to the Sioux. At the same time, smaller reservations were created in Colorado, Utah, Montana, and elsewhere for lesser tribes. Several wars were fought between 1868 and 1874 before the Indians could be herded onto these reservations.

B. The Later Wars, 1875-1890. Indian resentment at reservation life was responsible for a series of wars fought between 1875 and 1890. These forced another shift in Indian policy.

1. The Sioux War of 1875-1876. This was touched off by the Black Hills gold rush into the Sioux reservation. A number of the Indians under Chiefs _Sitting Bull_ and Crazy Horse were finally surrounded by federal troops on the Little Big Horn River in southeastern Montana, but were defeated only after destroying a small detachment of soldiers under _Colonel George A. Custer_ at the _Battle of the Little Big Horn._ Most of the Sioux surrendered a short time later, although Sitting Bull and a few others fled to Canada.

2. The Nez Percé War (1877) was fought in the Pacific Northwest by the Nez Percé tribe under _Chief Joseph._ After heroic resistance the Indians were finally defeated and assigned a reservation in Oklahoma.

3. The Apache War (1871-1885) was fought against the Apache Indians of New Mexico and Arizona under their great chief _Geronimo._ Eventually the shattered remnants of the tribe were assigned small reservations in the Southwest.

  4. The Ghost Dance War (1890) occurred on the Black Hills Reservation, when Indian resentment at unjust treatment by the government was whipped to war pitch by religious revivalism. The massacre of some 200 Sioux at the *Battle of Wounded Knee* ended the uprising.

  C. Federal Indian Policy. The continuing wars convinced Congress that a new Indian policy was needed. Reformers insisted that assimilation would be hurried if the natives were treated as individuals rather than in tribal units. Through the 1880's steps were taken to break the power of tribal chiefs, while educational opportunities were provided for younger Indians. The policy was climaxed by the passage of the *Dawes Severalty Act* (1887), which provided that all tribal lands should be divided among the Indians, with each receiving an adequate farm. As the Dawes Act was applied to tribe after tribe the reservations were broken up and the Indians absorbed into American society. In 1924 Congress bestowed citizenship on all of them.

  III. THE CATTLE KINGDOM. Indian removal opened the Great Plains to the cattlemen. Cattle to stock this giant pasture were available in Texas, where they had multiplied rapidly after being introduced by the Spaniards. By the close of the Civil War 5,000,000 longhorns could be purchased for $3 or $4 a head, while similar beeves brought $40 a head on the northern market. This price differential was responsible for the spread of the cattle kingdom.

  A. The Long Drives. These began in 1866 when drovers started northward from Texas with 226,000 cattle, in bands of 1000 head each, bound for the railroad at *Sedalia,* Missouri. Few reached their destination, for the resistance of Missouri farmers, and the difficulty of driving wild cattle across the rough Ozark Plateau, proved to be nearly insurmountable obstacles. To overcome these an Illinois meat dealer, *Joseph M. McCoy,* in 1867 built a new terminal point for the Long Drive at *Abilene,* Kansas, on the Kansas Pacific Railroad. In the next four years 1,500,000 cattle were driven over the *Chisholm Trail* to that town. After 1871 most of the drives were to

Ellsworth or Newton, Kansas, and after 1875 to Dodge City, Kansas. In all, some 4,000,000 cattle reached those _cow towns_ between 1867 and 1879.

B. Spread of the Cattle Kingdom. The Long Drive was economically wasteful, as cattle lost weight on the trail. Hence many longhorns driven northward were used to stock the northern range. Ranches soon covered Kansas and Nebraska, then spread westward into Colorado, where a million cattle were grazed by 1869. The occupation of Wyoming and Montana followed during the next decade. The cattlemen made no attempt to buy land, pasturing their stock on the public domain. Having no recourse to law, they worked out a rough system of justice which was backed with the universally worn Colt six-shooters. A herder who appropriated a spot along a stream was understood to have a "range right" to all land running back as far as the "divide" that separated one waterway from another. The roundup was introduced to separate cattle that drifted across these imaginary "range lines," while cowboys guarded the herds to keep them on their own ranges.

C. End of the Open Range. High profits led to an overstocking of the range during the 1880's; returns of 30 and 40 per cent attracted so much eastern capital that more cattle were introduced than could be fed on the dwindling grass supply. Attempts to limit grazing were made by cattlemen's organizations such as the _Wyoming Stock Growers' Association_, but with little success. An excessively cold winter in 1886-1887 and a series of dry years thereafter killed off thousands of beeves and ruined hundreds of ranchers. Those ranchers who survived retreated to the High Plains of the West, where they bought land, fenced their fields, and provided for winter feeding of hay or grain.

IV. THE ADVANCE OF THE FARMERS. The last western area to be occupied by farmers was the Great Plains province, which was settled between 1870 and 1900.

A. Opening the Great Plains. The advancing agricultural frontier was halted by the semiarid Great Plains until man-made inventions made their conquest possible. Before they could be farmed, cheap fencing had to be perfected, farm machinery and agricultural techniques improved, and a land system devised.

1. Fencing. This was needed as each advance of the farmers was made at the expense of cattlemen whose herds trampled crops; the wooden fences used in the East were too expensive in this treeless area. The problem was solved by an Illinois farmer, _Joseph F. Glidden,_ who in 1874 began manufacturing _barbed wire fence._ By 1880 he was producing 600 miles daily.

2. Farm Machinery. As the lack of rainfall reduced the productivity of the Great Plains, each farmer had to till many acres to produce the same crop that could be grown on a few acres in the more humid East. Labor-saving machinery was necessary for him to do this in the short planting and harvesting seasons. This was provided by many inventors. In 1868 _James Oliver_ patented the _chilled steel plow;_ by 1873 sulky gang plows allowed the farmer to ride and plow several furrows at once. _Grain drills_ for planting were in use by 1874, and the hay loader was invented in 1876. Reapers for harvesting grain were already known, but they were not satisfactory in the West until 1878 when the twine _binder_ was introduced. The _header,_ which cut the heads from grain while leaving the stalks standing, was added in the 1880's. Threshing machines were also improved during that decade by the addition of blowers and steam power. These inventions allowed a farmer to work only three hours to produce an acre of wheat in 1890, while in 1860 sixty-one hours were required.

3. Scientific Agriculture. Farm experts devised two ways to use the semiarid land of the Great Plains:

a. IRRIGATION was used in some areas where water was available from underground wells or mountain streams.

b. DRY FARMING was employed elsewhere. The farmer plowed deeply to bring subsurface water upward, then created a dust mulch on the surface to prevent evaporation. Progress in scientific agriculture was made possible by government aid. The _Morrill Act_ (1862) offered land grants to states that founded agricultural schools, while the _Hatch Act_ (1877) subsidized state experiment stations to carry on agriculture research.

4. *The Land System*. A satisfactory land system was essential to the advance of the frontier. This was apparently provided by the <u>Homestead Act</u> (1862), which offered every actual settler 160 acres of government land free of charge. Actually the Homestead Act did not solve the West's problem.

a. DEFECTS OF THE HOMESTEAD ACT. The law was poorly suited to the Great Plains, where a farmer needed either from 360 to 640 acres if he intended to practice extensive agriculture, or from 40 to 60 acres if he planned to use irrigation.

b. SPECULATIVE ACTIVITY. Despite the Homestead Act, speculators continued to control the best land in the West. They obtained this in several ways:

I. *Loopholes in the Land Laws.* The Homestead Act applied only to surveyed land; speculators moving ahead of surveying parties could pre-empt the best sites. Others hired dummy entrymen to take out homesteads on choice locations. About 100,000,000 acres were obtained by speculators in this way.

II. *Railroad Land Grants.* The railroads received 181,000,000 acres of land, most of which was desirable, as it was near transportation facilities. This was sold at an average price of $5 an acre.

III. *Grants to States.* Under the Morrill Act (1862) the states were given 140,000,000 acres of western land as endowments for agricultural schools. This land was then sold to speculators.

IV. *Reservation Lands.* As reservations were taken over by the government, the former Indian lands were sold, usually in large blocks to speculators. Not until 1887 did the Dawes Severalty Act rule that Indian lands must be sold in 160-acre plots to actual settlers. In the meantime 100,000,-000 acres were disposed of to speculators.

c. RESULTS OF DEFECTS IN LAND SYSTEM. While speculators secured 521,000,000 acres of land, homesteaders obtained only 80,000,000 acres. Thus most farmers were still required to pay high prices for their western farms.

B. Occupation of the Northern Plains.

1. Reasons for Settlement. Despite the defects of the land system, the Great Plains were peopled rapidly after 1870. This was because:

a. SURPLUS POPULATION had piled up in the Mississippi Valley, held back for a generation before 1870 by the hostile environment of the Plains.

b. RAILROAD ADVERTISING. Nearly all land-grant railroads set up bureaus of immigration to dispose of their lands. These advertised for immigrants throughout the East and Europe, provided free transportation and loans to prospective farmers, and did much to publicize the West everywhere.

c. ASSURED MARKETS for western produce attracted farmers. The northern plains were ideally suited to growing hard spring wheat, while hard winter wheat could be grown from Kansas southward. Mills to turn this wheat into flour by the efficient *New Process* method of milling were built at Minneapolis, Kansas City, and St. Louis during the 1870's. This process employed a succession of rollers, each set closer together than the last, to reduce the grain to flour gradually.

2. The Advance of Settlement. Population moved out first over Kansas and Nebraska, following rivers and railroads westward; both states were filled by 1880. Another stream of settlers turned northward to settle Dakota territory, where giant *Bonanza Farms* established by railroads in the Red River Valley after the Panic of 1873 demonstrated the richness of the soil. Wyoming and Montana, although less well suited to agriculture, also attracted pioneers during the 1880's. A demand for statehood from all of these newly settled regions was met in 1889 when Congress admitted North Dakota, South Dakota, Montana, and Washington to the Union. Idaho and Wyoming objected so strenuously to their admission that they were added a year later. These six states were known as the *omnibus states* because they were admitted by an "omnibus bill" rather than individually.

C. Occupation of the Southern Plains. The peopling of the northern plains left only the Indian Territory (Oklahoma) without white settlers.

1. Opening the Indian Territory. As the country about Oklahoma was occupied, pressure was exerted on the government to open this region to homesteaders. This pressure came from two sources: 1) the railroads that penetrated the area and were eager to develop agriculture there, and 2) frontiersmen who wanted to obtain land before all the West was settled. The latter were known as *Boomers*. Led by *David L. Payne,* the Boomers invaded the Indian Territory by force during the early 1880's, only to be driven out by federal troops. Congress, sensitive to this pressure, in 1885 authorized the Indian Office to secure title to two parts of the Indian Territory not actually occupied by any tribe, the *Cherokee Outlet* and the *Oklahoma District,* a triangle of land in the center of the territory. When this was done, the President announced that the Oklahoma District would be opened to settlers at noon on April 22, 1889.

2. Settlement of Oklahoma. When the deadline arrived, 100,000 Boomers lined the edge of the Oklahoma District, held back by troops who guarded the border. At noon officers sounded bugle blasts and the greatest land rush in history was on. By nightfall the whole district was settled, including the cities of Guthrie and Oklahoma City. During the next few years other reservations were opened as the Dawes Severalty Act was applied to tribe after tribe. Oklahoma became a state in 1907.

3. Settlement of the Southwest. The last two states in the Southwest, New Mexico and Arizona, entered the Union in 1912. Both were notable for their progressive constitutions, which provided for the initiative and referendum, direct primaries, short terms for elected officials, women's suffrage, limited executive power, and even—in the case of Arizona—the popular recall of judges. With their admission as states the political organization of the nation was completed.

V. THE CLOSING OF THE FRONTIER. The director of the census announced in 1890 that a frontier no longer existed. While much unoccupied land remained in the West, the areas of settlement were so broken that for the first time in history no line could be drawn separating occupied and unoccupied regions. This important date marked the close of one era in the nation's development.

A. Effect of the Closing of the Frontier. After three hundred years of expansion, the American people were forced to adjust themselves to a closed-border existence. This had important effects on their economy and psychology.

1. Economic Effects. These were lessened by the fact that the westward movement went on despite the "end" of the frontier. The West was only thinly settled before 1890, while improved agricultural methods continuously opened areas considered unfertile. Hence four times as many acres were homesteaded after 1890 as before, and between 1900 and 1920 a million Americans moved on to the Prairie Provinces of Canada. Despite this, the approaching end of the era of cheap lands stimulated a rush of farm buying which sent the price of agricultural lands up 118 per cent between 1900 and 1910. At the same time the price of farm produce rose sharply, reaching a peak during World War I. This advance was not due to the closing of the frontier, but to: 1) gold discoveries that inflated currency, 2) lagging farm production because of drought during the 1890's, and 3) new industrial uses for corn and cotton. Yet the rising commodity and land prices stimulated two developments:

a. AGRICULTURAL SPECIALIZATION. As land prices mounted, farmers tended to plant only the one crop best suited to their soil, thus obtaining the higher returns needed to carry their heavy investment. By 1920 the one-crop system was firmly planted in South and West. The South specialized in cotton, the upper Great Plains region in spring wheat, the lower Great Plains in winter wheat, the Iowa area in corn, and the urbanized portions of Wisconsin, Illinois, and southern Minnesota in dairy products. This system reduced the self-sufficiency of farmers, and endangered their security in periods of drought or depression.

b. FARM TENANCY increased as eastern capitalists, seeking a sure investment, poured money into land. By 1920, 40 per cent of the farms of Iowa and 50 per cent of those of Illinois were owned by absentee landlords.

2. Psychological Effects. For two centuries Americans had believed that the United States was prosperous because cheap land drained surplus labor westward, thus keeping wages and living standards high. Now they must learn to live within closed borders. The result was two-fold:

a. THE CONSERVATION MOVEMENT of the early twentieth century was based on the belief that natural resources could no longer be squandered as in the past.

b. THE QUEST FOR SECURITY became a paramount concern of the people and their government. Statesmen such as Theodore Roosevelt, Woodrow Wilson, and Franklin D. Roosevelt built their political systems on the belief that the federal government must provide its citizens with the social welfare and economic opportunity formerly provided by cheap land.

ADDITIONAL READING

The whole story of western settlement during this period is briefly told in Ray A. Billington, *Westward Expansion* (1949). Scholarly but readable accounts of the California gold rush are in Rodman W. Paul, *California Gold* (1947), and John W. Caughey, *Gold is the Cornerstone* (1948). Glenn C. Quiett, *Pay Dirt* (1936), reconstructs the advance of the whole mining frontier in popular form. An excellent account of early western transportation is in Oscar O. Winther, *Via Western Express and Stagecoach* (1945), while plains freighting is the theme of Raymond W. and Mary L. Settle, *Empire on Wheels* (1949). A colorful biography of a leading expressman is J. V. Frederick, *Ben Holladay* (1940). Several chapters in Frederic L. Paxson, *Last American Frontier* (1910), deal with Indian removal from the Great Plains; the resulting wars are popularly described in Paul I. Wellman, *Death on Horseback* (1947). Ernest S. Osgood, *The Day of the Cattleman* (1929), tells the story of the cattle frontier. The settlement of the Great Plains is interpreted in Walter P. Webb, *The Great Plains* (1931), and described in Fred A. Shannon, *The Farmers' Last Frontier* (1945).

CHAPTER IV

Business and Politics

1868-1890

⟪ BUSINESS CONTROL OF POLITICS

The years from 1868 to 1890 were the most drab in the nation's political history. At no time during this period did the parties take clearcut stands on the vital questions facing the people; instead they obscured major issues while giving voters a choice between nonentities for elected offices. This was because the true political rulers were captains of business who had no wish to solve the pressing problems facing the United States: the relations of capital and labor, the threat of industrial monopoly, the tariff issue, the farm problem, and the role of the nation in world relationships. Instead, their sole concern was to perpetuate a laissez-faire system that left them free to amass profits, at the same time winning special favors from the government for business.

I. THE GRANT ADMINISTRATION, 1869-1877. The degradation in politics was shown in the administration of _Ulysses S. Grant_. Inexperienced politically and blindly worshipful of anyone who had made money, Grant became the tool of unscrupulous industrialists and scheming grafters, although he was personally honest. Of the second-raters in his cabinet only his Secretary of State, _Hamilton Fish_ of New York, had any ability.

A. Domestic Problems. In addition to the problem of Reconstruction (see Chap. I) Grant was forced to deal with the currency situation, tariff revision, and civil service reform.

1. The Currency Problem. In 1868, $400,000,000 of the legal-tender *greenbacks* issued during the Civil War were still in circulation. Their inflationary effect was favored by farmers and debtor groups, but opposed by business leaders, who demanded that Congress take steps to redeem the greenbacks in gold, thus placing the country on a firm gold basis. For a time Grant seemed to side with the inflationists in this controversy, particularly in his handling of the Supreme Court in the *Legal Tender Cases.* In the first of these, *Hepburn v. Griswold* (1870), the Court held that greenbacks were not legal tender for obligations entered into before they were issued, and even questioned their constitutionality. When Congress increased the number of judges from seven to nine, Grant named two additional justices favorable to greenbacks. Hence in the second case, *Knox v. Lee* (1871), the Court reversed itself to hold Greenbacks constitutional. Business pressure finally prevailed when Congress passed the *Resumption Act* (1875), which provided that after 1879 all greenbacks would be redeemable in gold.

2. The Tariff Problem. High protective tariffs had been enacted during the war as part of the general taxation program. Instead of lowering duties after fighting ended, Congress responded to pressure from lobbyists and between 1867 and 1870 raised levels on numerous items. Western dissatisfaction was so great that Republican leaders, fearing defeat in the election of 1872, pushed through a general 10 per cent reduction in the *Tariff of 1872.* No sooner was the law passed, however, than the Panic of 1873 created a need for additional governmental revenue. To obtain this the *Tariff of 1875* restored high duties once more.

3. Civil Service Reform. Grant's mediocre appointees aroused such resentment that the President in 1871 asked Congress to provide that certain offices must be filled by qualified candidates selected through competitive examinations. This system, which was already in use in Europe, had been advocated for some years by a group of reformers under *Carl Schurz.* Congress adopted such a law in 1871, but it was never enforced.

B. The Election of 1872. Grant's sorry record

aroused such dissatisfaction that the Republican Party split over his renomination. Reformers under _Carl Schurz_ broke away to form the _Liberal Republican Party_ with _Horace Greeley_ of New York as their standard bearer. Greeley's long association with such eccentric causes as vegetarianism and temperance alienated many people, while his advocacy of protective tariffs made him unacceptable to Democrats. The Democratic Party, however, reluctantly accepted Greeley as its candidate. The _Republicans_ nominated _Grant_ on a platform that praised high tariffs and paid lip service to civil service reform. He was re-elected by an electoral vote of 286 to 62, receiving 56 per cent of the popular vote.

C. Panic and Corruption. The little popularity that Grant had enjoyed declined rapidly during his second administration. This was due largely to the Panic of 1873 and the evidences of corruption that came to light.

1. Panic of 1873. The wartime boom came to a sudden end in September, 1873, when the failure of a leading investment house, _Jay Cooke and Company,_ touched off a major panic. Stocks were dumped on the market, banks and factories closed, and business failures multiplied. Within a few months the nation was almost paralyzed economically, with 3,000,000 persons unemployed. Hard times continued for five years.

2. Corruption. A series of revelations during Grant's second administration laid bare a record of fraud and corruption that involved many of the President's close friends and even came close to the President himself.

a. THE GOLD CONSPIRACY. Two unscrupulous financiers, _Jay Gould_ and _James Fisk,_ decided to "corner" the nation's gold supply, drive the price up, and then sell out at a profit. To make this possible, Gould convinced Grant that the farmers would benefit if the government withheld its gold from the money markets for a time. Then, with the support of certain treasury-department officials, Gould and Fisk began buying metal in September, 1869. In four days they ran the price up from 140 to 163. Then, on Friday, September 24, the Secretary of the Treasury began selling gold once more. The effect of that _Black Friday_ on business almost resulted in a premature depression.

b. THE CREDIT MOBILIER SCANDAL. The builders of the Union Pacific Railroad created the Crédit Mobilier as a construction company to build the road, then awarded it such profitable contracts that the railroad nearly went bankrupt while the Mobilier paid dividends of several hundred per cent. Fearing the exposure of their scheme, the backers of the Mobilier placed blocks of their company's stock in the hands of several Republican congressmen, using *Oakes Ames,* a congressman from Massachusetts, as their agent. A congressional investigation eventually exposed the whole unsavory affair.

c. THE SALARY GRAB. In March, 1873, Congress doubled the salary of the President, and increased the salaries of congressmen by 50 per cent. Grant signed the bill but public indignation forced the next Congress to repeal the law.

d. THE SANBORN CONTRACT. A deal between the Secretary of the Treasury and J. D. Sanborn, a minor politician, allowed the latter to collect $427,000 in unpaid taxes, keeping half the sum as his commission. An investigation showed that most of this sum was used to pay Republican party workers.

e. THE WHISKEY RING FRAUD. This involved a ring of liquor dealers in St. Louis who defrauded the government of millions in excise taxes through connivance with treasury officials and even with the President's personal secretary. Grant was hurt rather than shocked by this revelation, and went so far as to defend his secretary against investigators.

D. Foreign Problems. The constructive foreign policy of Grant's administrations was not shaped by the President but by his able Secretary of State, *Hamilton Fish* of New York.

1. Territorial Expansion. This was begun under William E. Seward, Secretary of State under Lincoln and Johnson, who in 1867 purchased *Alaska* from Russia for $7,200,000 and annexed the Midway Islands west of Hawaii. Seward also tried to buy the Danish West Indies (Virgin Islands) from Denmark, but the Senate refused to ratify the agreement. Grant was eager to add *Santo Do-*

mingo to the United States, largely because American speculators with interests there convinced the President's secretary that this was advisable. Ignoring the State Department, Grant sent his secretary to negotiate a treaty of annexation. This was defeated in the Senate, largely through the efforts. of *Charles Sumner*.

2. Relations with England. Hamilton Fish's expert diplomacy allowed the peaceful settlement of two conflicts with England.

a. THE FENIAN UPRISING. Irish patriots in the United States planned to use ex-Union troops for the conquest of Canada, which would then be returned to England in exchange for Ireland's independence. With an army of 1500 Irish soldiers, they crossed the Niagara River in 1866 and fought an engagement with Canadian militiamen before fleeing back to New York. The United States curbed further attempts at invasion but never reimbursed Canada for losses suffered in this attack.

b. THE ALABAMA CLAIMS. The United States charged that British negligence allowed the Confederate cruisers *Alabama, Florida,* and *Shenandoah* to put to sea during the Civil War, thus making England liable for all damage the three ships did to American shipping. Extremists on both sides frustrated early attempts to settle the issue; an arbitration treaty drafted in 1869 was defeated in the Senate when Senator Charles Sumner charged that England's action had prolonged the war two years and cost the United States $2,000,000,000. Canada, he suggested, should be offered in payment. In contrast, Hamilton Fish worked quietly with British diplomats to arrange the *Treaty of Washington* (1871). England expressed regret for her action and agreed to submit the question of damages to an international tribunal. This tribunal eventually awarded the United States $15,500,000. The settlement was a triumph for the cause of arbitration and a landmark in international law.

II. THE HAYES-ARTHUR ADMINISTRATIONS, 1877-1885. Hard times after 1873, combined with the disclosures of corruption in Grant's second administration, threatened to defeat the Republicans as the election of 1876 approached.

A. The Disputed Election of 1876.

1. The Party Conventions. The <u>Republican</u> convention was split between "regular" Republicans who supported either Grant or <u>James G. Blaine</u> of Maine, and "liberal" Republicans who favored <u>Rutherford B. Hayes</u> of Ohio, a colorless three-time governor of the state who stood for honest government and civil service reform. Middle-roaders in the party, realizing that Grant's unsavory reputation must be offset, finally cast their votes for Hayes, giving him the nomination. The <u>Democrats</u>, determined to make reform the campaign issue, chose New York's progressive governor, <u>Samuel J. Tilden</u>, as their candidate. Tilden enjoyed a national reputation as a reformer for his part in overthrowing the notorious <u>Tweed Ring</u> which had fleeced the taxpayers of New York City. He was essentially a conservative, however, favoring "hard money" as did Hayes.

2. Results of the Election. Tilden won 184 electoral votes to 165 for Hayes. Twenty electoral votes were in dispute, however. These were from South Carolina, Louisiana, and Florida—where Republican-dominated election boards, refusing to accept the apparent Democratic majorities, certified that the states had gone Republican—and from Oregon, where, on a technicality, the Democratic governor had replaced one Republican elector with a Democratic one. Each of these four states submitted two sets of returns, one giving Hayes the vote, the other Tilden. If all twenty disputed votes were awarded Hayes he would have the 185 electoral votes necessary for election; if only one went to Tilden then Tilden would become President.

3. The Election Commission. The problem of deciding which candidate should have the disputed votes was complicated by the fact that the Senate was Republican and the House Democratic. They finally agreed on an <u>Election Commission</u> of fifteen, with five members from the House, five from the Senate, and five from the Supreme Court. Seven were to be Democrats and seven Republicans, while the fifteenth was Judge Davis of Illinois, who was nonpartisan. At the last minute Judge Davis resigned from the Supreme Court to enter the Senate, and a Republican judge was named in his place. By an eight to seven vote the Commission gave all twenty disputed votes—and the election—to Hayes. The justice of the dispute is hard to determine. Tilden had a popular majority of 250,000, but many southern Negroes who would have voted for Hayes were kept from the polls by force.

B. Problems of the Hayes Administration.

1. Civil Service Reform. Hayes' principal ambition as President was to end the *spoils system* through which men were named to government offices because of their political loyalty rather than their merit. His efforts were frustrated by both his own cabinet and Congress. Despite instructions from Hayes, only *Carl Schurz,* the Secretary of the Interior, and *John Sherman,* the Secretary of the Treasury, filled their departments without regard to the political allegiance of the appointees. Congressional opposition to reform came into the open when Hayes removed from office *Chester A. Arthur,* collector of the port of New York, who was a political friend of Senator *Roscoe Conkling.* The Senate refused to confirm the President's nominee for the position, even though his qualifications were unquestioned, because its members resented interference with their control of political spoils. Their attitude doomed effective civil service reform for the time.

2. Resumption of Specie Payments. The Resumption Act of 1875 provided that after January 1, 1879, all greenbacks were to be redeemable in gold; that is, that anyone could take a greenback to the Treasury Department and exchange it for a gold dollar. In anticipation of this day the government had accumulated a gold reserve of $100,-000,000 by selling bonds for gold. As $400,000,000 in greenbacks were in circulation this was deemed sufficient to satisfy all who cared to make the exchange. Actually few did so, and the greenbacks continued to circulate on a gold basis.

C. The Election of 1880. Hayes' refusal to run for a second term gave the "regular" Republicans, or *Stalwarts,* a chance to reverse the trend toward reform. When supporters of U. S. Grant and James G. Blaine could not agree, however, the convention nominated a dark horse, General *James A. Garfield* of Ohio, who was affiliated with the "liberal" or _Halfbreed_ faction of the party. His humble birth in a log cabin and his military record were counted on to attract voters. To appease the Stalwarts, _Chester A. Arthur,_ the New York spoilsman, was nominated for the vice-presidency. The _Democrats,_ seeking to regain popularity in the North, selected as their candidate a Union general, _Winfield S. Hancock_ of Pennsylvania. Their campaign stressed the need for civil service reform. Returning prosperity after the Panic of 1873 doomed their chances, and Garfield was elected by an electoral vote of 214 to 155. His popular vote, however, was only 7000 more than that for Hancock.

D. The Triumph of Civil Service Reform.

1. Garfield's Appointments. True to his Halfbreed principles, Garfield followed Hayes' example in attacking the spoils system. When he named an efficient administrator as collector of the port of New York, the senior Senator from that state, _Roscoe Conkling,_ resigned in protest, as did the junior Senator, Thomas C. Platt (who was thereafter known as "Me-too" Platt). Both hoped to be vindicated by re-election, but, to the amusement of the nation, the New York legislature refused to return them to Washington. Garfield also showed his honesty in handling the _Star Route Frauds._ These involved contracts to carry the mails over western routes where stagecoaches or riders were used instead of railroads. Investigation showed that the contracts were awarded only after substantial bribes to many influential men, including the secretary of the Republican National Committee. Yet the President disclosed the fraud fearlessly, forcing the guilty parties out of office.

2. Assassination of Garfield. After only four months in office Garfield was shot by a crazed office-seeker. This focused attention on the need for civil service reform, but few expected progress under the new President, _Chester A. Arthur,_ a leading Stalwart and proponent of the patronage system. To the delight of the people the responsibilities of office sobered and changed the former spoilsman. One result was an effective civil service law.

3. The Civil Service Law of 1883. In his messages to Congress in 1881 and 1882 Arthur pleaded for civil service reform. His pleas fell on deaf ears until the _election of 1882_ returned a Democratic majority to the House. Then both parties joined in adopting the _Pendleton Act_ (1883). This authorized the President to appoint three civil service commissioners with power to conduct competitive examinations for officeholders in branches of the public service that were "classified" by the President or Congress. Only a few offices were classified at first but each succeeding President extended the list, partly to protect his own appointees against removal by the next executive.

III. THE ADMINISTRATION OF GROVER CLEVELAND, 1885-1889. By 1884 the time was ripe for a Democratic victory because: 1) the Civil War generation was passing from the scene, making less effective the Republican device of winning votes by _waving the bloody shirt_, or boasting that they had saved the Union; 2) the Republicans were still believed to be the party of fraud and corruption; and 3) the emergence of the _Solid South_ guaranteed the Democrats a sure block of votes.

A. The Election of 1884.

1. The Republican Candidate. Stalwarts, revolting against Arthur's reforming record, nominated _James G. Blaine_. Although Blaine's long service in Congress and as Secretary of State made him the leader of the party, he was handicapped by two things: 1) his affiliation with the Stalwart wing of the party damned him in the eyes of all reformers; and 2) he had in 1876 used his political influence to obtain a land grant for an Arkansas railroad, receiving in return the privilege of selling the road's bonds at a high profit. Proof of this transaction was contained in letters that he had written to one James Mulligan. When Blaine obtained these letters by a ruse, the _Mulligan Letters_ became an important issue in the campaign.

2. The Democratic Candidate. The Democrats were encouraged to nominate a reforming candidate when liberal Republicans, led by _Carl Schurz_ and George William Curtis, announced that they would bolt their party if a suitable choice was made by the opposition. Although derisively labeled _Mugwumps_ by the Stalwarts, these progressives promised to control the election. Hence the Democrats selected *Grover Cleveland,* whose reforming activity as mayor of Buffalo and governor of New York had won him national fame.

3. The 1884 Campaign and Election. Despite the clear-cut division between the two candidates, two minor issues helped decide the election. 1) Cleveland was charged with having fathered a seven-year-old illegitimate child in Buffalo. He admitted the truth of the charge, but announced that he had done everything possible financially to rectify a moral error. Republican emphasis on his immorality, however, doubtless influenced many middle-class voters. 2) Just before the election Blaine was visited by a delegation of Protestant ministers whose spokesman, Dr. Samuel Burchard, referred to the Democrats as the party of *"rum, Romanism, and rebellion."* Blaine's failure to refute this insulting phrase cost him the votes of many Roman Catholics, particularly in New York, where Cleveland's popular vote was only 1149 more than Blaine's. The importance of these minor issues was revealed by the closeness of the final vote. Cleveland's plurality was only 23,000 and the electoral vote 219 to 182. The Democrats won control of the House but Republicans still dominated the Senate.

B. Reform Under Cleveland. Fundamentally conservative, Cleveland was interested in increasing the administrative efficiency of the government. This, rather than a desire to improve the welfare of the people by positive action, accounted for most of the laws that he sponsored.

1. Civil Service Reform. Cleveland's belief in civil service was demonstrated when he added 12,000 offices to the classified list, yet members of his party exerted great pressure on him to place Democrats in office, pointing out that loyal politicians deserved some reward after being out of power for twenty-four years. Cleveland responded reluctantly but completely; by the close of his term two-thirds of the nonclassified offices were held by Democrats. This cost him the support of many reformers.

2. Pensions. During the Civil War Congress had authorized pensions for Union soldiers suffering disabilities while in service, and for widows and children of veterans. Those unable to obtain benefits under this law usually asked their congressmen to introduce private pension bills, which were always passed without question, even though the applicant had no legal claim to a pension. The 500,000 members of the Union veterans' organization, the *Grand Army of the Republic* (G.A.R.), served as a pressure group in behalf of such laws. Cleveland offended this organization and all veterans by: 1) rigorously scrutinizing all private pension bills and vetoing hundreds where no disability claim was warranted; 2) vetoing a *Dependent Pension Bill* (1887) which would have granted pensions to all disabled veterans, whether or not their disabilities were suffered while they were in the armed services; and 3) ordering the return of captured Confederate flags to their original states. The uproar resulting from this last step was so great that Cleveland withdrew his order and the flags remained in the North until 1905, when they were returned by a Republican Congress—without uproar.

3. Conservation. Cleveland's Secretary of the Interior uncovered a record of fraud in the disposal of the public domain. Acting vigorously, the President forced the return of lands illegally granted to railroads, lumber and mining interests, and cattlemen. In all he restored 81,000,000 acres to the public domain.

C. The Tariff Issue. This was the most important problem faced by Cleveland.

1. Background of the Problem. The Tariff of 1875, which continued the protective principle accepted during the Civil War by leveling 40 per cent duties on imports, was not questioned until the 1880's, when a new problem emerged.

a. PROBLEM OF THE SURPLUS REVENUE. Beginning in 1880 the federal government each year took in $100,000,000 more than it needed for operating expenses. This was highly undesirable, for in those days government funds were stored in vaults rather than banks. As money was removed from circulation, business suffered the effects of deflation. All agreed that the surplus was bad, but the government faced difficulties in either spending the excess sums or stopping their flow into the treasury.

ı. *Spending the Surplus Revenue.* The surplus could be spent in only two ways, neither desirable: 1) By paying off the national debt. This debt was largely in the form of government bonds which were held by national banks. As these banks issued paper money (national bank notes) on the basis of the bonds they held, any sudden repurchase of the bonds by the government would dangerously contract the currency. 2) By spending money recklessly through *pork barrel* bills to improve rivers and harbors. Cleveland was too honest to sanction such waste.

II. *Preventing the Growth of Surpluses.* Equally impossible was the task of stopping money from flowing into the national treasury. This money came from two sources: 1) excise taxes on liquor and tobacco, which moral reformers insisted on retaining; and 2) the tariff, which businesses demanding protection wanted to keep high.

b. REPUBLICANS AND THE TARIFF. President Arthur recognized the seriousness of the problem and named the *Tariff Commission of 1882* to recommend some means of dealing with the surplus revenue. Although the Commission was packed with protectionists—its chairman was secretary of the National Association of Wool Manufacturers—it recommended a general reduction in duties to the 20 per cent level. When Congress undertook to carry out its suggestions lobbyists swarmed in to plead for their special interests. The resulting *Mongrel Tariff of 1883* differed little from the Tariff of 1875, but did stamp the Republican Party as favoring high levels.

2. Cleveland and the Tariff.

a. ATTITUDE OF DEMOCRATIC PARTY. While southern and western Democrats generally favored lower tariffs, a strong group of eastern Democrats under *Samuel J. Randall* of Pennsylvania were archprotectionists. Their influence was shown in 1884 when Representative W. R. Morrison of Illinois tried to push through a 20 per cent reduction. Forty-one Randall Democrats joined with Republicans to defeat the measure.

b. TARIFF MESSAGE OF 1887. Cleveland made up his mind slowly on the issue, but by 1887 he was convinced that the surplus revenue could be wiped out only by lowering duties. In 1887 he devoted his entire presidential message to the subject, asking Congress to enact a lower tariff as the only way to deal with the surplus. Cleveland knew that any measure would be defeated in the Republican Senate, but he hoped the Democratic House would favor reduction, thus providing an issue for the election of 1888.

c. RESULTS OF TARIFF MESSAGE. Cleveland's plan succeeded. The _Mills Bill_, providing for wholesale reductions, was adopted by the House with only four Democrats in opposition. In the meantime, Senate Republicans under _Nelson W. Aldrich_ met the challenge by proposing even higher tariffs. As neither bill could pass, there the matter rested until the election of 1888.

IV. THE ADMINISTRATION OF BENJAMIN HARRISON, 1889-1893.

A. The Campaign of 1888. The _Democrats_ renominated _Cleveland_ and pledged themselves to carry out his program. The Republican nominee was _Benjamin Harrison_, an Indiana lawyer with few attributes for the office. Capitalizing on manufacturers' fears of tariff reduction, Harrison's supporters raised a vast campaign fund from industrialists. This, plus a solid G.A.R. vote against Cleveland, gave Harrison the election. His popular vote, however, was 100,000 less than Cleveland's. Both houses of Congress were Republican by narrow majorities, with "Czar" _Thomas B. Reed_, Speaker of the House, in a position to push through a legislative program.

B. Minor Political Issues.

1. Civil Service. Harrison, ignoring the civil service laws, filled government offices with party hacks. His commissioner of pensions, for example, remarked on taking office, "God help the surplus revenue." Harrison did name the youthful _Theodore Roosevelt_ to the Civil Service Commission.

2. Pension Legislation. A _Dependents' Pension Act_ similar to the one vetoed by Cleveland was adopted by the Republicans in 1889. This provided pensions for all Union veterans suffering any physical or mental disability, no matter how or where contracted, as well as increased allowances to widows and children of veterans.

3. The Federal Elections Bill. This measure, which was designed to restore the vote to southern Negroes, gave the federal government a measure of control over national elections. It passed the House but was defeated in the Senate. The results were the opposite of those sought by Republicans, for the southern states responded with still more discriminatory laws. All provided for literacy tests for voters, limiting the franchise to those who could read and interpret a section of the state constitution. As these tests eliminated many poor-white voters, they were soon displaced by laws restricting voting to descendants of those able to vote before 1867. Until 1915, when these *grandfather clauses* were declared unconstitutional by the Supreme Court, they remained on the statute books of most southern states.

C. The Tariff Problem. Republicans set out to devise a tariff that would continue protection but cut down the surplus revenue. Their answer was the *McKinley Tariff* (1890), which raised duties to such high levels that imports virtually ceased, thus lowering the amounts received from customs duties. The bill also placed raw sugar on the free list. As sugar imports had paid duties of $50,000,000 yearly, about half the surplus revenue was eliminated by this one item. Louisiana sugar growers were placated by a bounty of two cents a pound, which cared for still more of the surplus. At the insistence of Secretary of State *James G. Blaine,* the McKinley Tariff contained provisions designed to stimulate trade with Latin America. These included: 1) placing molasses, tea, coffee, and other items on the free list; and 2) authorizing the President to impose duties on these items whenever another nation levied unjust duties on American goods. This backhanded reciprocity aroused only resentment in Latin America. Popular reaction to the higher prices resulting from the McKinley Tariff was expressed in the *Congressional elections of 1890.* Three-fourths of the Representatives elected were Democrats, while even William McKinley of Ohio, the author of the bill, was defeated.

V. THE BANKRUPTCY OF POLITICS. Why was the political record of the postwar years so drab? And how did this record influence the future?

A. Reasons for Political Degradation. The principal reason for the lack of progress was the failure of the political parties, both Republican and Democratic, to provide the people with a means of expressing the majority will. Neither developed any clear-cut program on major social or economic issues; instead, both became loose confederations or local machines bent only on seizing power. For this two things were responsible: 1) Local politicians, who were in real control of the parties, were too afraid of offending their constituents to take an open stand on any important question; 2) Party lines did not accurately reflect the basic issues. This was shown in the tariff controversy where eastern Democrats voted with eastern Republicans for protection, while even western and southern Democrats fought for high duties on goods produced in their districts. This allowed organized minorities to win political victories that did not reflect the will of the people.

B. Lessons for the Future. Astute political observers who were in their youth during those years—men such as Theodore Roosevelt and Woodrow Wilson—saw the solution to the problem. Among parties constituted as were those of the United States, strong executive leadership was necessary for positive results. Cleveland, although by no means an outstanding leader, demonstrated this when his dramatic tariff message of 1887 temporarily welded his party together on this issue. The statesmen whose forceful leadership made the Progressive Period possible learned their lesson during this period.

ADDITIONAL READING

Matthew Josephson, *The Politicos, 1865-1896* (1938), deals in popular fashion with the interaction of business and politics. The politics of the Grant administration are best considered in William B. Hesseltine, *Ulysses S. Grant* (1935), while foreign problems during the same period are stressed in Allan Nevins, *Hamilton Fish* (1936). E. D. Ross, *The Liberal Republican Movement* (1919), and P. L. Haworth, *The Hayes-Tilden Disputed Presidential Election of 1876* (1906), deal satisfactorily with those topics. The political history of the period after 1876 is best told in the biographies of leading figures: H. L. Eckenrode, *Rutherford B. Hayes* (1930); George F. Howe, *Chester A. Arthur* (1934); and Allan Nevins, *Grover Cleveland* (1934). An understandable treatment of the financial problem is in A. D. Noyes, *Forty Years of American Finance* (1909), while civil service reform is described in Carl R. Fish, *Civil Service and the Patronage* (1905).

Chapter V

The Assault on Laissez Faire

1868-1890

⟪ THE REVOLT AGAINST RUGGED INDIVIDUAL-ISM

Despite the barren political record of the postwar era, the basis for reform was laid during those years. Those responsible were farmers and workers who, driven to rebellion by the growing power of Big Business, organized to support a new theory of government. They held that the state should assume a positive role in men's lives. If railroad rates were too high, they argued, the government should protect shippers by forcing roads to lower their charges; if a business became so monopolistic that it could charge unreasonable prices, it should be broken down into competing units. The gradual acceptance of this theory revolutionized political thought, for Americans had long maintained that private property was immune to governmental interference.

I. THE ATTACK ON THE RAILROADS.

A. The Granger Movement. The theory of government regulation was first advanced by the most individualistic of all Americans—the farmers. They were goaded into action by deep-seated discontent with the status quo.

1. Causes for Agrarian Unrest. Agricultural prices broke sharply in 1868, then tumbled further downward after the *Panic of 1873*. This was due to overproduction, for new farming areas opened in Canada, Australia, Argentina, Russia, and India flooded the world's markets with produce. American farmers insisted, however, that the cause was not overproduction, but underconsumption. If easterners purchased food according to their full capacity to consume, there would be no surpluses. They did not, it was maintained, because prices were kept high by middlemen who exacted too high a profit for transferring goods from producer to consumer. Chief among these were:

a. RAILROADS. Farmer grievances against western railroads were many: 1) As monopolies they charged all the traffic would bear. In proof of this, farmers cited the lower rates on eastern railroads where competition existed. 2) The land-grant railroads were looked upon as speculators which withheld territory from settlement for selfish ends. 3) The long-and-short-haul device was resented. By this railroads charged more for a short haul in areas where they enjoyed a monopoly than for a long haul where they faced competition. 4) The roads were charged with granting rebates to large shippers, giving free passes to politicians, and corrupting state legislatures.

b. GRAIN ELEVATORS. As only one elevator existed in each farm community, farmers had no choice but to sell their grain in a monopolistic market. Most elevator operators kept their prices in line with national prices, but they were charged with corrupt methods of grading and weighing grain that cheated farmers.

c. MANUFACTURERS. Farmers believed that monopolistic corporations producing farm machinery and other necessities charged prices that bore no relation to production costs.

2. The Advent of the Grange.

a. ORIGINS OF THE GRANGE. The farmers' answer to the problem of monopoly was to win political control of state legislatures, then pass laws regulating freight rates and elevator charges. Seizing on a social organization, the *National Grange of the Patrons of Husbandry,* which had been organized in 1867 by *Oliver H. Kelley,* a clerk in the Department of Agriculture, they joined in such numbers that by 1874 the Grange had 1,500,000 members. Grangers soon dominated the legislatures of Illinois, Wisconsin, Iowa, and Minnesota.

b. THE GRANGER PROGRAM. The Granger legislatures adopted a twofold program:

I. *Rate Regulation* was the weapon used against railroads and grain elevators. Laws were passed setting maximum rates for carrying or storing grain, and commissions were established to enforce the measures.

II. *Cooperative Buying* was employed to lower the price of goods purchased. By pooling their orders farmers found that they could buy farm machinery for about half the retail price. Thus encouraged, they began establishing cooperative grain elevators, insurance companies, flour mills, banks, and factories. Most of these failed because of inadequate managerial skill and cut-throat competition from industrialists.

3. The Granger Cases.

a. LEGALIZATION OF RATE SETTING. Railroad and elevator operators insisted that the Granger Laws violated the *Fourteenth Amendment* by depriving them of property without due process of law. Their objections led to the *Granger Cases* (1876-1877). In the most famous of these, *Munn v. Illinois,* the Supreme Court passed on an Illinois statute setting rates for storing and handling grain. The Court upheld the law, stating that property was no longer completely private when it was "affected with a public interest." This occurred when it was "used in a manner to make it of public consequence, and affect the community at large." Elevators, railroads, gristmills, and the like were defined as "clothed in a public interest" and hence subject to regulation.

b. THE PROBLEM OF INTERSTATE COMMERCE. In a second group of cases, of which *Peik v. Chicago and North Western Railroad* was the most important, the Court not only applied this doctrine to railroads, but held that the Granger Laws did not violate the *interstate commerce clause* of the Constitution which gave Congress sole authority over commerce between the states. Until Congress acted, the Court ruled, the states were free to adopt legislation necessary to the welfare of the people.

c. Results of the Granger Cases. These decisions marked the first successful attack on the doctrine of laissez faire in post-Civil War America. They laid the basis for all subsequent state regulatory activities, and eventually for the federal regulation of interstate carriers. Despite this success, the Grange declined rapidly after 1877, partly because its success convinced farmers their battle was won, partly because its cooperative ventures collapsed. The railroads soon reverted to their old practices.

B. The Advent of Federal Regulation.

1. Undoing the Granger Laws. With the decline of the Grange and the growing conservatism of the Supreme Court, the Granger Laws were virtually nullified in two important cases:

a. The Wabash Case. In the case of *Wabash, St. Louis and Pacific Railway v. Illinois* (1886) the Court reversed its decision in the Peik Case, ruling that states had no right to fix rates on shipments passing beyond their borders. In effect this ended state regulation, for nearly all traffic crossed state lines.

b. The Minnesota Rate Case. In the case of *Chicago, Milwaukee and St. Paul Railroad v. Minnesota* (1889) the Court decreed that the reasonableness of any rate set by a state commission was a matter to be determined by the courts. This allowed railroads to protest any rate, then fight the matter through the courts for years before a decision was reached.

2. Demand for a Federal Law. If the states could not regulate railroad rates, progressives agreed that the federal government must do so. Its power was clear under the *commerce clause*. This was emphasized in two Senate committee reports:

a. The Windom Committee (1874) recommended that the United States build and operate competing railroads to force private lines to keep their rates down. At the same time a bill authorizing federal rate regulation was passed by the House but defeated in the Senate.

b. The Cullom Committee (1886) disclosed that railroads were guilty of *pooling* tactics: that is, that com-

peting lines formed pools to set high rates or end competition
in a region. As three-fourths of the roads were interstate
carriers that could not be regulated by the states under the
Wabash Case decision, the committee recommended immediate federal regulation.

3. The Interstate Commerce Act (1887) was passed
by Congress in response to this demand. It: 1) established
an *Interstate Commerce Commission* of five to enforce the
measure; 2) required railroads to post their rates publicly
and decreed that these must be "reasonable and just"; 3)
forbade such practices as pooling, rebates, and rate discrimination among shippers; 4) prohibited higher charges for a
short haul than for a longer haul over the same line; and 5)
authorized the Commission to investigate complaints against
railroads and hand down rulings which would be enforceable
through the courts.

4. Failure of Federal Regulation. The Interstate Commerce Act was rendered ineffective by judicial hostility. As
the Commission could enforce its rulings only through the
courts, their friendship was essential. Instead, they handed
down hostile decisions in fifteen of the sixteen cases tried
before 1905. The decision in one of these, the *Maximum.
Freight Rate Case* (1897), ruled that the Commission did
not have power to fix rates, while another, in the *Alabama
Midlands Case* (1897), virtually nullified the long-and-short-
haul prohibition. By 1900 the act was noneffective.

**II. THE ATTACK ON INDUSTRIAL MONOP-
OLY.** Big business was subjected to an attack from: 1)
labor unions, and 2) reformers who demanded governmental
regulation.

A. The Organization of Labor. The ineffectual local
trade unions of the prewar era were transformed into powerful national unions during these years. This unity was
forced on the workers by the problems they faced in an
industrialized America.

1. Causes for Labor Unrest.

a. RISE OF CORPORATIONS. These ended all personal
relationships between employers and employees, as corporations were governed by distant boards of directors who were

in no position to look after the welfare of workers. Managers of corporations, moreover, were primarily interested in producing profits for stockholders rather than in protecting the rights of laborers in their factories. Workers therefore felt that they must protect their own interests.

b. MECHANIZATION OF INDUSTRY. As machines took over the tasks formerly performed by men, individual skills became less and less important. This tended to place workers at the mercy of employers who no longer had to placate the small number of skilled artisans available for a particular trade. Instead, they could draw upon the inexhaustible pool of unskilled or semiskilled labor provided by immigration. To protect their jobs laborers felt that they must organize.

c. NATIONALIZATION OF INDUSTRY. This made competition among workers nation-wide; industries could take advantage of cheap labor wherever it existed rather than depending on a local supply. At the same time the power exerted by national business organizations suggested that national labor organizations could wield a similar influence.

d. WORKING CONDITIONS. Wages did not increase as rapidly as living costs during this period. In 1890 the average pay for unskilled workers was $10 a week, and for skilled $20. This did not allow an average family to exist unless the wife and children also worked, as was usually the case. Hours of labor were from ten to twelve each day, six days a week. Factories were badly lighted and ventilated, with no attempt made to guard employees against dangerous machinery. Compensation for death or injury were virtually unknown.

e. NEED FOR ORGANIZATION. Workers could not turn to politics to obtain better conditions as had farmers. This was because the doctrine of laissez faire was so entrenched that any demand for the federal regulation of industry would have been ineffective. Workers felt that they must protect themselves, and that this could only be done by forming nation-wide unions strong enough to combat nation-wide corporations.

2. Stages of Organization. Labor organization went through three stages between the close of the Civil War and 1890:

a. The National Labor Union. This was established in 1866 by a combination of local craft unions, reform groups, and trades assemblies. Built on the "federal" principle, its individual unions continued their separate existence but sent delegates to national conventions where a common policy was shaped. This policy embraced such diverse objectives as the eight-hour day and producers' co-operatives. The National Labor Union collapsed after the Panic of 1873 because its leaders failed to realize that the worker did not want idealistic panaceas but better wages, hours, and working conditions.

b. The Knights of Labor.

I. *Rise of the Knights of Labor.* Formed in 1869 by *Uriah S. Stephens,* a Philadelphia tailor, the Knights of Labor attempted to unite workers of all skills, colors, and creeds into *One Big Union* that could wrest from employers a more equitable share of the nation's wealth. It gained membership rapidly, especially after the *Panic of 1873,* but its golden period did not begin until 1878 when *Terence V. Powderly,* a Pennsylvania machinist, became Grand Master. Although Powderly was an idealist who believed in long-term objectives rather than strikes, the Knights under his direction won their first great victory in 1884 when a strike on the Missouri Pacific Railroad forced a restoration of wage cuts. This brought the Union such prestige that its membership grew to 700,000 by 1886.

II. *Decline of the Knights of Labor.* The union's decline began in 1886 and was caused by two events: 1) the failure of a strike against the Texas and Pacific Railroad; and 2) the *Haymarket Riot* in Chicago. This followed a nation-wide strike on May 1, 1886, for the eight-hour day. In Chicago the strike was supported not only by the Knights but also by a handful of foreign-born anarchists who preached the forceful overthrow of the government. When one of their number was addressing strikers at the McCormick Harvester Works on May 3 the meeting was charged by police, who killed several workers. The anarchists called a protest meeting at Haymarket Square the next evening. Although the 1500 people attending were orderly, a column of police marched into the square just as the meeting was breaking up. Someone threw a bomb into the column, killing seven of the police and wounding sixty more. Public resentment was so great that seven anarchists were sentenced to death on the grounds that they had advised violence, even though no one could show that they were connected with the bomb throwing. Anarchism and labor were now so associated in the popular mind that the Knights declined rapidly in membership. Skilled workers especially withdrew to protect themselves from _blacklisting_ by employers. This was done by sending names of union members to all factories employing men of their skills. They could then not find employment anywhere in the country.

c. THE AMERICAN FEDERATION OF LABOR. Formed in Pittsburgh in 1881, the A.F. of L. did not become important until it received the influx of skilled workers who deserted the Knights of Labor after 1886. This new organization was composed of self-governing craft unions, united on the federation principle through an elected governing board which set national policy. Membership was restricted to skilled workers who were as much interested in protecting themselves from the competition of the unskilled as in protecting labor from capital. The objectives of the organization were completely realistic; disregarding long-term panaceas, the A.F. of L. worked for an eight-hour day, a six-day work-week, better wages, job tenure, and the abolition of child labor. It sought to obtain these ends by using the _strike_ and the _boycott_. This practical program, combined with the excellent leadership of its long-time president, _Samuel Gompers_ (1885-1924), won the A.F. of L. 500,000 members by 1900. These were successful in winning the _closed shop_ (plants hiring only union workers) and the abolition of _yellow-dog contracts_ (labor contracts forcing workers to agree they would not join a union), as well as better pay, shorter hours, and better working conditions in many industries. Yet by its nature the A.F. of L. excluded 90 per cent of the American workers who did not have the craft or skill to qualify for membership in one of its affiliated unions.

3. _Industrial Strife._ Moderate as were the demands of organized labor, public opinion and employers were so hostile

that those demands could be achieved only after a long period of industrial strife. Between 1881 and 1900 strikes numbered 24,000 and involved 128,000 establishments. Several attracted national attention:

a. THE RAILROAD STRIKE OF 1877. Protesting wage cuts following the Panic of 1873, railroad workers went on strike, then attempted to stop the roads from operating. The conflict was so bitter that federal troops were called out to quell riots in Pennsylvania, Maryland, West Virginia, and Illinois. The greatest disorders occurred at Pittsburgh after militiamen killed twenty strikers. Some $5,000,000 worth of property was destroyed before the strike was broken, the workers returning at the lower wages set by the railroads.

b. THE HOMESTEAD STRIKE (1892). This was staged at the Homestead, Pennsylvania, plant of the Carnegie Steel Company in July, 1892, following a company threat to cut wages and smash the Amalgamated Association of Iron and Steel Workers. When workers picketed the plant, Carnegie's lieutenant, _Henry C. Frick,_ imported 300 guards from the Pinkerton Detective Agency. As the _Pinkertons_ landed from barges they were captured by a mob and run out of town, several on both sides being killed in the process. Frick's appeal to the state for aid resulted in an invasion of militiamen that turned Homestead into an armed camp. The strikers held out for nine months, but when public opinion turned against them they resumed work at company terms. The strike crushed the Amalgamated, leaving the steel industry unorganized for forty years.

c. THE PULLMAN STRIKE (1894). A drastic wage cut at the Pullman Palace Car Company of Chicago following the Panic of 1893 led to a strike of the _American Railway Union_ under the leadership of _Eugene V. Debs._ This soon spread to other railroads when trainmen were discharged for refusing to operate trains carrying Pullman cars. As bitterness increased, mobs representing both contestants did $80,000,000 worth of damage in the Chicago area. This led the railroads, operating through the _General Managers' Association,_ to appeal to President Grover Cleveland for protection, despite the insistence of Governor _John P. Altgeld_ of Illinois that the situation was under control. Cleveland responded, even though the Constitution stated that federal soldiers could be sent into a state only at the request of the governor or legislature, justifying his action on the grounds that the army was needed to safeguard the mails. The 2000 troops that arrived on July 3, 1894, soon broke the strike. One far-reaching result was an extended use of the federal *injunction.* Such a writ was issued against Debs, ordering him to do nothing that would prolong the strike. When he disregarded this order he was tried for violating the injunction and sentenced to six months in jail. The Supreme Court upheld his conviction in the case of *In Re Debs* (1895). The decision gave employers a new weapon against all strikers who interfered with interstate commerce.

4. Results of Labor Organization. Apparently, labor made few gains during the period; public opinion and the courts remained hostile to unions while the mass of workers was still unorganized. Actually, some progress was made:

a. ATTITUDE OF EMPLOYERS. A few employers realized that industrial peace could be secured only by co-operating with unions. These firms showed a willingness to bargain collectively with workers or to submit disputes to impartial arbitration; they also set up old-age pension plans, death benefits, and profit-sharing programs. Among the corporations adopting such an attitude were the Pillsbury Mills, the Baltimore and Ohio Railroad, and one hundred others.

b. ATTITUDE OF GOVERNMENT. National laws favorable to labor included: 1) an act (1868) setting the eight-hour day on public works; 2) the creation of the Bureau of Labor (1884); 3) the prohibition of the importation of contract labor (1885); 4) an act (1892) establishing the eight-hour day for all government employees; and 5) the Erdman Act (1898) providing for the arbitration of disputes on interstate carriers. State laws of the same nature were also passed, although most were disallowed by conservative courts. Massachusetts established a ten-hour day for women and children in 1879 and other industrial states soon followed. Acts were also passed to assure better working conditions. At the end of the century, however, 70 per cent of the men still worked from ten to twelve hours a day, six or seven days a week.

B. Trust Regulation. During the postwar years the federal government made its first attempts to regulate business as well as transportation. While these were largely unsuccessful they set a pattern that changed the whole nature of American life in the twentieth century.

1. Background of the Problem.

a. GROWTH OF INDUSTRIAL MONOPOLIES. Public sentiment against monopolies, or *trusts,* began to develop in the 1880's, following the formation of the Standard Oil Company and other giant combinations (See pp. 21-22). The Standard Oil trust particularly was singled out for attack. In 1882 this company owned fourteen other companies outright, as well as holding a majority interest in twenty-six others. All were operated by nine trustees who held the stock of the individual companies, the stockholders receiving in return "trust certificates" which entitled them to a share in the profits. The oil trust was so successful that before 1887 others were formed in cottonseed oil, linseed oil, lead, whiskey, sugar, and other products.

b. OBJECTIONS TO THE TRUSTS. It was charged that these trusts: 1) set high prices which had no relation to the cost of production; 2) forced producers of raw materials to sell at a low price as they controlled the market; 3) ruined small businesses by obtaining rebates from railroads in return for their business; 4) mistreated workers by blacklisting those who joined unions, thus denying them a chance to obtain other jobs where they could use their skills; and 5) bribed legislatures to obtain special favors from state and national governments. This was especially the case after 1886 when the Supreme Court, in the case of Santa Clara County v. Southern Pacific Railroad, ruled that corporations were "persons" within the meaning of the Fourteenth Amendment, and hence that states could not deprive them of "life, liberty or property without due process of law." In effect this ruling forbade the states to tax or regulate corporations without the approval of conservative federal courts.

2. Demands for Trust Regulation. It was popularly believed that the public could be protected only by forcing the monopolistic trusts to break up into competing units. This could best be accomplished by the federal government through the use of its power over interstate commerce; Congress could forbid monopolies to ship their produce across state lines. A demand for federal action was voiced in the 1880's by: 1) an Anti-Monopoly Party which in the 1884 election won few votes but called attention to the problem; 2) popular writers who attacked the trusts in books and magazine articles; 3) farmer and labor organizations which demanded reform; and 4) state legislatures which passed laws forbidding agreements that would restrain free competition. Fifteen such laws were passed in 1889 and 1890.

3. The Sherman Antitrust Act (1890). This important measure, passed by Congress in response to popular pressure, provided: 1) that every contract, combination, or conspiracy in restraint of trade among the states or with foreign countries was illegal, and 2) that any person who monopolized trade or commerce among the states or with foreign countries was guilty of a misdemeanor and subject to a fine of $5000 and one year's imprisonment.

4. Failure of the Sherman Antitrust Act.

a. DEFECTS OF THE ACT. The measure was so loosely worded that it proved unenforceable. Thus, although trusts were forbidden and disappeared rapidly, they were replaced by *holding companies,* through which a single corporation owned and voted the controlling shares of the stock of a large number of companies. Organizations of this character proved immune to federal attack.

b. HOSTILITY OF THE COURTS. Conservative federal courts removed most of the teeth from the Sherman Act by defining "trade" narrowly. The outstanding example was the decision in *United States v. E. C. Knight Company* (1895) which held that an exchange of stock which gave the E. C. Knight Company control of 95 per cent of sugar refining was not an act of "trade" and hence not forbidden. After this rebuff, government attorneys made few attempts to enforce the law. Only eighteen suits were brought between 1890 and 1900, and some of these were designed to restrain labor unions rather than industries.

c. GROWTH OF CORPORATIONS. Encouraged by the courts' attitude, industry organized more rapidly after 1890 than before. Between 1860 and 1890 twenty-four combinations were formed, capitalized at $436,000,000; between 1890 and 1900, 157 were created with a total capitalization of $3,100,000,000.

III. GOVERNMENT AND BUSINESS: AN APPRAISAL.

A. Results of the Attack on Laissez Faire. Big business ruled America in 1900 as it had in 1870, but by that time business was bigger and the rule more complete. Farmers were still at the mercy of monopolistic railroads, workers (other than a few skilled craftsmen) were unprotected by effective organizations, and both industry and transportation were dominated by a few individuals who held the real reins of government. Equally important was the fact that the courts still placed property rights above human rights on their scale of values.

B. Results of the Attack on Big Business. A generation of agitation bore some fruit, however. Farmers and workers had demonstrated that they could unite for a common end; only time was needed before their organizations would give them a more equitable share of the national wealth. Even more important was the fact that the Interstate Commerce Act and the Sherman Antitrust Act demonstrated the federal government's power to take positive steps in behalf of the general welfare of the people. Later generations of lawmakers had only to improve these basic measures to make them effective instruments for human betterment.

ADDITIONAL READING

The Granger Movement is popularly treated in Solon J. Buck, The *Agrarian Crusade* (1921), and more fully in the same author's *The Granger Movement* (1913). W. E. Clark, *The Trust Problem* (1929), deals with the beginnings of federal regulation, as do Eliot Jones, *The Trust Problem in the United States* (1921), and Burton J. Hendrick, *The Age of Big Business* (1920). Norman J. Ware, *The Labor Movement in the United States, 1860-1895* (1929), is the best study of the Knights of Labor, although

Terence V. Powderly, *Thirty Years of Labor* (1889), contains much colorful information. The history of the American Federation of Labor is satisfactorily told in L. L. Lorwin, *The American Federation of Labor* (1933), and in the reminiscences of its perennial president, Samuel Gompers, *Seventy Years of Life and Labor* (1925). Samuel Yellen, *American Labor Struggles* (1936), tells the story of the nineteenth-century industrial disputes, while a more colorful account of the same strikes is found in Louis Adamic, *Dynamite* (1934).

CHAPTER VI

The Urban Impact
1870-1890

❡ THE CITY IN AMERICAN CIVILIZATION

The city was a product of the machine age. As men left their farms to cluster about factories, more and more they felt the impact of an urban environment which reshaped their lives and their thought. Some found in the city an inspiration for cultural expression. The remarkable progress in literature, music, art, and architecture was traceable to the urbanization process. Others were aroused by the evils and sin that centered in the cities; the reform movements that flourished in the late nineteenth century all stemmed from a desire to wipe out the poverty, slums, and immorality which appeared in magnified form among city dwellers. The important changes that occurred in American society during these years were largely the products of urbanization.

I. THE RISE OF THE CITY. In 1860 one in every six Americans lived in cities (compact units of 8000 inhabitants or more); in 1890 three out of every ten. New York was the largest with 2,500,000 inhabitants, but both Chicago and Philadelphia had more than 1,000,000, and St. Louis, Boston, and Baltimore more than 500,000. Others were growing rapidly: Kansas City and Detroit grew fourfold between 1860 and 1890, Cleveland sixfold, and Los Angeles twenty-four fold.

A. Reasons for Urbanization.

1. *Economic and Social Factors.* Industrialization was

71

principally responsible, as men grouped themselves around machines. Also important were: 1) railroads that allowed large populations to be fed and supplied with fuel; 2) the influx of immigrants; and 3) the exodus of men from farms as declining profits and labor-saving machinery released agricultural workers.

   2. Physical Factors. Cities could not become important until mechanical devices allowed men to live in large groups. Sewers, garbage disposal plants, and trolley cars were not romantic, but they were indispensable.

   a. TRANSPORTATION. Horse cars, in use before the Civil War, were first displaced by cable cars, invented by Andrew S. Hallidie and installed in San Francisco in 1873. These gave way to electric *trolley cars,* which were developed by Frank J. Sprague and used in Richmond, Virginia, in 1887-1888. New York opened its first *elevated railroad* in 1878, and Boston the first *subway* in 1895. Bridges to span rivers on which cities were built were also essential. The leading builder was *John A. Roebling* who, with his son Washington A. Roebling, completed the *Brooklyn Bridge* in 1883. This was the engineering marvel of the age.

   b. LIGHTING. Gas lights were gradually displaced by *arc lights,* invented by Charles F. Bush of Cleveland in 1878. The *incandescent lamp,* perfected by Thomas A. Edison in 1880, solved the problem of home lighting.

   c. PUBLIC HEALTH. Public water works, garbage disposal plants, and efficient sewage systems were gradually developed, helping solve the problem of contagious diseases. Equally important was the announcement of the germ theory of disease by *Louis Pasteur* of France. This allowed doctors to check the epidemics that had previously wiped out city populations.

   II. WEALTH AND POVERTY. The rise of the city called attention to the growing gulf between rich and poor that accompanied industrialization. This discrepancy, made clear by the spreading slums in urban America, aroused humanitarians to strenuous efforts that were designed to restore economic democracy in the United States.

   A. The Gospel of Wealth. Industrialization increased the national wealth from $16,000,000,000 to $65,000,000,-

000 between 1860 and 1890, but was also responsible for the uneven distribution of that wealth. Nine per cent of the people owned 71 per cent of the nation's money by 1890; at the other extreme 88 per cent of the families owned only 14 per cent of the wealth. This inequality was defended by spokesmen for the gospel of wealth, of whom _Andrew Carnegie_ was the leader. In magazine articles and books they argued that: 1) the fortunate few deserved extra compensation for making the United States the world's leading nation; 2) all eventually benefited as wealth seeped down to the masses; and 3) the concentration of riches supported education and culture.

B. The Problem of Poverty. The concentration of wealth meant that millions of city-dwelling Americans would live in poverty. In spreading slums, tenements housed masses of workers amidst unhealthy conditions; the death rate among New York's 1,500,000 tenement dwellers was 62 per 1000 while elsewhere the rate was only 20 per 1000. By 1890, 10 per cent of all the population lived in slums. Their plight was revealed by such widely read books as Jacob A. Riis, _How the Other Half Lives_ (1890), and John Spargo, _The Bitter Cry of the Children_ (1906). Aroused by such revelations, humanitarians suggested numerous panaceas:

1. Social Reformers. One group sought to remedy the plight of the poor by social action.

a. ORGANIZED CHARITY. Reformers launched a threefold attack on the problem: 1) State _boards of charities_ were created to supervise local almshouses, orphanages, and insane asylums. Massachusetts created such a board in 1864, and half the states had imitated its example by 1900. 2) The Society for the Prevention of Cruelty to Children was organized in 1874 to campaign against child labor and similar evils. 3) _Social Service Centers_ were set up in slum areas. These provided pleasant recreational surroundings for youth and adults, as well as club facilities, training in arts and crafts, education, and the like. The most famous was _Hull House_ in Chicago, founded in 1889 by _Jane Addams._ In all, one hundred were established between 1886 and 1900.

b. PRISON REFORM. To assure more equitable treatment for those driven to crime by poverty, reformers developed the theory, then novel, that prisons should be used to regenerate rather than punish lawbreakers. The theory was first applied at the New York *Elmira State Prison,* opened in 1877 under the direction of *Zebulon R. Brockway.* Youthful offenders were separated from hardened criminals, sentences reduced for good conduct, a parole system installed, and educational opportunities provided. The example was imitated in other prisons before 1900.

c. RELIGIOUS INSTITUTIONS. The Young Men's Christian Association (1851), the Salvation Army (1879), and the city mission (1887) sought to combine social and religious regeneration.

2. Critics of the Social Order. Those not satisfied with these palliatives analyzed the nature of the social structure in their effort to reform society. In this group were social critics, utopian novelists, and political radicals.

a. SOCIAL CRITICS. Of the many who suggested social readjustments, none was more prominent than *Henry George.* In his *Progress and Poverty* (1879) George argued that as land was the basis of all wealth, its unequal distribution forced the many who owned no land to slave for the few who did. This situation could be remedied not by a redistribution of property, but by a *single tax* on land to replace all other taxes, thus depriving owners of unearned profits stemming from the increase in land values. George's book sold 2,000,000 copies before 1905, and almost elected its author mayor of New York in 1886.

b. UTOPIAN NOVELISTS. Of those who used fiction to picture the ideal society of the future, the most outstanding was *Edward Bellamy,* whose *Looking Backward, 2000-1887* (1887) described the United States as it would be in the year 2000. All production facilities were owned by the people through their government. The greater efficiency resulting allowed much leisure time, which was used for cultural advance. The book sold 400,000 copies in ten years, while one hundred and fifty *Nationalist Clubs* were formed to advocate Bellamy's system.

c. POLITICAL RADICALISM. Anarchism and socialism were advocated in the late nineteenth century.

I. *Anarchism.* This flourished briefly in the 1880's, largely among immigrants from southwestern Europe, where the philosophy had many followers. Anarchists, through such journals as *The Alarm* (1883), advocated a forceful overthrow of government and the substitution of a ruleless social order.

II. *Socialism.* German and French immigrants introduced Marxian Socialism to the United States just after the Civil War. They advocated an orderly change to a system of government ownership of facilities for production and distribution, with the nonprofit-making exchange of commodities. The Panic of 1873 gave them sufficient strength to form the *Socialist Labor Party* (1877), but membership was confined largely to immigrants. American labor, capitalistic in philosophy, wanted a larger share of profits rather than any change in the system. Not until the close of the century was discontent among workers widespread enough to foster a native socialist movement. Formed in the 1890's by *Eugene V. Debs,* the *Socialist Party* polled 95,000 votes in the election of 1900, and nearly a million in the election of 1912. Many were the protest votes of middle-class intellectuals, but more were cast by workers who no longer felt that the United States was a land of infinite opportunity.

III. THE REVOLUTION IN RELIGIOUS THOUGHT.

Urbanization and the concentration of wealth posed a problem for churchmen. Accustomed to dealing with a rural, middle-class society, they were forced to revise theology and remake the churches as social institutions under the impact of industrialization.

A. Theological Readjustment.

American Protestantism traditionally based its teachings on the assumption that the Bible must be literally interpreted. This belief suffered a threefold attack after the Civil War.

1. The Attack on Orthodoxy.

a. THE EVOLUTIONARY HYPOTHESIS. The English scientist, *Charles Darwin,* in his *Origin of Species* (1859) and *Descent of Man* (1871), showed that life forms had evolved slowly from primitive ancestors, rather than being created suddenly as stated in the Book of Genesis. After the death in 1873 of *Louis Agassiz,* the Harvard biologist who was the last scientific opponent of Darwinism, all scholars accepted the hypothesis, while intelligent laymen were won over by such popularizers as _John Fiske._

b. The Higher Criticism. New methods of historical scholarship devised in Germany allowed scholars to subject the Bible to scientific criticism. This demonstrated that the Scriptures were not written at one time and under one inspiration, but were the product of many peoples who displayed the weaknesses and ignorance of all human beings. This was as shocking to the orthodox as the doctrine of evolution.

c. The Study of Comparative Religions. The sympathetic study of other religious systems disclosed that Christianity was not alone in prescribing an enlightened moral code. The people learned of other religions through such best-selling books as James Freeman Clarke, _Ten Great Religions_ (1871).

2. The Theological Revolution. For a time the churches resisted this assault by ridiculing or denouncing evolution and the higher criticism. As popular acceptance of the new theories spread, however, they were forced to adjust themselves. Leadership was supplied by progressive clergymen such as the Reverend _Washington Gladden,_ Congregational minister of Columbus, Ohio, and the Reverend _Henry Ward Beecher,_ Congregational pastor of Brooklyn, New York, who found no basic antagonism between the scientific concepts and the basic principles of Christianity. By the end of the century theological schools were teaching evolution and the higher criticism. This change was strenuously resisted by an orthodox minority, giving rise to a conflict between _Modernism_ and _Fundamentalism._ The center of fundamentalist thought was in rural areas of the South and West, although such revivalists as the Reverend _Dwight L. Moody_ attacked modernism in the Northeast.

B. Social Readjustment. The churches faced two problems as social institutions: 1) How could they combat the growing secular trend, and 2) Should they follow rich or poor as the redistribution of wealth divided the classes.

1. The Secular Trend. Churches lost membership rapidly as secular interests occupied more and more of men's time. The need for recreation in a speeded-up industrial society also lessened interest in worship. Although the churches did all in their power to combat this trend they accomplished little, as shown by the gradual secularization of the Sabbath day.

2. Wealth or Poverty? As the gulf between rich and poor widened, the churches at first followed the wealthy, building their edifices in upper-class neighborhoods and neglecting the slums. Ministers adopted such an unsympathetic attitude toward labor that workers felt unwelcome in many churches.

3. The Social Revolution. The solution of their dual problem—reversing the trend toward secularization and winning the workingmen back to the churches—was devised by such progressive clergymen as the Reverend *Washington Gladden* and the Reverend *Josiah Strong*. They proposed to make Christianity a part of the everyday life of the people, not simply a brief Sabbath episode. To this end they urged ministers to side with labor in the conflict with capital, to denounce the *"tainted money"* of corporations, and to make their churches into attractive social institutions. The latter was accomplished by adding reading rooms, club rooms, gymnasiums, and the like. These *socialized churches* gained membership far more rapidly than the nonsocialized churches, encouraging imitation. In line with this trend was the rise of a new religion, *Christian Science,* under the guidance of *Mary Baker Eddy.* By promising physical as well as spiritual salvation it appealed especially to urban workers. Even more indicative of the new religious spirit was the formation of the *Society of Christian Socialists* (1889) by clergymen who believed that the teachings of Jesus led directly to socialism. Efforts of this sort did much to restore the influence of the churches by 1900.

IV. THE REFORM MOVEMENTS. Urbanization accentuated the evils that had long troubled reformers, thus heightening the effort to stamp out political inequalities, the liquor traffic, and racial prejudice.

A. The Struggle for Women's Rights. Women had few legal or economic rights in 1865. Long considered creatures of the home, they were believed unequal to the task of competing in a male world.

1. The Basis for Equal Rights. Changed economic and social conditions stemming from industrialization prepared women for political equality:

a. ECONOMIC ACTIVITIES. Industry allowed women to demonstrate their ability by working in gainful occupations; between 1870 and 1900 the number employed increased from 1,800,000 to 5,300,000. These gains were made possible by inventions that allowed emancipation from the drudgery of the home: prepared foods, commercial bakeries, kitchen implements, and improved washing and ironing facilities.

b. SOCIAL ACTIVITIES. Women did yeoman service in social agencies. They also showed their organizing skill by forming women's clubs; the first was founded in 1868 and by 1889 the clubs were numerous enough to unite in the General Federation of Women's Clubs.

c. INTELLECTUAL ACTIVITIES. Women's colleges were opened at Vassar, Smith, and Wellesley between 1865 and 1875, with others following rapidly. More significant was the spread of coeducation, especially in the state universities. By 1900 about 70 per cent of all colleges admitted women. Thus trained, they were able to enter such professions as teaching. Two of every three teachers were women by 1900.

2. The Campaign for Equal Rights.

a. STRUGGLE FOR LEGAL EQUALITY. State after state liberalized its laws to allow women to own property, retain their earnings, make contracts, and sue or be sued. By the end of the century this battle was won.

b. STRUGGLE FOR POLITICAL EQUALITY. Agitation for the right to vote was carried on by such reformers as *Elizabeth Cady Stanton* and *Susan B. Anthony*, who organized the *National American Woman Suffrage Association*. By 1895 sixteen states allowed women to vote in school elections and four on taxation bills. *Wyoming* (1890) was the first state to grant full political equality; three other western states followed before 1900. Some sentiment developed for a constitutional amendment to bestow the franchise on women, but this was not secured for another generation.

B. The Attack of the Liquor Traffic. The rising power of the liquor industry, as shown through the _Whiskey Ring_ (see p. 44) strengthened the hand of reformers seeking prohibition. As support mounted, they organized the _Prohibition Party_ (1869) and the _Women's Christian Temperance Union_ (1874), the latter with _Frances E. Willard_ as its guiding spirit. _The Anti-Saloon League_ (1895) was designed to coordinate the efforts of smaller temperance societies. These organizations agitated for expensive licenses for saloons, school education against drinking, and complete prohibition. By 1890 seven states had passed dry laws, while smaller areas elsewhere banned liquor sales under local option. Yet the per capita consumption of liquor trebled between 1860 and 1900.

C. The Problem of Racial Minorities. Two minority groups felt the lash of discrimination: the Negroes and recent immigrants.

1. The Negro Problem. Southern states were left free to handle the Negroes after 1877 when federal troops were withdrawn. Their answer was a _Jim Crow_ system of segregation with separate schools, railroad cars, and the like. This was upheld by the Supreme Court in the _Civil Rights Cases_ (1883), which denied the federal government the right to interfere. After 1890 Negro rights were further restricted by voting requirements that effectively denied them the franchise (see p. 54). Efforts to better conditions were made by such outstanding Negro leaders as _Booker T. Washington,_ who held that the ex-slaves must be educated before they could demand equality. Washington was responsible for founding the Normal and Industrial Institute at Tuskegee, Alabama (1881). Northern philanthropists also provided funds for Negro education; the Peabody Fund (1867) and the Slater Fund (1882) helped establish many schools.

2. The Immigrant Problem. Anti-immigrant sentiment was directed largely against the _new immigration_ (see p. 17) and Orientals. Organized labor was especially insistent that aliens be barred to protect jobs in America. This feeling led Congress to: 1) ban the entry of paupers, criminals, and the insane in 1882, and of any diseased person in

1891; 2) forbid Chinese immigration (1879) in a law that violated the Burlingame Treaty (1868) which had guaranteed a free movement of peoples between the two countries. President Hayes vetoed the bill but drafted a new treaty with China (1880) allowing the United States to restrict immigration. This was done in 1882 for a ten-year period; in 1902 the restriction was made permanent.

V. THE CITY AND CULTURAL PROGRESS.

Urbanization stimulated cultural advance by: 1) allowing people of like interest to mingle for mutual stimulation; 2) providing such cultural facilities as libraries, schools, museums, orchestras, and theaters; 3) concentrating wealth which could then be used for cultural purposes.

A. The Educational Renaissance.

1. Spread of Public Schools. On the lowest school level was the *kindergarten*, which was introduced into the St. Louis school system in 1873 and spread rapidly. *Grammar school* education was made compulsory in state after state, although the rural South did not develop its educational system until after 1900. School enrollments more than doubled between 1870 and 1900, while illiteracy dropped from 20 per cent to 11 per cent. The increase in the number of *high schools* was especially notable as states recognized their obligation to provide secondary education; the 500 high schools operating in 1870 had swelled to 6000 by 1900. On all these levels teaching was greatly improved by: 1) the recognition of teaching as a profession, made possible by the establishment of normal schools in all states; and 2) the popularization of a new philosophy of education propounded by *John Dewey*. Dewey held that the function of a teacher was to interest the pupil in learning rather than to force him to learn. He also taught the need of training for life in the classroom. The better instruction resulting kept many pupils in school.

2. College Education.

a. IMPROVEMENTS IN THE COLLEGES. The renaissance enjoyed by the colleges after the Civil War was due to: 1) the rise of educational leaders who had been well trained in German universities; 2) the *Morrill Act* (1862) which offered federal land grants to states establishing agricultural and engineering schools, thus stimulating the growth of *state universities;* and 3) the financial resources made available by industrialization. Wealthy philanthropists used their fortunes to found such schools as Vanderbilt, Johns Hopkins, Leland Stanford, and the University of Chicago.

b. CHANGES IN THE COLLEGES. The colleges were modernized and improved by: 1) broadening the curriculum to place greater emphasis on practical rather than classical subjects, an innovation that led to the development of the *"elective system"* under Harvard's great president, *Charles W. Eliot;* 2) emphasizing graduate instruction and research, with a corresponding growth of professional training in law, medicine, and other fields. *Daniel Coit Gilman,* president of the *Johns Hopkins University,* was a pioneer in this type of instruction.

3. Adult Education. The *Chautauqua Movement* originated in 1874 when summer instruction was first offered on the banks of Lake Chautauqua in upstate New York. The meetings proved so popular that a four-year course of study and reading was worked out. By 1892 one hundred thousand people were enrolled. The movement soon spread over the United States, with a week of lectures during the summer and reading through the remainder of the year.

4. Public Libraries. All states after the Civil War authorized towns to use tax revenues for public libraries; by the close of the century these libraries existed everywhere. Their spread was stimulated by *Andrew Carnegie,* who began founding town libraries in 1881. By 1900 he had given away $10,000,000 for this purpose. At the same time library methods were improved under the guidance of the *American Library Association* (1876).

5. Newspapers. Daily newspapers increased from 700 in 1870 to 2500 in 1900, while circulation mounted from 2,500,000 to 15,000,000. This growth was partly the result of mechanical improvements, the most important being the invention of the *linotype* by Otto Mergenthaler in 1886. Newspapers also underwent a twofold change: 1) mounting production costs brought increasing control of the press by large corporations, leading to growing editorial conservatism as the papers' viewpoint reflected the attitude of the business office rather than the editor; 2) the nervous tensions of urban life created a demand for colorful and terse news accounts, leading to the rise of *yellow journalism.* The pioneer was *Joseph Pulitzer,* who in 1883 purchased the *New York World.* Using flaming headlines, cartoons, and stories of crime and scandal, he soon made his paper the nation's most profitable. Of his many imitators the most successful was *William Randolph Hearst,* who acquired the *New York Morning Journal* in 1895. The circulation war betwen Pulitzer and Hearst set a new low in journalistic sensationalism.

6. Magazines. Monthly magazines increased from 280 in 1860 to 1800 in 1900. Some were excellent literary or critical journals, the most influential being *The Nation* under the able editorship of *Edwin L. Godkin* (1865-1899). *Harper's Weekly* was also a major political force, largely because of the cartoons of *Thomas Nast.* The modern magazine age, however, did not begin until 1883 when Cyrus H. K. Curtis founded the *Ladies' Home Journal.* Its editor, *Edward W. Bok,* realized that advertising rather than subscriptions could pay printing costs, thus producing an excellent magazine for ten cents. This was the origin of the popular magazine.

B. The Gilded Age. Critics have characterized the postwar era as "The Gilded Age," implying a crassness and lack of taste that was typical of most middle-class Americans. This judgment, however, ignores the remarkable progress made in literature, art, and architecture under the stimulus of industrialization and urbanization.

1. Progress in Literature. In the United States, as in all countries, the advent of the machine age was marked by a gradual shift from romanticism to *realism* as the grim realities of urban life influenced authors. This transformation proceeded in three stages:

a. THE LOCAL COLORISTS. In the 1870's and 1880's a school of writers described pre-Civil War America in faintly realistic terms, although their descriptions were highly romanticized. Each section of the nation had its chroniclers to record the changes wrought by industrialization or to dwell lovingly on the rural past. For the West the principal writers were *Mark Twain, Bret Harte,* and Joaquin Miller. Life in

the Middle West was described by _Edward Eggleston_ and
James Whitcomb Riley. Southern authors who glorified the
plantation life of the prewar era were _Thomas Nelson Page_,
F. Hopkinson Smith, George Washington Cable, and _Joel
Chandler Harris_, author of the Uncle Remus stories. New
England's golden days were recaptured by _Sarah Orne Jew-
ett_ and Mary E. Wilkins Freeman.

     b. THE PSEUDO-REALISTS. Authors of the 1880's and
1890's wrote realistically of American society, but centered
their attention on the upper middle class. _William Dean
Howells_ and _Henry James_ were leaders of this school. Both
presented accurate and merciless pictures of a society adjusting itself to a machine civilization.

     c. THE REALISTS. By the turn of the century, authors
turned their attention to the sufferings of the lower class.
Their pioneer was _Hamlin Garland_, whose _Main-Travelled
Roads_ (1891) painted a savage picture of the drab life of a
Middle-Western farmer. _Stephen Crane's Maggie, A Girl of
the Streets_ (1892), which showed how society turned an
innocent girl into a prostitute, was the first novel to picture
the urban world realistically. Others who wrote in this tradition were _Frank Norris_ and _Jack London_.

     2. Progress in Painting and Sculpture. Scorning tra-
dition, artists executed bold, realistic treatments of the
American landscape and figure which bore little resemblance
to the romanticized portraits of an earlier generation.

     a. PAINTING. American painters trained in France be-
gan returning to the United States in the 1870's. The
Society of American Artists (1877) which they organized
to popularize their less conventional concepts included a
number of excellent artists. _George Inness_ was a leading
landscapist; _Winslow Homer_ was famed for his bold pictures of the sea; _James A. McNeill Whistler_ painted middle-
class portraits realistically. The leading muralist was _John
La Farge_.

     b. SCULPTURE. The foremost of many sculptors was
Augustus Saint-Gaudens, whose statues did much to beautify
the urban landscape. His figure on the tomb of Mrs. Henry
Adams is considered by some to be the best in the history of

American sculpture. *Daniel Chester French,* while less original, was also justly famed.

3. Progress in Architecture. The overornate homes and fantastic jigsaw ornamentation that made the hideous Victorian Gothic buildings of the period even more hideous helped characterize this as the "gilded age." Yet two important developments occurred:

a. RICHARDSON ROMANESQUE ARCHITECTURE was introduced by *Henry Hobson Richardson,* whose first important building was the Trinity Church in Boston (1877). The comparative simplicity of this style, which was based on French Romanesque architecture, set a good example that others eventually imitated.

b. THE SKYSCRAPER was America's unique contribution to architectural beauty. Resulting from the necessity of space saving in urban centers, skyscrapers were first built in Chicago, where tradition was less strong than in the East. The Home Insurance Building (1885) set the pattern by towering ten stories high. The leading skyscraper architect was *Louis Sullivan,* whose emphasis on functionalism as a basis for design has influenced building ever since.

4. Music. American contributions to music were few; only *Edward A. McDowell* earned his reputation as a composer. More significant was the spread of musical appreciation among the people. The *New York Symphony Orchestra* (1878) and the Boston Symphony Orchestra (1881) were followed by others in leading cities. The Metropolitan Opera House in New York was opened in 1883.

VI. THE RISE OF THE CITY: AN APPRAISAL. The city was the crowning monument to American industrialization. In it were focused the best and the worst innovations of the machine age:

A. Harmful Results of Urbanization. The slums, poverty, and class conflicts that centered in cities were the normal products of the transition taking place in American society. The humanitarians who expressed concern for the plight of the poor or who sought to improve the lot of workers did their best to convert the new social order to the uses of the many, but without success. Even today the United

States is seeking a means of adjusting itself to a form of civilization not yet fully understood.

B. Beneficial Results of Urbanization. The rise of the city stimulated cultural progress as had nothing in America's past. The ease with which men of like interests could meet in cities, the wealth made available by a concentration of property, and the educational opportunities offered in thickly settled communities laid the basis for a cultural upsurge of lasting benefit. Even more significant was the gradual adjustment of the arts to the popular taste. The democratization of culture was an American contribution of the machine age.

ADDITIONAL READING

The standard study of urbanization is Arthur M. Schlesinger, *The Rise of the City* (1933). The rise of a gospel of wealth is traced in Ralph H. Gabriel, *The Course of American Democratic Thought* (1940), while the relation of Darwinism to the subject is considered in Richard Hofstadter, *Social Darwinism in American Thought* (1944). R. W. DeForest and L. Veiller, *The Tenement House Problem* (1903), presents contemporary evidence on that subject, as does Jane Addams, *Forty Years at Hull House* (1935). The views of a leading social critic are well presented in G. R. Geiger, *The Philosophy of Henry George* (1933), and of the utopian novelists in Vernon L. Parrington, Jr., *American Dreams* (1948). Two scholarly but readable accounts on the impact of industrialism on the churches are Aaron I. Abell, *The Urban Impact on American Protestantism* (1943), and Henry F. May, *Protestant Churches and Industrial America* (1949). The struggle for women's rights is treated in E. A. Hecker, *A Short History of Women's Rights* (1911). Educational progress is traced in E. P. Cubberley, *Public Education in the United States* (1934), and C. F. Thwing, *History of Higher Education in America* (1909). The standard history of journalism is F. L. Mott, *American Journalism* (1941), while Percy H. Boynton, *Literature and American Life* (1936), gives a satisfactory account of literary developments. Oliver W. Larkin, *Art and Life in America* (1949), brilliantly relates progress in the arts to the social background.

~~~~~~~~~~~~~~~~~~~~~~~~~~~~~~~~

CHAPTER VII

The Populist Era
1890-1900

~~~~~~~~~~~~~~~~~~~~~~~~~~~~~~~~

ℭ THE TRIUMPH OF CONSERVATISM

The conflicts of the industrial age reached a climax during the 1890's. On the one hand farmers and workers, better organized than ever before, demanded a greater share of the national wealth. On the other the masters of capital insisted on the right to operate as they pleased without interference from society or government. In this struggle the industrialists were victorious. By 1900 labor unions had been rendered powerless by the use of the injunction; the Sherman Antitrust Act and the Interstate Commerce Act reduced to uselessness by hostile courts; and the farmers so decisively beaten at the polls that they were ready to abandon their battle for economic equality. Yet the conservative triumph led to an inevitable reaction in the form of the Progressive Movement of the early twentieth century.

I. THE AGRARIAN CRUSADE. Farmer unrest, which had died down after the collapse of the Granger movement in the late 1870's (see pp. 57-60), revived in the 1880's.

A. Causes of the Agrarian Unrest.

1. The Social Factor. The rise of the city made the farmer aware of his own grim existence. As he read of gay times in lighted streets, or at theaters and parties, he grew more discontented with the monotonous drudgery of his own calling.

2. Falling Prices. The price of agricultural staples declined steadily through the 1880's and 1890's, until wheat sold at sixty-three cents a bushel, corn at thirty cents, and cotton at six cents a pound. The prices paid farmers were even lower. They insisted that they could not make money, but each year went further and further into debt.

3. Inadequate Rainfall. For a decade after 1887 rainfall in the West was below normal. On the semiarid plains the resulting droughts ruined thousands of farmers. Even in the Mississippi Valley yields were poor.

4. Mounting Debts. These were acquired during a brief boom period from 1880 to 1887. At this time eastern capitalists, seeking safe investments, sent agents through the West who literally pleaded with farmers to borrow money. The temptation was too strong to resist, especially as farmers reasoned that better machinery or more land would offset falling commodity prices. During the decade, as a result, farm mortgage indebtedness almost doubled. By 1890 there was one mortgage for every two persons in Kansas and North Dakota; one for every three in South Dakota, Minnesota, and Nebraska. In the South the situation was made worse by the _crop-lien system;_ there a farmer mortgaged his growing crop at high interest rates to carry himself until harvest time. If the crop was not profitable, he lost his whole year's income.

5. Growth of Farm Tenancy. Mortgage foreclosures increased as low crop prices prevented farmers from paying their debts. By 1890 one-fourth of the farmers of Kansas were tenants or share croppers. In other western states the situation was nearly as bad. Apparently the United States was developing a peasant class.

B. The Farmers' Solution. Farmers reasoned that a more plentiful money supply would allow them to pay off their debts as well as increase the price of crops. Inflation was their principal demand through the 1880's and 1890's.

1. The Monetary Problem. Three types of money were in circulation in 1890: 1) _greenbacks_ to the set sum of $346,681,012. 2) _National bank notes_ issued by National banks on the basis of government bonds in their vaults. These decreased steadily as the retirement of the national debt canceled bonds; the number in circulation declined from $339,000,000 in 1873 to $168,000,000 in 1890. 3) *Gold coins* which increased in quantity only slowly; so little gold was mined during this period that newly minted coins barely replaced the National bank notes that were retired from circulation. Hence the nation's money supply, which amounted to $2,000,000,000 in 1865, was no larger in 1890 despite a doubled population and a tripled business activity. Farmers maintained that as debtors they suffered especially from the declining purchasing power of the dollar. They pointed out that a dollar that bought one bushel of wheat in 1865 paid for two bushels in 1890. Yet debts did not decline proportionately. This meant that a farm debtor had to produce two bushels of wheat (at fifty cents a bushel) to pay for a dollar he had borrowed when wheat was worth one dollar a bushel.

2. The Answer to the Problem. The farmers' solution was to increase the money supply either by printing more greenbacks or by coining silver dollars.

a. THE GREENBACK INTERLUDE. Congressional enactment of the Resumption Act of 1875, which made greenbacks redeemable in gold, aroused protest in the form of the *Greenback Party* (1878). This demanded the continued circulation of paper money and other reforms. Its nominee in the election of 1880, *James B. Weaver* of Iowa, polled only 300,000 votes, largely from among Mississippi Valley farmers. This meagre support doomed the party, although the fourteen congressmen that it elected joined with Democrats to prevent a further contraction of the number of greenbacks in circulation.

b. FREE SILVER. The farmer knew that large quantities of silver were mined in the West. He also knew that through most of the nation's history both gold and silver coins were minted, a system known as *bimetallism*. This required that the amount of precious metal in both types of coins be exactly balanced: that the gold in a gold dollar be worth just as much as the silver in a silver dollar. For some time this ratio had been 16 to 1; there had been sixteen times as much silver in a silver dollar as there was gold in a gold dollar. This ratio had been upset by the gold discoveries after 1849.

So much was mined that it became less valuable, in relation to silver, than this ratio recognized. Hence silver dollars disappeared from circulation as they were melted down for the commercial sale of the precious metal. Congress recognized this situation in 1873 by ordering that no more silver dollars be coined, placing the country on a gold basis. No sooner was this done than new silver mines were opened. This metal became so plentiful that, if coined into dollars, the money supply would be greatly inflated. Farmers realized too late that the *Crime of 1873* (the Coinage Act mentioned above) had deprived them of a cheaper circulating medium. They demanded that the law be repealed and the *free and unlimited coinage of silver at the ratio of 16 to 1* be restored.

C. Stages of Organization. Once more, as in the Granger period, farmers organized to agitate for *"free silver."*

1. The Farmers' Alliances. Organization began in the South with the formation of the National Farmers' Alliance (1879) and the Agricultural Wheel (1882). These were combined in 1887 as the *Southern Farmers' Alliance,* with three million members. In the meantime the *Northern Farmers' Alliance,* formed in 1880, attracted two million members by 1890. Delegates from the northern and southern Alliances met in 1889 to agree upon a common program. This included support for free silver, a graduated income tax, government ownership of the railroads, and other reforms. Independent local parties based on this platform placed Alliance candidates in many offices in the *elections of 1890,* as well as sending fifty-three congressmen to Washington. Their success was due to the fanatical enthusiasm of the farmers. This was engendered by such inspirational speakers as *Pitchfork Ben Tillman* of South Carolina, *Sockless Jerry Simpson* of Kansas, *Ignatius Donnelly* of Minnesota, *James B. Weaver* of Iowa, and *Mary Lease* of Kansas, who won a place in every history textbook by urging farmers to "raise less corn and more Hell."

2. The Populist Party. Encouraged by their success in 1890, representatives of northern and southern Alliances met at Cincinnati in May, 1891, to form a new party. This they called the *People's Party,* or Populist Party. A second convention held at Omaha on July 4, 1892, nominated *James B. Weaver* as the party's presidential candidate and adopted the *Omaha Platform,* which promised a long list of progressive reforms: 1) free silver at the ratio of 16 to 1; 2) a circulating medium of $50 a person; 3) economy in government; 4) a graduated income tax; 5) postal savings banks; 6) government ownership of railroads and telegraph lines; 7) the direct election of senators; 8) the use of the initiative and referendum. This platform remained the ideal of progressives for a generation.

II. POLITICAL DEVELOPMENTS, 1892-1896.

A. The Election of 1892. The two principal issues were the Tariff (see pp. 51-54) and the money question. The Democrats nominated *Grover Cleveland,* whose support for a lower tariff was made clear during his first administration (1885-1889). *Benjamin Harrison* was renominated by the Republicans, despite his mediocre record between 1889 and 1892. Cleveland was elected by 277 electoral votes to 145 for Harrison. The remaining 22 electoral votes went to *James B. Weaver,* the *People's Party* candidate, who received a million popular votes. Cleveland's election was due primarily to hatred of the *McKinley Tariff* (see p. 54) and to his reputation for honesty.

B. The Second Cleveland Administration. The tariff and money issues that had so influenced the election remained the principal problems.

1. The Tariff Problem. Cleveland interpreted his election as a popular mandate for a lower tariff, especially as the McKinley Tariff had turned a $100,000,000 surplus in 1890 into a $70,000,000 deficit by 1894. Administration views were incorporated in the *Wilson Bill,* drafted by William L. Wilson, chairman of the House Ways and Means Committee. As adopted by the House in February, 1894, this was designed to increase the revenue while decreasing protection. Basic raw materials used in manufacturing—sugar, lumber, wool, iron ore, etc.—were admitted duty free while duties on manufactured goods were lowered. To offset the loss of revenue, higher taxes were levied on liquor, tobacco, and other luxuries. The bill also included the country's first

income tax: a 2 per cent levy on incomes over $4000. The
senate quickly ended Cleveland's hope of tariff reform.
Under the influence of a swarm of lobbyists and such pro-
tectionist Democrats as *A. P. Gorham* of Maryland, 634
amendments were added, most of them revising levels upward. The *Wilson-Gorham Tariff* (1894) lowered duties
slightly, to about 40 per cent, but continued protection.
Cleveland's hopes suffered another blow when the Supreme
Court ruled in the case of *Pollock v. Farmers' Loan and
Trust Company* (1895) that an income tax was unconstitutional.

2. The Money Problem.

a. BACKGROUND OF THE PROBLEM. Before Cleveland's
election Congress had made two concessions to inflationists:
1) the *Bland-Allison Act* (1878) required the Secretary of
the Treasury to purchase from $2,000,000 to $4,000,000
worth of silver bullion monthly for coinage into dollars; and
2) the *Sherman Silver Purchase Act* (1890) increased the
amount of silver that the Treasury Department was forced
to purchase to 4,500,000 ounces a month—about double the
former quantity. This silver bullion was paid for in legal-
tender treasury notes, redeemable in either gold or silver as
the government decreed. The practice was always followed
of redeeming the notes in gold, thus preserving the gold
standard. Hence the measures did little to satisfy the silverites.

b. THE PANIC OF 1893. The money problem became
acute after the *Panic of 1893*. This was caused by: 1) the
decline of farmer purchasing power, which decreased the
demand for manufactured goods; 2) a European depression
which curtailed foreign markets; 3) speculative overinvest-
ment in railroads and industrial plants; and 4) fears created
among businessmen by the threat of free silver. This last
was the immediate cause of the panic. For some time financiers had agreed that the nation's finances would remain
sound only so long as the gold reserve—set up in 1879 to
redeem greenbacks—remained over $100,000,000. After
the passage of the Sherman Silver Purchase Act this reserve
was subjected to unusual pressure as both greenbacks and
silver certificates were redeemed. Only a few weeks after

Cleveland's inauguration it dipped below $100,000,000. As fear spread, people rushed to obtain gold for their Greenbacks or treasury notes, further depleting the fund. In the resulting panic, business failures mounted, banks closed, 156 railroads went into receivership, and unemployment mounted until 4,000,000 men were out of work by the summer of 1894. So desperate was their plight that an army of unemployed from the Middle West, led by "General" Jacob Coxey, marched on Washington to demand a work-relief program financed by noninterest-paying bonds. *"Coxey's Army"* aroused more ridicule than sympathy.

    c. CLEVELAND AND THE PANIC. Cleveland, a hard-money man, believed that the depression would end only when the public's confidence in the nation's currency was reestablished by banishing the threat of inflation. Hence he took two steps:

    I. *Repeal of Sherman Silver Purchase Act.* Congress was called into special session in August, 1893, to repeal the Sherman Silver Purchase Act (November, 1893), thus easing the strain on the gold reserve.

    II. *Bond Issues.* Gold was borrowed from private interests to rebuild the gold reserve. The first bond issue of $50,000,000 (January, 1894) failed to accomplish this purpose, for the Wall Street syndicate making the loan simply drew gold from the treasury to pay for their bond purchases. A second issue (January, 1895) succeeded when the government stipulated that half the gold must be obtained from abroad. When a third issue of $100,000,000 was floated in January, 1896, public confidence returned and the depression ended. Cleveland's action, however, convinced farmers and workers that he had sold out to Wall Street, preparing the way for a revival of Populism.

III. THE ELECTION OF 1896.

A. Western Discontent. The agrarian revolt reached a climax between 1894 and 1896. This was due to:

    1. Western Drought. Conditions were at their worst in 1894 and 1895.

    2. Falling Farm Prices. Prices hit new lows as a result of the Panic of 1893, until wheat sold at forty-nine cents a bushel and cotton at six cents a pound.

3. Government Conservatism. Events of 1894-1895 seemed to indicate that both major parties were acting in the interests of Wall Street rather than those of the common people. These included: 1) passage of the Wilson-Gorham Tariff; 2) the smashing of the Pullman strike; 3) the outlawing of the income tax by the Supreme Court; 4) the judicial negation of the Sherman Antitrust Act in the Knight case; 5) the treatment suffered by Coxey's Army; and 6) Cleveland's repeal of the Sherman Silver Purchase Act and his reliance on Wall Street in ending the panic. Many ordinary people were convinced by these events that only the Populist Party had their interests at heart.

4. Effective Propaganda. In the West a small book by William H. Harvey, *Coin's Financial School* (1894), argued for free silver in a language that the common man could understand. It sold 100,000 copies monthly during this period. In the East Henry Demarest Lloyd's *Wealth Against Commonwealth* (1894) convinced thousands that the democratic process had broken down under pressure from Wall Street.

B. Growth of Populist Strength. Under the influence of these forces, enthusiasm for Populism took on some of the fervor of a holy crusade. In the West and South speakers such as *Tom Watson* of Georgia and *Ignatius Donnelly* of Minnesota were cheered by excited thousands. The Populist popular vote in the 1894 elections was half again as large as in 1892, and six Populist senators were sent to Washington. The real gainers, however, were the Republicans, who capitalized on lower-class dissatisfaction with Cleveland to win control of both House and Senate. The Populists, encouraged by their showing, looked forward to the election of 1896.

C. The Nominating Conventions. Populist leaders were aware that large "free-silver blocs" existed in both major parties. Hence they decided to let the Republicans and Democrats stage their nominating conventions first, confident that these silverites would bolt when the parties endorsed a gold standard. The People's Party would then gather in the malcontents, increasing its own strength.

MAJOR POLITICAL PARTIES IN POWER   1853-1881

1853   1857   1861   1865   1869   1873   1877   1881

LINCOLN-JOHNSON   GRANT   HAYES

REPUBLICAN

PIERCE   BUCHANAN

DEMOCRATIC

1. The Republican Convention. The Republicans, confident of victory over the depression-discredited Democrats, assembled in June. Their convention was dominated by *Marcus A. Hanna,* a wealthy Ohio industrialist who had entered politics to satisfy a lust for power. Under his tutelage they nominated *William McKinley* of Ohio, author of the McKinley Tariff and an unwavering conservative. The platform denounced Cleveland's record, praised protection, and advocated a gold currency. On its adoption thirty-four *Silver Republicans,* led by Senator *Henry M. Teller* of Colorado, walked out, announcing that they would support any party favoring free silver.

MAJOR POLITICAL PARTIES IN POWER   1897-1921

1897   1901   1905   1909   1913   1917   1921

REPUBLICAN

McKINLEY·   T. ROOSEVELT   T. ROOSEVELT   TAFT

DEMOCRATIC

WILSON

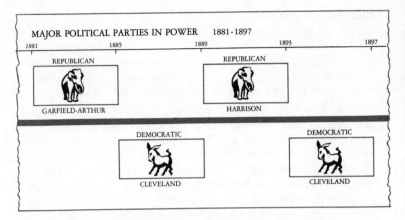

MAJOR POLITICAL PARTIES IN POWER 1881-1897

1881   1885   1889   1893   1897

REPUBLICAN
GARFIELD-ARTHUR

REPUBLICAN
HARRISON

DEMOCRATIC
CLEVELAND

DEMOCRATIC
CLEVELAND

2. The Democratic Convention. The Democrats were divided when they met in Chicago on July 7, 1896. Southern and western delegates, led by _William Jennings Bryan_ of Nebraska, had been agitating for free silver since 1894, while eastern representatives favored a sound money. The inflationists showed their strength when the platform committee proposed "the free and unlimited coinage of both gold and silver at the present legal ratio of sixteen to one." After supporting this proposition vigorously, they finally carried the day when Bryan delivered his _Cross of Gold speech,_ in which he told the delegates: "You shall not press down upon the brow of labor this crown of thorns; you

MAJOR POLITICAL PARTIES IN POWER   1921-1953

1921   1925   1929   1933   1937   1941   1945   1949   1953

REPUBLICAN
HARDING-COOLIDGE HOOVER

DEMOCRATIC
F. D. ROOSEVELT-TRUMAN

Charts by *Graphics Institute, N. Y. C.*   From: Muzzey—*A History of Our Country,* New Edition, Ginn & Co.

shall not crucify mankind upon a cross of gold." Swept away by this oratory, the convention endorsed free silver and nominated the thirty-six-year-old Bryan as its candidate. The platform was a progressive document that stole much Populist thunder by favoring reduced tariffs, antitrust legislation, and the outlawing of the injunction in labor disputes.

3. The Populist Convention. Populist leaders faced a dilemma: if they nominated their own candidate they would split the silverite vote and hand the election to the Republicans; if they endorsed Bryan's nomination they would submerge their own party. Believing that the nation's salvation depended on a more flexible currency, they did not hesitate. Bryan was selected as the party's nominee, but Tom Watson of Georgia was named vice-presidential candidate rather than the Maine banker, Arthur Sewall, selected by the Democrats. The platform not only advocated free silver but many of the liberal reforms contained in the Omaha Platform of 1892.

D. Campaign and Election.

1. The Campaigns. The *Battle of the Standards*—silver and gold—was bitterly fought. Party lines were ignored as silver Republicans supported Bryan and gold Democrats favored McKinley. Bryan gave thousands of speeches on an 18,000-mile tour, while the Republicans used a $4,000,000 fund to spread advertisements, tracts, and other propaganda everywhere. Newspapers reflected the conservatism of their owners by ridiculing Bryan; industrialists warned their workers that factories would be closed if the Democrats were successful. To make matters worse for Bryan, farm prices advanced sharply during the autumn of 1896, driven upward by grain failures in Russia and Argentina. This, combined with bountiful harvests in the United States, convinced many farmers that their fears were unjustified.

2. Results of the Election. The result was a decisive Republican victory. McKinley's popular vote was 600,000 greater than Bryan's, while the electoral vote was 271 to 176. Republicans carried the Northeast and Middle West; Democrats the South and West.

IV. THE McKINLEY ADMINISTRATION, 1897-

1901. Foreign affairs occupied most of McKinley's attention (see pp. 105-110), but two domestic issues were settled:

A. The Tariff Question. McKinley interpreted his victory as a mandate for protection. With both houses Republican, he called a special session of Congress immediately after his inauguration to enact the _Dingley Tariff_ (1897), which raised duties to a 57 per cent average—the highest in history. Returning prosperity after the Panic of 1893 allowed the Republicans to boast that the tariff was responsible, thus removing the issue from politics for a decade.

B. The Money Question. Prosperity also allowed the Republicans to deal firmly with the currency problem, especially as farm prices continued to rise through 1897 with crop failures in Europe. Sensing the decline of agrarian discontent, McKinley urged Congress to settle the currency issue forever. The result was the _Gold-Standard Act_ (1900) which made all forms of money redeemable in gold, at the same time increasing the gold reserve to $150,000,000.

V. AN APPRAISAL OF A DECADE OF CONSERVATISM.

A. The Triumph of Conservatism. The Populist era closed with conservatism completely triumphant. McKinley's election was only one part of a broad pattern of victory that included protective tariffs, the defeat of the income tax, judicial approval of the labor injunction, the negation of the Sherman Antitrust Act, and the imperialism of the Spanish-American War (see pp. 105-107). Farmers and workers had some reason to feel by 1900 that the cause of progressivism was permanently lost.

B. Nature of the Issues. Actually the battles of the 1890's were not fought between "conservatives" on the one hand and "radicals" on the other, nor was the progressive defeat more than temporary. Considered broadly, the farmers who supported Bryan were more conservative than the industrialists who espoused McKinley's cause. Their inspiration was not Karl Marx but Thomas Jefferson. They wanted a return to an earlier day when farmers shaped the nation's policies in the interest of agrarianism, when free competition rather than monopolistic greed regulated prices, when natural economic laws rather than a "money power" governed the flow of currency, and when the people rather than lobbyists for special interests controlled the government. In their insistence on a return to the practices of an earlier day the Populists were the true "conservatives."

C. Implications for the Future. Because the Populists' demands were in keeping with the American tradition, they could not be long denied. After the turn of the century, when the Progressive Period allowed the people to regain partial control of their nation's government and economy, the liberal program outlined in the Omaha Platform was gradually realized.

ADDITIONAL READING

Solon J. Buck, *The Agrarian Crusade* (1921), deals with the whole history of agrarianism, but a more satisfactory account of this period is in John D. Hicks, *The Populist Revolt* (1931). The economic backgrounds of Populism are considered in Fred A. Shannon, *The Farmer's Last Frontier* (1945). Chester McA. Destler, *American Radicalism* (1946), relates Populism to the broader postwar discontent, as does Nathan Fine, *Labor and Farmer Parties in the United States* (1928). Fred E. Haynes, *James Baird Weaver* (1919), deals fully with the Greenback Party, while two excellent biographies of Populist leaders are C. Vann Woodward, *Tom Watson* (1938), and Francis B. Simkins, *Pitchfork Ben Tillman* (1944). Allan Nevins, *Grover Cleveland* (1934), presents the viewpoint of the conservative wing of the Democratic Party. The complicated financial story is clearly presented in Davis R. Dewey, *Financial History of the United States* (1922). A colorful contemporary account of the 1896 election is in William Jennings Bryan's *The First Battle* (1896).

CHAPTER VIII

America and the World

1877-1900

⟪ **THE END OF GEOGRAPHIC ISOLATION**
Industrialization was responsible for a transformation in American foreign policy; each year after the Civil War the United States played a larger role in world affairs until by 1900 it had become an imperialistic nation, with colonies scattered over the globe and a prominent voice in international affairs. The overseas areas that interested the people, however, remained those of the prewar era. Americans were still indifferent to Europe and Africa, but increasingly concerned with Latin America and Asia. Interest in the southern hemisphere resulted from the application of the Monroe Doctrine to that region; interest in the Pacific area followed a pattern established by the China traders of the early Republic and implemented by such diplomatic steps as the commercial treaty with China of 1844 and Commodore Matthew Perry's opening of Japan to American trade in 1853.

I. THE ORIGINS OF AMERICAN IMPERIAL-ISM. America's new world role was forced on the nation by developments at home and abroad.

A. Causes for Growth of Imperialism.

1. The International Scene.

a. WORLD TRADE. Industrialization led to a demand for markets and raw materials. Hence the foreign trade of the United States increased from $400,000,000 in 1865 to $1,600,000,000 in 1890. More important than this expansion was the fact that more and more manufactured goods were exported. These could best be sold in the "underdeveloped" countries, whose primitive peoples were in constant danger of being engulfed by Europe's imperialistic powers unless the United States took them first. Diplomacy was needed to keep these markets open.

b. CAPITAL INVESTMENTS. Industrialization increased the amount of American capital available for investment. Financiers, seeking high interest returns, turned to underdeveloped areas where the risk was greatest and the rates correspondingly higher. Having made these investments they called on the government to protect their capital. Between 1870 and 1900 the sums invested abroad increased from nothing to $500,000,000.

c. THE EUROPEAN EXAMPLE. After the Franco-Prussian War (1871), newly united Germany and Italy entered the rush for colonial possessions, grabbing off such extensive territories in Africa and Asia that the other powers moved into action. In the scramble that followed, most of the primitive areas of the world were appropriated. The United States, increasingly aware of its physical pre-eminence among nations, hurried to get its share before everything was taken.

2. The Domestic Scene.

a. THE CLOSING OF THE FRONTIER. The gradual exhaustion of western lands, climaxed by the announcement in 1890 that the frontier no longer existed, bred expansionistic sentiment among the American people. With their own frontier closed they demanded lands elsewhere to which they could move.

b. IMPERIALISTIC PROPAGANDA. Numerous writers during the 1880's and 1890's urged overseas expansion. Typical was the Reverend Josiah Strong, whose book, *Our Country* (1885), proclaimed Anglo-Saxon superiority and stressed the nation's duty to extend its civilization over "backward" peoples everywhere. Equally important was Captain *Alfred T. Mahan,* a retired naval officer, whose numerous books glorified a large navy and preached the *Manifest Destiny* of the United States to rule "lesser" people.

c. Missionary Pressure. Overseas missionaries had been active since the 1820's, particularly in the Pacific area. Now they demanded government aid, pointing out that the conversion of the "benighted heathen" would be easier under American rule. Their appeal was backed by many religious people.

d. Naval Pressure. America's modern navy originated in 1883 when Congress authorized the first steel cruisers. From that time on construction proceeded rapidly, until by 1893 the United States stood fifth in naval strength among the world's powers, and in 1900, third. Such a weapon tempted the people to test its strength.

B. Growth of Internationalism. The new global consciousness of the United States was shown by its willingness to enter into:

1. Collective Treaties. Between 1865 and 1900 fifteen treaties were signed dealing with such matters as cables, weights and measures, patents, etc.

2. International Agreements. Most famous of these was the _Geneva Convention_ (1882) to establish the International Red Cross. This was largely the result of personal efforts by an American woman, _Clara Barton,_ who was also responsible for the "American Amendment" (1884) allowing the Red Cross to undertake peacetime relief programs.

II. AMERICAN POLICY IN THE PACIFIC, 1877-1895.

A. The Hawaiian Islands.

1. Origins of Hawaiian Policy. American traders, whalers, and missionaries first interested the United States in the Hawaiian Islands during the early nineteenth century. In 1842 the State Department announced that the islands would not be open to colonization by any other nation, but a treaty of annexation was defeated by the Senate a few years later. The next important step was the _Reciprocity Treaty of 1875_ which gave sugar and other native products the right to enter the United States duty free in return for a pledge by the Hawaiian king not to dispose of his territory to any other power. In 1884 the United States leased the excellent naval base at Pearl Harbor.

2. Steps Toward Annexation.

a. SUGAR AND THE TARIFF. The Reciprocity Treaty of 1875 stimulated sugar production. By 1890 sugar plantations owned by Americans were valued at $25,000,000 while the island's exports of $20,000,000 yearly all went to the United States. This thriving trade was upset by the _McKinley Tariff_ (1890), which placed all sugar on the free list and provided for bounties to American sugar growers. Moreover, a native ruler, Queen Liluokalani, or _Queen Lil_ as she was called, who had just ascended the Hawaiian throne, determined to confiscate all plantations and drive foreigners from the islands. Under these circumstances the sugar planters determined to seek American annexation; this would protect their estates from Queen Lil and also place their sugar within the tariff wall.

b. PROBLEM OF ANNEXATION. The planters, probably with the aid of the American minister, staged a revolution in January, 1893, then asked to be annexed. President _Benjamin Harrison_ was willing, but before a treaty could be negotiated _Grover Cleveland_ became President (March 4, 1893). A foe of imperialism, he withdrew the annexation treaty after investigation showed that the revolution did not represent native wishes. He did extend _recognition_ to the American-dominated government of the _Republic of Hawaii._

B. The Samoan Islands.

1. Origins of American Interest.
The Samoan Islands of the South Pacific had been visited by sailors and missionaries since the 1830's. In 1872 a naval officer negotiated an agreement that gave the United States the fine harbor of _Pago Pago_ on the island of Tutuila; this arrangement was embodied in a formal treaty in 1878.

2. Efforts Toward Annexation.
The United States showed no desire to annex the islands until the 1880's when Germany and England also became interested in them. A musical-comedy war between adherents of these three powers reached a climax in 1889 when a German threat of annexation drew naval vessels of the three powers to the harbor at Pago Pago. The threat of conflict passed when a hurricane wrecked the fleets. Instead, the three nations entered into a _tripartite protectorate_ over the islands, the first "entangling

alliance" in the history of the United States. This was terminated in 1899 when the islands were divided between Germany and the United States, England receiving compensation elsewhere.

III. LATIN-AMERICAN POLICY, 1877-1895.

A. Pan-Americanism. Until the 1870's the United States interpreted the *Monroe Doctrine* in a negative way: as an instrument to keep European nations from meddling in the western hemisphere. After that time the doctrine was transformed into a positive device to secure for the United States political primacy and economic favoritism among the American Republics.

1. International Arbitration. The United States first displayed its new aggressivism by offering to serve as mediator in disputes between Latin-American countries. Thus a boundary dispute between Argentina and Paraguay was settled in 1876, another between Mexico and Guatemala considered in 1881, and an attempt made to stop a war between Chile, Peru, and Bolivia over the nitrate districts of Tacna and Arica. England and the United States also arbitrated (1891) the *Bering Sea Controversy* between Canadian and American seal fishermen.

2. Pan-American Congresses.

a. ORIGINS OF THE CONGRESSES. The originator was *James G. Blaine,* Secretary of State under Garfield (1881) and Harrison (1889-1892). Knowing that the Latin-American countries sold most of their raw materials to the United States, yet purchased their manufactured goods in Europe, he proposed to secure a share of this market for American manufacturers by setting up a customs union. This would give Latin-American goods reciprocal preference in American ports in return for similar concessions by South American countries. His purpose in calling the first Pan-American Congress was to arrange this reciprocity.

b. THE FIRST CONGRESS. Blaine called the first Congress in 1889 when delegates from eighteen countries met at Washington. His proposal of a customs union aroused no interest among the Latin Americans, who knew that 87 per cent of their goods entered the United States duty free.

Hence the sole result of the conference was the creation of the _Pan-American Union_ to serve as a clearing house for commercial information. Blaine obtained acceptance for his reciprocal trade plan when the McKinley Tariff (1890) included provisions for reciprocity with ten countries, but the policy was not generally adopted until the administration of Franklin D. Roosevelt.

B. Threats to Latin-American Friendship. Two incidents upset any international good will created by Blaine's Pan-Americanism:

1. The Chilean Episode. The United States minister to Chile, _Patrick Egan_, adopted a hostile attitude toward a new government that took control of the country after a revolution in 1890-1891. The controversy reached a climax in October, 1891, when two American sailors were killed and eighteen wounded during a barroom brawl in Valparaiso. President Benjamin Harrison treated this fight as an international incident, demanding satisfaction which the Chilean government was unwilling to give. War was averted by the election of a new government in Chile, but the attitude of the United States left a bad impression throughout Latin America.

2. The Venezuelan Boundary Dispute. An ancient boundary dispute between Venezuela and British Guiana assumed new importance with the discovery of gold in the disputed area. Venezuela was willing to arbitrate, but England refused. Acting on the assumption that Britain's attitude violated the Monroe Doctrine by threatening the territory of a Latin-American power, President _Grover Cleveland_ through his Secretary of State, _Richard Olney_, on July 20, 1895, warned that "grave consequences" would follow unless the British acceded. They answered in a blunt message (November 26, 1895) stating that the Monroe Doctrine was not involved and that the United States had no right to intervene. Cleveland then asked Congress to appoint a boundary commission whose findings the United States would enforce in any way necessary. Although Congress responded to this request, the President was condemned by newspapers and business leaders for creating a war scare. English opinion was also outspoken for peace.

This popular attitude, combined with the approach of the *Boer War* in Africa, forced England to back down and submit the dispute to arbitration. A tribunal eventually awarded most of the disputed area to British Guiana (1899). The incident not only strengthened the Monroe Doctrine but gave the United States new prestige in European eyes. The unexpected show of power, however, alarmed Latin Americans.

IV. THE SPANISH-AMERICAN WAR. The final break in cordial relations between the United States and Latin America came with the Spanish-American War.

A. The Cuban Question.

1. Background. The United States had been interested in Cuba for half a century. Its attitude was shown in the *Ten Years' War* (1868-1878) in which Cubans fought to free their island from Spain. During this struggle many filibustering expeditions from American ports aided the rebels. One vessel, the *Virginius,* was captured by Spain (1873) and eight Americans executed. War threatened until Spain apologized and paid an indemnity. The Ten Years' War ended with the Spanish victorious and the Cubans burdened with even heavier war taxes.

2. Changing American Attitude. Between the Ten Years' War and the 1890's the United States became much more interested in Cuba. This was due to:

a. ECONOMIC PENETRATION. American capital flowed into Cuba during the 1880's until investments there totaled $50,000,000 by 1893, while trade with the island amounted to $100,000,000 yearly. Moreover, the United States was dependent on Cuban sugar.

b. STRATEGIC INTERESTS. The growth of the navy made strategists aware of the need for Caribbean naval bases, especially as plans matured for a canal across Central America. Cuban bases would be necessary to protect this.

c. SPIRIT OF MANIFEST DESTINY. As Americans wakened to the fact that the United States was a major power, they paid increasing attention to the plight of "backward" people. The country's imperialistic destiny was the theme of Congressional orators such as *Albert J. Beveridge* and *Henry Cabot Lodge,* and of such scholars as Frank H. Giddings and John W. Burgess. Jingoistic newspapers also preached the need of expansion into "backward" areas. As a result the American people were far more ready to accept war with Spain in the 1890's than in the 1870's.

d. NEWSPAPER PROPAGANDA. Led by the *New York World* of *Joseph Pulitzer* and the *New York Journal* of *William Randolph Hearst,* the nation's "yellow press" was ready to use sensationalism as a circulation-builder, no matter what the cost. Warfare in Cuba allowed papers to print atrocity stories that aroused a demand for intervention.

3. The Cuban Revolution. A new revolt against Spain began in Cuba in February, 1895. This was caused by: 1) the continued autocratic rule of Spain; 2) the exploitation of Cuban peasants by Spanish landlords; and 3) the *tariff policy* of the United States. The latter was important. The McKinley Tariff (1890), which placed sugar on the free list, encouraged the expansion of sugar growing on the island. This was followed by the Wilson-Gorham Tariff (1894) which levied a 40 per cent duty on Cuban sugar, ruining the island's economy. The suffering that resulted drove the Cubans to revolt. In the fighting that followed, the insurgents adopted a policy of guerrilla warfare. The Spanish army, unable to capture the actual rebels, threw thousands of peasants into *Reconcentrados,* or concentration camps, where they died like flies. In one province alone, 50,000 perished.

4. American Interest in the Revolution.

a. SYMPATHY WITH THE CUBANS. This was fanned by newspaper accounts of suffering in the concentration camps. The *New York World* and the *New York Journal* particularly vied with each other in printing atrocity stories under blazing headlines. War was also demanded after a Spanish gunboat fired on an American ship, the *Alliance*.

b. POLICY OF GROVER CLEVELAND. Cleveland, who was President when the Cuban revolution began, did all in his power to preserve neutrality. Although recognizing a state of rebellion in Cuba, he refused to recognize the revolutionists as belligerents, despite a congressional resolution favoring such a step (1896).

c. POLICY OF WILLIAM McKINLEY. McKinley was elected (1896) on a platform calling for Cuban independence.

I. _Events Leading to War._ McKinley's firm attitude toward Spain forced that country to modify its _reconcentración_ policy (1897) and to offer the Cubans a larger share of self-government. The Cubans refused, insisting on independence. At this point two events occurred that plunged the United States into war : 1) the publication of the _De Lome Letter_ (February, 1898), written by Dupuy de Lome, the Spanish minister to Washington. In this private letter, which was stolen from the Havana post office, he called McKinley a would-be politician interested only in the plaudits of the crowd. Spain's refusal to disavow the letter aroused great indignation. 2) The _sinking of the battleship Maine_ in Havana Harbor on February 15, 1898. The vessel was sunk by an external explosion with a loss of 260 men.

II. _Preparation for War._ The sinking of the _Maine_ united American opinion behind war. Congress appropriated $50,000,000 for military purposes, but McKinley still sought to maintain the peace desired by financial and business interests. On March 27, 1898, he sent an ultimatum to Spain, asking an immediate armistice, the end of the _reconcentración_ policy, and American mediation of peace terms. The Spanish queen accepted the armistice proposal on April 9, apparently ending the threat of war.

III. _Declaration of War._ Despite Spain's retreat, the popular clamor for war was so great that McKinley feared he would sacrifice the leadership of his party unless he acceded. Hence he sent a message to Congress on April 11 that ignored Spain's concessions and asked for a declaration of war. Congress responded on _April 17._ At the same time it adopted the _Teller Amendment_ which pledged the United States to acquire no Cuban territory and to turn the island over to its people as soon as their independence was won.

B. The Defeat of Spain. The war was so popular in the United States that a special bond issue of $200,000,000 was subscribed at once and additional taxes accepted without protest. These funds were used to raise the regular army from 28,000 to 62,000 men and to equip 200,000 volunteers.

Spain still enjoyed a military advantage, with an army of 200,000 men in Cuba and a navy that outranked that of the United States.

1. The War in Cuba. An expeditionary force of 15,000 Americans landed near Santiago, Cuba, between June 20 and June 25, 1898. The 1700 Spanish troops opposing them were defeated at the battles of El Caney and _San Juan Hill._ In the latter, volunteer cavalry recruited by _Colonel Theodore Roosevelt,_ the "Rough Riders," gained the fame that helped make Roosevelt president. _Santiago_ fell on July 13, 1898. The seven Spanish vessels in the harbor fled, but all were destroyed by a blockading American squadron. At the same time the bloodless conquest of Spanish Puerto Rico was begun by troops under General Nelson A. Miles.

2. The War in the Pacific. As soon as war was declared, Commodore _George Dewey,_ with six cruisers, set out from Hong Kong for the Spanish-owned Philippines. On May 1, 1898, he ran the guns at _Manila Bay_ and destroyed the entire Spanish fleet of seven vessels without losing an American life. The city of Manila was then besieged with the help of natives under _Emilio Aguinaldo_ who were fighting for Filipino independence. Manila fell on August 13. In the meantime a lone cruiser captured _Guam_ and other tiny islands scattered widely over the Pacific.

3. Cost of the War. Only 289 Americans were killed in battle, yet for every one of these, thirteen died of disease. At one time 75 per cent of the troops in Cuba were sick with yellow fever or malaria, despite the efficiency of the Red Cross. Improper clothing, inadequate health measures, and faulty medical knowledge were responsible. Public criticism led to an important discovery. In 1900 an army medical board under Major _Walter Reed_ proved that yellow fever was transmitted by the bite of a species of mosquito. This knowledge allowed the subsequent American penetration of Central America with a minimum of risk from disease.

4. The Peace Terms.

a. THE TREATY OF PEACE. After three months of war, Spain began peace negotiations which ended in an armistice on August 12, 1898. The final peace treaty was signed at

Paris on December 10, 1898, after being dictated by the American commissioners. Cuba was handed over to the United States until it was ready for independence, while Puerto Rico and Guam were also annexed. The Philippines were taken but Spain was paid $20,000,000 in return.

b. THE PHILIPPINE QUESTION. The annexation of the Philippines marked a break with tradition. They were part of the Asiatic coast line, inhabited by an alien people, offered no room for American expansion, and could never expect statehood. McKinley apparently did not intend taking them when the war ended, but changed his mind between August and December, 1898, because: 1) the American people, who had been made imperialistically minded overnight by their military victories, demanded annexation; 2) businessmen awakened to the possibility of trade with millions of Orientals through the Philippine gateway; 3) missionaries who wanted the islands to safeguard their efforts emphasized the "white man's burden"; and 4) strategists insisted that if the United States did not take them, Germany or Japan would. The latter danger was made clear during the war when the presence of a German fleet near Manila precipitated a series of incidents that made scare headlines in the United States.

c. THE CONTEST OVER RATIFICATION. Anti-imperialistic sentiment was first shown when the treaty was placed before the Senate. The spokesman for this point of view was *George F. Hoar* of Massachusetts, a Republican, who argued that annexation of the Philippines would submit the natives to rule without their own consent. Imperialists, led by *Albert J. Beveridge* of Indiana, stressed the commercial and strategic advantages of ownership, and deplored *"hauling down the flag."* Their arguments triumphed when the treaty was ratified (February 6, 1898) by a two-vote majority.

V. THE NEW PACIFIC POLICY, 1895-1900. Ownership of the Philippines committed the United States to a more aggressive policy on the Far East. That this met popular favor was shown in July, 1898, when the *Hawaiian Islands* were annexed with scarcely a dissenting voice raised. The nation's destiny now required naval bases, no matter how acquired.

A. The Chinese Problem. The Sino-Japanese War (1894-1895), in which the Japanese wrested Formosa and other areas from China, demonstrated to European powers the weakness of the Chinese Empire. The result was a mad scramble for territorial concessions there; during the next five years England, France, Germany, and Russia obtained naval bases, ports, and spheres of influence. This alarmed the United States, where businessmen realized that the Philippines would be valueless if all China was closed to American trade. Missionaries also insisted that they could continue to operate in the Far East only with government protection.

B. The Open Door Policy. Great Britain was as concerned as the United States, for her trade with China was also threatened. In 1898 she proposed a joint alliance to protect trading rights, but this was rejected. Instead, _John Hay_, McKinley's able Secretary of State, in September, 1899, issued a series of notes to the powers, asking them to accept an _Open Door Policy_ in China. This meant that all nations controlling portions of China would grant free trading opportunities—including equal tariffs, railroad rates, and harbor duties—to all nations. When all but Russia agreed, Hay announced the Open Door Policy to be in operation.

C. The Boxer Rebellion. Aroused by the plunder of their nation, some of the more nationalistic Chinese formed a secret society, the _Boxers_, to drive out the "foreign devils." In June, 1900, the members laid siege to the foreign legations of Peiping and massacred three hundred people. A joint expeditionary force, including 2500 Americans, was sent to the aid of the beleagured residents. At the same time Secretary of State Hay announced that the United States would oppose any attack on the territorial integrity of China. Hay carried out this policy with great difficulty after the rebellion was crushed, but in October, 1900, England and Germany agreed to the Open Door and the preservation of Chinese independence. He could not, however, prevent the powers from laying heavy indemnities on China. Of the $25,000,000 awarded the United States, the government returned $17,000,000. The Chinese showed their gratitude by setting aside money to send their students to American colleges.

VI. IMPERIALISM: GOOD OR EVIL? Did the nation—and the world—benefit from the altered foreign policy of the United States? What were the results of the new imperialism?

A. The Myth of Isolationism Was Shattered. Although never actually isolated from Europe or Asia, the American people had clung to the belief that they could remain aloof from world affairs. This feeling took root between 1815 and 1898 only because no major war was fought during that time; had such a struggle occurred, the Americans would have been involved as they were in the Napoleonic Wars or in World Wars I and II. With the Spanish-American War this myth was discredited, allowing the country to play a larger world role than in the past.

B. The Democratic Principle Was Threatened. Government by consent of the governed had been a fundamental axiom of the American people for a century. Yet in annexing the Philippines, Hawaii, Guam, and Puerto Rico the United States ignored that basic concept. The cause of democracy suffered as a result.

C. American Nationalism Was Intensified. One tragedy of the shrinking world was that the machines which brought men closer physically also created the differences that drove them apart. Antagonisms resulting from friction between nations as they struggled for world possessions laid the basis for the wars of the twentieth century.

D. America's New-World Supremacy Was Confirmed. The expulsion of Spain from Cuba ended a period of history that began with Columbus' voyage. From 1899 on, the United States dominated the western hemisphere.

ADDITIONAL READING

A brief and readable account of foreign policy during this period is in Thomas A. Bailey, *A Diplomatic History of the American People* (1940). Relations with Hawaii and Samoa are considered in Foster Rhea Dulles, *America in the Pacific* (1932). David S. Muzzey, *James G. Blaine* (1935), deals with the origins of Pan-Americanism, while the early controversies with Latin America are described in Dexter Perkins, *The Monroe Doctrine, 1867-1907* (1937), or more popularly in the same author's *Hands Off: A History of the Monroe Doctrine* (1941). The rise of imperialism is traced in A. K. Weinberg, *Manifest Destiny* (1935), and Julius W. Pratt, *Expansionists of 1898* (1936). Claude H. Bowers, *Albert Beveridge and the Progressive Era* (1932), deals with the career of the leading imperialist. A readable and sound summary of the causes of the Spanish-American War is in Walter Millis, *The Martial Spirit* (1931). The struggle over the ratification of the treaty is described in W. S. Holt, *Treaties Defeated by the Senate* (1933). A. W. Griswold, *The Far Eastern Policy of the United States* (1938), and Tyler Dennett, *John Hay* (1933), are concerned with the origin of the Open Door Policy.

CHAPTER IX

The Progressive Period
1900-1917

⫷ **THE PROMISE OF PROGRESSIVISM**

The triumph of conservatism and imperialism in the 1890's forced middle-class Americans to ask an important question. Should the results of industrialization be farm peasantry, worker poverty, and the exploitation of colonial peoples? And how could these evils be remedied? The answer, they believed, was two-fold; they must: 1) restore the government to the hands of the people, and 2) use that popularly controlled government to regulate industry, finance, transportation, agriculture, and foreign policy in the interest of the many rather than the few. As they carried out that program in the early twentieth century, the United States entered on that phase of its history known as the Progressive Period.

I. THE ORIGINS OF PROGRESSIVISM.

A. European Background. In Europe, where the impact of industrialism was felt earlier than in the United States, the need for government control of business was recognized by the middle of the nineteenth century. Particularly rapid strides were made in the 1880's when *Germany* under Prince Bismarck adopted a national program of social security—workingmen's compensation, old-age pensions, government care of the sick, etc.—as an answer to the radical Marxian socialists. *England* followed in the early twentieth century with a New Liberalism responsible for health acts, national housing legislation, social security, accident compensation, minimum-wage laws, old-age pensions, and the like. Similar measures in France and Italy provided an example that the United States could not ignore.

B. American Background.

1. Conditions Demanding Reform.

a. BREAKDOWN OF THE MORAL CODE. As soulless corporations assumed control of American enterprise, the moral code that had assured decency in the individualistic society of the past no longer sufficed. Corporate directors, shifting responsibility for sin from themselves to their companies, engaged in practices they would not have condoned as individuals: the sale of impure food or drugs, use of inferior materials, corrupt weighing of merchandise, fraudulent advertising of stocks, employment of children, and other things harmful to society. Government action was needed to protect the people from exploitation.

b. GROWTH OF MONOPOLIES. The trend toward monopoly continued into the twentieth century, despite the Sherman Antitrust Act (1890). By 1903, 185 monopolies, capitalized at $3,000,000,000, controlled much of the nation's production. These stifled competition from small businesses, charged exhorbitant prices, and exploited workers.

c. CONCENTRATION OF WEALTH. By 1900, as a result of the continued growth of industrial fortunes, 1 per cent of the people owned 50 per cent of the nation's wealth, while the top 12 per cent controlled 90 per cent. The growth of a wealthy class threatened political democracy, for rich industrialists could buy up legislatures or subsidize candidates to protect their interests. Reformers believed that a redistribution of wealth was necessary to restore true democracy.

d. CORRUPTION OF POLITICS. Progressives soon found that before they could work through government to reform business they must reform government itself. This was partly because institutions adopted by an earlier agrarian society proved incapable of functioning in an industrialized civilization, and partly because the mediocre politicians who held office could be bribed or otherwise controlled by industry. Reform of government was as much a part of Progressivism as was the attack on monopoly.

2. Propaganda for Reform.

a. PROTEST OF THE INTELLECTUALS. Intellectuals who diagnosed the ills of society laid the basis for Progressivism. Their pioneer was *Lester F. Ward,* the father of American sociology, whose *Dynamic Sociology* (1883) urged social planning to equalize opportunity for mankind. Equally important was *Thorstein Veblen,* author of *The Theory of the Leisure Class* (1899) and other economic classics, who exposed the inefficiencies of laissez-faire capitalism that retarded the maximum employment of men and machines. Even more influential was *John Dewey,* academic philosopher and educator, who taught that educational, economic, and governmental institutions should be used to change man's environment and thus improve his behavior. Herbert Croly, *The Promise of American Life* (1909), decried "chaotic individualism" and pleaded for government regulation through democratic processes. All these intellectuals, and others like them, had in common their rejection of laissez faire and their belief in *progress through social planning.* This was the theory that underlay Progressivism.

b. THE MUCKRAKERS. Between 1902 and 1908 a group of writers exposed the evils of business monopoly and government corruption in terms understandable to laymen. First of the muckrakers was *Ida M. Tarbell,* whose *History of the Standard Oil Company* appeared in *McClure's Magazine* during 1902-1903. This work set the pattern by describing the way in which Standard Oil fleeced consumers and ruined competitors. It was followed by numerous exposés of other corporations in magazine and book form. Most important among these were: Thomas W. Lawson, *Frenzied Finance,* which exposed the business methods of Amalgamated Copper; *Lincoln Steffens, The Shame of the Cities,* which dealt with corruption in city governments; David Graham Phillips, *The Treason of the Senate,* which revealed corruption in that body; Burton J. Henrick, *The Story of Life Insurance;* and *Upton Sinclair, The Jungle* which laid bare conditions in the meat-packing industry with such realism that half the nation ate vegetables for months.

c. ORGANIZED LABOR. The American Federation of Labor, which grew from 550,000 to 2,400,000 members during this period, threw its weight behind Progressive reform. In 1906 it departed from precedent by endorsing political candidates favorable to labor, thus increasing its national influence. Less important, but more in the public eye, were the *Industrial Workers of the World*, a militant union formed in 1905 by *"Big Bill" Haywood* to unite unskilled workers. Its object was to abolish capitalism by the strike, boycott, and sabotage. Although never boasting more than 60,000 members, the I.W.W. kept the West in turmoil for a decade, and in 1912-1913 staged strikes in eastern textile mills. It lost influence rapidly after 1917 when it opposed American participation in World War I.

d. RADICAL THINKERS. Criticism of the established order was effectively voiced by the *Socialist Party* under *Eugene V. Debs*. While demanding public ownership of facilities for production and distribution, the Socialists exposed the evils of American capitalism so persuasively that they polled nearly a million votes in 1912. One Socialist, *Victor L. Berger*, was elected mayor of Milwaukee in 1910. The support for this party convinced many politicians that reform was needed to prevent the further spread of radical theories.

II. PROGRESSIVISM IN CITIES AND STATES.
Reform began in local governments, which were closest to the people. It was directed toward: 1) restoring popular rule, and 2) obtaining social legislation to benefit the masses.

A. The Striving for Democracy. The problem of giving the people a more direct voice in their government was attacked on two levels:

1. City Government. Reformers directed their attention to wiping out corruption and scrapping archaic political institutions.

a. THE ATTACK ON CORRUPTION. The attack on *bossism* was led by civic-minded mayors who gained control in city after city. Most famous among them were *"Golden Rule" Jones* of Toledo and *Tom Johnson* of Cleveland, who fought for the public control of utilities, abolished corruption, and made their cities models for reformers.

b. POLITICAL REFORM. Reformers realized that efficient city administration could be secured only by substituting a managerial type of government for the archaic system of mayors and councils. This was achieved by: 1) *Municipal Home Rule,* which was adopted in fifteen states by 1915, allowing cities to frame their own charters without state interference; 2) the *commission plan,* first used in Galveston in 1900, which placed city government in the hands of a commission of experts; 3) the *city manager plan,* inaugurated by Dayton, Ohio, in 1913, which employed a specially trained city manager.

2. State Government. Corruption was attacked by such reforming governors as *Charles Evans Hughes* of New York, *Robert M. LaFollette* of Wisconsin, *Woodrow Wilson* of New Jersey, and *Hiram Johnson* of California, all of whom later became national progressive leaders. Their reforms, most of which originated in the western states, included:

a. DIRECT PRIMARIES. These allowed party members to name candidates rather than simply to choose between those selected by bosses. Two-thirds of the states followed Wisconsin's example by adopting direct primaries after 1903.

b. INITIATIVE, REFERENDUM, AND RECALL. The *initiative* allowed voters to propose laws directly, either for legislative action or for submission to the electorate. The *referendum* was a device to let the people approve or reject, by popular vote, laws passed by the legislature. The *recall* permitted voters to remove an elected official before his term expired.

c. DIRECT ELECTION OF SENATORS. By allowing state legislators to elect Senators, as the Constitution provided, wealthy men were able to bribe their way into that national body. To offset this, the states, beginning with Nevada in 1899, required candidates for the state legislatures to endorse a Senatorial candidate chosen in a state-wide primary election. By 1912 thirty states had such laws. The *Seventeenth Amendment* (1913), which provided for the direct election of Senators by popular vote, simply recognized a democratic change already completed.

d. WOMEN'S SUFFRAGE. A movement to enfranchise

the feminine half of the population was already under way before 1900 (see pp. 77-78). During the progressive period additional political rights were extended to them, until by 1914 they enjoyed full equality in eleven states, all in the West. National women's suffrage, however, had to wait until 1920 when the *Nineteenth Amendment* was ratified in grateful recognition of women's work in World War I.

B. Social Legislation.

1. Protection of Workers. *Child-labor laws* were passed in thirty-eight states by 1912, limiting the hours of work for children, raising the age limit for employment, and forbidding night work. Twenty-eight states set *maximum working hours* for women, while twenty-four established the *eight-hour day* for men laborers on public works. Many also limited the working day for men in mining, transportation, and other hazardous employments. Maryland (1902) pioneered in a *workingmen's compensation law,* making the employer liable for injuries suffered by employees; by 1917 all but ten states had such laws.

2. Regulation of Business. Laws setting railroad rates were passed by many states in 1906 and 1907. Other measures used the states' taxing power to limit profits of corporations and to redistribute wealth through income and inheritance levies.

3. Social Legislation and the Courts.

a. EARLY CONSERVATIVE DECISIONS. At first, courts invalidated most of the state progressive laws. This was done under the *Fourteenth Amendment,* which forbade any state to deprive a person of life, liberty, or property without due process of law. The courts held that laws setting minimum wages or maximum hours, forbidding child labor, and providing for workingmen's compensation either deprived the employer of his property or the employee of his liberty. Thus in *Lochner v. New York* (1905) the Supreme Court outlawed a New York statute limiting bakers to a ten-hour day on the grounds that the measure was not essential to the health of either the baker or the community.

b. JUDICIAL APPROVAL. Under the influence of progressivism the Supreme Court gradually liberalized its views. In *Muller v. Oregon* (1908) it approved an Oregon law setting a ten-hour day for women workers. The Court's decision departed from precedent by showing the harmful social results of excessive labor for women. In *Bunting v. Oregon* (1917) the principle was extended to a ten-hour law for all factory workers.

III. THEODORE ROOSEVELT AND PROGRESSIVISM.

A. Roosevelt as President. In the *Election of 1900* McKinley was re-elected over William Jennings Bryan in a contest that hinged largely on Republican imperialism. Scarcely had he taken office when he was assassinated by a crazed anarchist, elevating to the presidency *Theodore Roosevelt*, who launched national progressivism.

1. Character of Roosevelt. Although honest and efficient, Roosevelt was not a real progressive. He was so aristocratic in background that his faith in democracy was intellectual rather than instinctive, so unschooled in economics that he often failed to understand important issues, so thoroughly a politician that he was willing to compromise rather than fight for reform. His contribution to progressivism was his ability to dramatize issues and lead men. Like Jackson or Lincoln before him, or Wilson or F. D. Roosevelt after him, he provided the executive leadership necessary for progress. This was shown in his dealings with Congress.

2. Roosevelt and Congress.

a. THE INAUGURAL MESSAGE. Roosevelt's first message to Congress horrified Republican conservatives. In it he asked for: 1) an attack on the "serious social problems" facing the nation; 2) legislation to allow the regulation, rather than the prohibition, of business combinations; 3) broader power over the railroads; and 4) the conservation of natural resources. Congress, dominated by such conservatives as Speaker *Joseph Cannon* in the House and *Mark Hanna* in the Senate, refused to respond to this plea. Roosevelt then carried his case to the people in a speaking tour in behalf of his *Square Deal*. Although arousing popular support in this way, Roosevelt would not have stirred Congress into action except for a fortunate incident: the coal strike of 1902.

b. THE ANTHRACITE COAL STRIKE OF 1902. This began in May, 1902, when the _United Mine Workers_ walked out to obtain a shorter day, better wages, and union recognition. The mine owners refused to negotiate or to submit the issues to arbitration, despite the threat to public welfare as winter approached. In October, Roosevelt offered to serve as peacemaker, but while the union was willing to submit its case to arbitration, the owners denied his right to interfere in any way. Not until the President threatened to call out troops to operate the mines did the owners submit. The strike was settled on October 23, 1902, when a presidential arbitration board granted the miners a nine-hour day and a 10 per cent pay increase, but not recognition of their union as a bargaining agency. The indifference of the mine owners to public welfare greatly influenced public opinion. Hence Congress was forced to make grudging concessions to Roosevelt's demands.

3. The Election of 1904. Roosevelt did not really control Congress, however, until after he was elected in his own right. His popularity forced the _Republicans_ to renominate him in 1904, although the platform contained few references to his progressive program. The _Democrats,_ having lost faith in Bryan's liberalism, nominated Judge _Alton B. Parker_, a conservative New York lawyer. The voters had their choice between a conservative party with a liberal candidate and a liberal party with a conservative candidate. In this situation Roosevelt's personal magnetism proved decisive. His electoral-college majority was 336 to 140 and his popular vote even greater than that achieved by McKinley over Bryan. With this mandate Roosevelt was able to launch his progressive program.

B. Roosevelt and the Trusts.

1. The Roosevelt Trust Program. Roosevelt knew that the election of 1900 was a decision against trust regulation, but he was also aware of the popular clamor against monopoly. Hence his "trust busting" was more verbal than real. His actual purpose was not to dissolve monopolies but to do away with their evils. To this end he asked Congress to create a _Department of Commerce and Labor_ (1903) and a _Bureau of Corporations_ (1903), both authorized to investigate business combinations and to warn them against harmful practices.

2. *Enforcement of the Sherman Act.* Roosevelt won his first victory as a "trust buster" when his Attorney General brought suit against the Northern Securities Company, a holding company controlling the Northern Pacific, Great Northern, and Chicago Burlington and Quincy railroads. In *Northern Securities Company v. United States* (1904) the Supreme Court held this to be a combination in restraint of trade, reversing its decision in the *Knight Case* (see p. 68). Thus encouraged, Roosevelt pushed other prosecutions, obtaining twenty-five indictments during his administrations.

C. Railroad Regulation. Despite the Interstate Commerce Act (see p. 61), railroad consolidation had gone on so rapidly that by 1904 six systems controlled three-fourths of the nation's mileage. Roosevelt attacked railroad monopoly in two acts passed by Congress:

1. *The Elkins Act (1903).* This made illegal the granting or accepting of secret *rebates,* and provided that both the road granting the rebate and the shipper accepting the lower rate could be punished. Under the law the Standard Oil Company was fined $29,000,000 in 1907, although the sentence was set aside by a higher court.

2. *The Hepburn Act (1906).* This measure was accepted by the roads as a means of checking progressive demands for rate-fixing powers for the Interstate Commerce Commission. It: 1) gave the I.C.C. power to reduce unreasonable or discriminatory rates subject to review by the courts; 2) increased the size of the I.C.C. from five to seven members and extended its jurisdiction over pipe lines, terminals, ferries, and express companies; 3) placed on the railroads the burden of showing that a rate was not unreasonable; 4) forbade free passes to all but employees; and 5) forbade the roads to carry commodities in the production of which they were interested. The Hepburn Act gave the I.C.C. real power for the first time since it was created in 1887. Yet it did not satisfy such reformers as *Robert M. LaFollette,* who wished it to have power to evaluate railroad property as a preliminary to setting rates that would give roads a fair return on their investment.

D. The Conservation Movement. By 1900 the United States faced the exhaustion of its mineral and timber lands. Roosevelt's interest in the West allowed him to make his greatest contribution by protecting these natural resources.

1. Timber Conservation. Acting under a _Forest Reserve Act_ that had been passed in 1891, Roosevelt withdrew 150,000,000 acres of timber land from sale, in addition to 85,000,000 acres in Alaska. This land was transformed into national forests under the able administration of _Gifford Pinchot._ In addition, a national conference on conservation (1908) inspired forty-one states to create conservation commissions. A National Conservation Commission (1909) also stressed the preservation of resources.

2. Land Reclamation. The _Newlands Reclamation Act_ (1902) authorized the use for irrigation purposes of money obtained from land sales in sixteen semiarid states. Under this law dams were built and the task of reclaiming the area begun.

E. Public Health Measures. In 1906 Roosevelt secured from Congress a _Pure Food and Drugs Act,_ which banned the use of harmful drugs, chemicals, or preservatives in food or medicine shipped in interstate commerce. The measure was passed partly because of Upton Sinclair's revelations of meat-packing plants in his novel, _The Jungle,_ and partly because of the muckrakers' crusade against adulterated foods and drugs.

IV. THE TAFT ADMINISTRATION.

A. The Election of 1908. _William Howard Taft_ of Ohio was Roosevelt's choice as successor. He was nominated by the _Republicans_ on a platform calling for trust regulation and a tariff that would recognize the difference between the cost of production at home and abroad. The _Democrats,_ returning to the progressive camp, selected _William Jennings Bryan_ once more. Their platform stressed the tariff question and the autocratic powers of the speaker of the House. Taft was chosen with 321 electoral votes to 162 for Bryan, but Bryan's popular vote was a million greater than Parker's in 1904.

B. Taft as President. Fundamentally conservative, Taft lacked Roosevelt's power to dramatize issues or lead Congress.

1. The Tariff Question. Bryan's emphasis on the tariff during the campaign forced Taft to endorse lowered duties. The House responded with the Payne Bill which followed the President's suggestions, but the Senate made 847 amendments, most of them upward. The *Payne-Aldrich Tariff* (1909) was bitterly opposed by progressive Republicans like *LaFollette* and *Beveridge.* Taft, however, not only signed the measure but in his *Winona Speech* declared it "the best the Republican Party ever passed." His popularity declined rapidly as a result.

2. The Ballinger-Pinchot Controversy. Gifford Pinchot, chief forester, in 1909 accused Richard A. Ballinger, Secretary of the Interior, of a lack of zeal in protecting natural resources from private exploitation. When Taft decided that the charges were unjust, he dismissed Pinchot, giving rise to the impression that he was undermining Roosevelt's conservation program.

3. Contest Over the Speakership. Democrats and Progressive Republicans alike objected to the autocratic powers of *Joseph Cannon,* Speaker of the House. Through his power to appoint committees and to dominate the rules committee he prevented progressive measures from reaching the floor of the House. In 1910 Republican insurgents under *George W. Norris* of Nebraska joined with Democrats to deprive Cannon of his power to appoint the rules committee or serve as a member. A year later, all committees were made elective. Taft's refusal to support the progressives in this controversy contributed to his unpopularity.

4. Canadian Reciprocity. Taft's inept handling of these problems led to a Democratic victory in the *Congressional elections of 1910.* To regain lost strength, the President drafted a reciprocity treaty with Canada which lowered the American duty on foodstuffs in return for similar Canadian reductions on manufactured goods. The measure passed Congress in 1911 with Democratic help. This not only cost Taft farmer support, but when Canada rejected the agreement he lost face.

C. Taft and Progressivism. Taft's political blunders concealed the fact that his record as a progressive was as outstanding as Roosevelt's. He sponsored:

1. Railroad Legislation. The *Mann-Elkins Act* (1910) remedied defects in the Hepburn Act. It: 1) gave the I.C.C. jurisdiction over telephone and telegraph lines; 2) authorized the I.C.C. to suspend rate increases until satisfied that they were reasonable; and 3) created a Commerce Court to hear appeals from the I.C.C.

2. Trust Busting. Under Taft twice as many suits were brought against trusts as under Roosevelt. Most important were those against the *Standard Oil Company* of New Jersey and the *American Tobacco Company,* both decided in 1911. In these the Supreme Court redefined the Sherman Act by deciding that it did not forbid all combinations, but only those that unduly or unreasonably restrained trade. This doctrine was called the *rule of reason.*

3. Minor Progressive Laws. These included: 1) a measure creating a *postal savings bank* and a *parcel post service;* 2) the division of the Department of Commerce and Labor into two departments; 3) laws limiting the amounts that could be spent on political campaigns and requiring the publication of all contributions; and 4) the *Sixteenth Amendment* (1913) which authorized income taxes. Taft also showed his support of *conservation* by withdrawing oil lands from sale, creating new national forests, and setting up the *Bureau of Mines.*

V. THE ELECTION OF 1912.

A. The Revolt of the Insurgents. The split between Republican Progressives (or Insurgents) and conservatives decided the election of 1912. Organized as the *Progressive Republican League* (1911) under Senator *Robert M. LaFollette* of Wisconsin, the Insurgents cast about for a standard bearer who could unseat Taft in the Republican convention. After a period of indecision, *Theodore Roosevelt,* in February, 1912, announced that he would be their candidate. He laid down the principles of his *New Nationalism* in a series of speeches: honesty in government, the regulation of business, conservation of natural resources, and the reconstruction of society by political action. *LaFollette* also announced his own candidacy.

B. The Nominating Conventions.

1. The Republican Convention. The contest between Taft, Roosevelt, and LaFollette was bitter. *Taft,* however, controlled the machines so completely that all disputed delegates were awarded to the President, who was renominated on the first ballot. The platform avoided a stand on all vital issues.

2. The Progressive Convention. Roosevelt and his followers, reassembling at Chicago as the Progressive Party, chose the ex-president as their candidate on a platform embodying the New Nationalism. They adopted the *bull moose* as their symbol to match the elephant and donkey of the other parties.

3. The Democratic Convention. The jubilant Democrats recognized the chance of victory over a divided opposition. After a spirited contest between liberal and conservative factions, the liberals triumphed with the nomination of *Woodrow Wilson,* a scholar and college president who had gained fame as the progressive governor of New Jersey. The platform pledged tariff reform, enforcement of the Sherman Act, outlawing of the labor injunction, and better banking and currency laws.

C. Outcome of the Election. Wilson was elected with 435 electoral votes to 88 for Roosevelt and 8 for Taft. His popular vote was only 42 per cent of the total. This did not mean that Wilson's principles were endorsed by a minority of the people. Instead, the progressive measures supported by Wilson, Roosevelt, and Eugene V. Debs (who polled nearly a million votes on the Socialist ticket) commanded the support of three-fourths of the voters.

VI. THE WILSON ADMINISTRATION. Under Wilson, Progressivism reached a climax. A trained political scientist and author of a monumental work on *Congressional Government* (1885), the President realized that strong executive leadership was necessary for progress. Hence he went beyond Roosevelt in imposing his will on Congress, even abandoning a practice used since the days of Jefferson when he read his own messages to that body. The

result was a mass of legislation unequalled in any administration to that time.

A. Tariff Reform. When lobbyists descended on the special session of Congress that Wilson called to revise the tariff downward, he exposed their tactics to the newspapers. The resulting *Underwood Tariff* (1913), while retaining certain protective features, lowered duties on more than one hundred items, including food, textiles, iron, and steel. To offset the loss in revenue a graduated *income tax* (authorized by the *Sixteenth Amendment*) was adopted.

B. Currency Reform.

1. Background of Reform. Progressives had demanded modernization of the archaic currency system ever since the Populist era. Their demands were given weight by the Panic of 1907 and by disclosures of a "money trust":

a. PANIC OF 1907. This "Bankers' Panic" occurred while the national economy was sound, and resulted from overspeculation in securities by a few financiers. The business failures and unemployment that followed called attention to: 1) the unreasonable control over the country's money supply exercised by private banks; and 2) the inelasticity of the currency. Many business failures occurred because national banks, unable to enlarge the volume of national bank notes they issued, could not supply tottering firms with loans. The *Aldrich-Vreeland Act* (1908) attempted to meet this situation by allowing national banks to issue additional notes in periods of emergency, but this was only a stopgap.

b. THE "MONEY TRUST." Two congressional investigations disclosed the need for reform: 1) the *National Monetary Commission* (1908-1912) listed seventeen defects in the banking and currency system, including such a concentration of funds in New York City that business elsewhere was handicapped. It recommended a complete revision of the banking laws and the establishment of a central reserve bank. 2) *The Pujo Committee* (1911), a special committee of the House, disclosed that a few financiers controlled not only the finances but much of the business of the United States, through a series of interlocking directorates.

2. The Federal Reserve Act (1913). Wilson's financial program aimed at three objectives: 1) a more elastic currency; 2) greater cooperation among banks in times of crisis; and 3) less concentration of money power in the hands of a few bankers. His recommendations were embodied in the *Federal Reserve Act* (1913), which was drafted by Senator *Carter Glass* of Virginia and other congressmen. Its provisions were these: 1) The country was divided into twelve districts with a *Federal Reserve bank* in each. 2) These banks were to serve as depositories for the cash reserves of national banks in their districts and such state banks as cared to join the system. They carried on no private business, serving instead as banks for banks. 3) The Federal Reserve banks were authorized to issue *Federal Reserve notes* on the basis of securities deposited with them by member banks. 4) The Federal Reserve banks could loan money to member banks when needed to prevent a crisis. 5) The system was administered by a *Federal Reserve Board*.

3. Other Financial Reforms. Easier credit for farmers was obtained by the *Federal Farm Loan Act* (1916), which created twelve Farm Loan banks similar to the Federal Re-

HOW THE FEDERAL RESERVE SYSTEM

1. STABILIZES MEMBER BANKS

MEMBER BANK · DISTRICT RESERVE BANK · COMMON RESERVE

2. MAKES CURRENCY SUPPLY ELASTIC

Currency in circulation · Rediscount rate

MEMBER BANK · DISTRICT RESERVE BANK

3. INHIBITS RECKLESS SPENDING

Currency in circulation · Rediscount rate

MEMBER BANK · DISTRICT RESERVE BANK

From: Muzzey—*A History of Our Country*, New Edition, Ginn & Co.   Chart by *Graphics Institute, N. Y. C.*

serve banks. These were authorized to loan money on farms, buildings, and improvements up to 70 per cent of their value at interest rates not over 6 per cent.

C. The Regulation of Business. In a special congressional message (January, 1914) Wilson called for five measures to break up monopolies: 1) a law prohibiting interlocking directorates; 2) authority for the I.C.C. to regulate railroad rates; 3) an exact definition of "combinations in restraint of trade"; 4) a federal trade commission to correct harmful business practices; and 5) penalties for individuals as well as firms that violated the antitrust acts. Congress responded with:

1. The Federal Trade Commission Act (1914). This created a *Federal Trade Commission* empowered to issue "cease and desist" orders to any firm found guilty of unfair methods of competition.

2. The Clayton Act (1914). This: 1) defined the "unfair methods of competition" that the Federal Trade Commission was empowered to forbid; these included interlocking directorates, acquisition of a corporation's stock by a competing concern, price discrimination tending to create a monopoly, tying agreements, and the like; 2) made officers of corporations liable for illegal acts of those corporations; 3) exempted labor unions from the antitrust acts and forbade the use of the labor injunction except where necessary to protect property. Workers hailed this provision as the *Magna Charta of Labor*.

D. Further Social Legislation. A number of measures were adopted after the Democrats regained control of Congress in the *Elections of 1914.* These included: 1) the *LaFollette Seamen's Bill* (1915) which required better living and working conditions for ocean and lake sailors; 2) the *Adamson Act* (1916) setting an eight-hour day for railroad workers; and 3) the *Keating-Owen Act* (1916) excluding from interstate commerce the products of firms employing children under fourteen. This last measure was declared unconstitutional in the case of *Hammer v. Dagenhart* (1918).

VII. AN APPRAISAL OF PROGRESSIVISM. The progressive period demonstrated:

A. The Need for Executive Leadership. The progressive period showed that party responsibility was so lax that progress was possible only with strong executive leadership. This was the case because congressmen, once they were elected, succumbed to the lure of lobbyists or reverted to the conservatism of their class. This left the parties, which were essentially combinations of local machines without strong national cohesion, powerless to carry out programs promised in presidential platforms. Realizing this, Wilson made himself virtually a prime minister by combining the functions of executive and party leader. The impressive legislative record of his administration was the result.

B. The Persistence of Liberalism. The achievements of the progressives were virtually those demanded by Populists a generation before. They had asked for a more flexible currency, the direct election of senators, a parcel post service, postal savings banks, a graduated income tax, the initiative and referendum, outlawing of the labor injunction, and other reforms, all of which were secured by 1916. Especially significant was the fact that these Populist planks were adopted by both Democrats and Republicans, indicating the basic unity of liberal platforms, which had little to do with party labels.

C. The Need for Continued Liberal Action. Within a few years after 1916 the Clayton Act was virtually a dead letter, with business again endulging in "unfair" practices and labor restricted by injunctions. The same fate waited most of the measures of the progressive period. This was largely the result of the American tendency toward inertia; mistaking success in battle for victory in the war, liberals relaxed their vigilance, only to lose much that they had gained.

ADDITIONAL READING

The entire period is admirably described in Harold U. Faulkner, *The Quest for Social Justice* (1931). Excellent accounts of the reforming spirit underlying Progressivism are in John Chamberlain, *Farewell to Reform* (1932), C. C. Regier, *The Era of the Muckrakers* (1932), and Louis Filler, *Crusaders for American Liberalism* (1939). The best account of Theodore Roosevelt's role is George E.

Mowry, *Roosevelt and the Progressive Movement* (1946), although the biography by Henry Pringle, *Theodore Roosevelt* (1931), is colorful. The Taft administration is fully treated in Henry Pringle, *The Life and Times of William Howard Taft* (1939). The growth of Republican Insurgency is traced in Claude G. Bowers, *Beveridge and the Progressive Era* (1932). Wilson's first administration is carefully appraised in Frederic L. Paxson, *The Pre-War Years, 1913-1917* (1936), and in such biographies as W. E. Dodd, *Woodrow Wilson and His Work* (1920), and H. C. F. Bell, *Woodrow Wilson and the People* (1945). A fuller study of Wilson's life is being prepared by Arthur Link, and the first volume has appeared: *Wilson, the Road to the White House* (1947).

CHAPTER X

Foreign Policy
of the Progressive Period
1900-1917

ℂ THE NATIONALISTIC SPIRIT

The liberal domestic program of the Progressive presidents
contrasted strongly with their foreign policy. Between 1900
and 1917 the United States warred ruthlessly on subject
peoples, dominated weaker neighbors, and exerted its power
over much of the world. This nationalistic spirit could be
traced to: 1) the sense of national superiority that followed
the easy victory in the Spanish-American War; and 2) the
situation in Europe. There the major powers were guilty of
the same integral nationalism; they built large navies,
launched armament programs, engaged in power politics,
and expanded their colonial empires. Their clashing interests
bred the tensions that finally resulted in World War I.

I. SHAPING A COLONIAL POLICY. The United
States emerged from the Spanish-American War with outright possession of the Philippines, Puerto Rico, and the
Hawaiian Islands, as well as responsibilities toward Cuba.
How should these dependencies be governed? Should their
people be prepared for self-rule? Should they be allowed to
govern themselves as states? The Courts and Congress tried
to answer these questions.

A. The Courts and Colonial Policy. During 1900 and 1901 the Supreme Court was asked to decide whether the Constitution followed the flag—that is, whether America's colonial peoples had the same Constitutional rights as native Americans. Its answer was given in the *Insular Cases,* of which the most important were *Downes v. Bidwell* (1900) and *De Lima v. Bidwell* (1901). The Court held that certain *fundamental rights* were common to all people under American jurisdiction, but that *formal rights* (such as trial by jury) could be extended to colonials by act of Congress only. In effect this ruling stated that colonial peoples were not citizens of the United States until citizenship was conferred upon them, thus giving Congress a free hand to administer the colonies as it chose.

B. Congressional Policy.

1. The Hawaiian Islands and Alaska. An *Organic Act* (1900) incorporated *Hawaii* as a territory of the United States, granted citizenship to its inhabitants, and authorized an elective legislature and a governor appointed by the President. *Alaska,* which had been neglected since its purchase in 1867, attracted attention when the Klondike Gold Rush (1896) increased its population. Territorial status, with the usual elected assembly and appointed governor, was granted in 1912. In 1958, Alaska became the 49th state and in 1959, Hawaii became the 50th state.

2. Puerto Rico. By the *Foraker Act* (1900) Congress made the people citizens of Puerto Rico but not of the United States, and provided for a legislature with an elected lower house and an appointed upper house. The governor was also appointed in Washington. In 1917 the *Jones Act* conferred citizenship on Puerto Ricans as well as making the upper house elective. Puerto Rican demands for home rule continued, largely because of the poverty of the island.

3. The Philippines.

a. THE INSURRECTION. When the Philippines were annexed, the Senate adopted the *McEnery Resolution* (1899) declaring that the islands would not be kept permanently. The natives, however, were so desirous of independence that when a commission (1899) reported that they were not ready for self-government a revolt began. With *Emilio*

Aguinaldo as their leader they fought bitterly until 1902, when the insurrection was crushed by methods that aroused criticism from anti-imperialists in the United States.

b. GOVERNMENTAL BEGINNINGS. A *Philippine Commission* (1901) of three Filipinos and five Americans under *William Howard Taft* was appointed to devise a government for the islands. Its recommendations were embodied in the *Organic Act of 1902.* This: 1) granted the suffrage to literate males over twenty-three, 2) made the Filipinos citizens of the Philippines but not of the United States, and 3) extended to them most of the constitutional guarantees enjoyed by Americans. *Taft* was made governor-general, and ruled with the Commission. In 1907 an elected legislature was added, with the appointed Commission serving as the upper house.

c. ECONOMIC DEVELOPMENT. Taft and his successors improved the lot of the Filipinos. Extensive holdings were purchased from three Catholic orders and the land sold on easy terms to small farmers. Public works were built, a currency system installed, and health improved. Spectacular gains in educational facilities increased the number of pupils from 5000 in 1898 to 1,000,000 in 1920, while the University of the Philippines (1909) provided for higher education. This benevolent system was responsible for a population gain of three million between 1900 and 1917.

d. MOVEMENT FOR INDEPENDENCE. The Filipinos still wanted independence, and their cause was sponsored by the Democratic Party. When Woodrow Wilson was elected President he urged Congress to allow them more self-rule as a step toward freedom. The resulting *Jones Act* (1916) made both houses of the legislature elective, extended the franchise to all men over twenty-one, and promised independence as soon as the Filipinos were capable of caring for themselves. The Republican victory in 1920 ended their hopes until the administration of F. D. Roosevelt.

4. Minor Possessions. Guam, Samoa, and other Pacific islands were ruled by governors appointed by the Navy Department. The *Danish West Indies* or *Virgin Islands,* which were purchased from Denmark in 1917, were also placed under an appointed governor. Local self-rule was gradually extended there until 1927, when the people were made citizens of the United States.

II. FOREIGN POLICY OF THEODORE ROOSEVELT, 1900-1909.

A. Building the Panama Canal.

1. Background of the Canal Project. As early as 1850 the *Clayton-Bulwer Treaty* between the United States and England provided that any canal across Central America should be jointly built and not fortified. Although a triumph at the time, this treaty later lessened American interest in a waterway, for by the late nineteenth century the United States was determined to build and fortify its own canal. Hence the first efforts were made by a French company headed by *Ferdinand De Lesseps,* builder of the Suez Canal, which obtained a franchise from Panama in 1879. After sinking $26,000,000 the company failed, transferring its franchise to the *Panama Canal Company.* An American company, the Maritime Canal Company, also went bankrupt in 1893 while trying to dig a canal across Nicaragua. The United States was unwilling to aid either so long as international control was necessary. In 1901, however, Roosevelt's Secretary of State, *John Hay,* negotiated with England the *Hay-Pauncefote Treaty* which granted the United States exclusive control.

2. Selection of a Route. Two routes were possible, one across the Isthmus of Panama, which was owned by Colombia, the other across Nicaragua. A congressional commission named to choose a site preferred the Panama route, but recommended the route across Nicaragua as the price asked by the French Panama Canal Company for its franchise was too high. When the French company cut its price in half, the *Spooner Act* (1902) was passed, authorizing Roosevelt to proceed with the Panama route.

3. Canal Diplomacy.

a. NEGOTIATIONS WITH COLOMBIA. In January, 1903, the Colombian minister in Washington signed the *Hay-Herran Treaty* which leased a ten-mile strip across Panama to the United States in return for $10,000,000 and an annual rental of $250,000. In August the Colombian senate rejected the treaty, feeling 1) that it surrendered too much power to the United States, and 2) that the compensation was inadequate. Roosevelt was outraged and made his feelings clear.

b. THE PANAMA REVOLUTION. Especially alarmed by Colombia's action were members of the French Panama Canal Company, who would lose $40,000,000 if they did not sell their rights to the United States before their franchise expired in 1904. Using as their agent a Panamanian revolutionist, *Philippe Bunau-Varilla,* they planned a revolution to free Panama from Colombia. Roosevelt was probably informed of their plans; in October, 1903, he ordered a naval vessel to Panama with orders to keep the railroad across the isthmus open. The planned rebellion broke out on November 3, 1903, in the city of Panama. A day later United States troops were landed to keep Colombian soldiers from reaching the scene, and on November 6 Secretary of State Hay formally recognized the *Republic of Panama.* On November 18 a treaty with the new republic gave the United States perpetual control of a ten-mile zone across the isthmus. Roosevelt's conduct was virtually without precedent as an example of international bad taste. Not until 1921 were Colombia's ruffled feelings soothed by a grant of $21,000,000.

4. Constructing the Canal. Work began in 1906 under the direction of Colonel *G. W. Goethals* of the army, and was completed in 1914. Equally important was the sanitary work of Colonel *W. C. Gorgas,* who reduced tropical diseases among workers to a minimum.

B. Roosevelt's Caribbean Policy. Once the Panama Canal was built, American naval strategy depended on shuttling the fleet between the Atlantic and Pacific oceans. As the canal was vital to national defense, no European nation could be allowed a foothold in the Caribbean. Hence the United States adopted a new aggressive policy toward the Caribbean, designed to prevent any nation from gaining an excuse to intervene in the region.

1. Policy Toward Cuba. Mounting imperialistic sentiment soon caused the United States to regret the *Teller Amendment* (see p. 107), in which it had promised freedom for the Cubans as soon as they could care for themselves. Instead, its policy was directed toward keeping Cuba under its own thumb.

a. GOVERNMENTAL BEGINNINGS. A military commission under Major General *Leonard Wood* (1899) brought order to the chaotic island preliminary to the calling of a constitutional convention (1900) which drafted a constitution modeled on that of the United States. This document, however, made no mention of Cuban-American relations. Angry at this slight, Congress responded by adopting the *Platt Amendment* (1901) and instructing the President to prolong military occupation until its provisions were inserted in the Cuban constitution. These provided that: 1) Cuba could make no international commitments impairing its sovereignty without the consent of the United States; 2) Cuba could contract no debts that could not be paid from its ordinary revenues; 3) the United States could intervene whenever necessary to preserve Cuban freedom or orderly government; and 4) two naval bases were granted the American navy. These provisions were reluctantly accepted and in 1902 independent Cuba installed its government.

b. APPLICATION OF THE PLATT AMENDMENT. The Cubans, untrained in self-government, were guilty of political misconduct that gave the United States several excuses to intervene. In 1906 civil disorders following an election led to a three-year occupation. Marines were landed in 1912 to protect American interests, and in 1917 more troops were sent to quell election disorders.

c. ECONOMIC PENETRATION OF CUBA. American investments in Cuba increased from $80,000,000 in 1901 to $1,500,000,000 thirty years later. Most of this went into sugar plantations which were controlled by a few banking houses, the National City Bank of New York being most important. This economic vassalage proved as objectionable to most Cubans as the Platt Amendment, and helped account for the rise of a spirit of Cuban nationalism that complicated relations between the two governments. On the other hand, the American policy resulted in political stability and a measure of economic prosperity.

2. The Venezuelan Crisis.

a. ORIGINS OF THE VENEZUELAN INCIDENT. In 1902 England, Germany, and Italy blockaded Venezuela to force that country to pay its long-standing debts. President Roosevelt, alarmed by the presence of European fleets in the Caribbean, brought secret pressure on Germany to withdraw and accept arbitration. His efforts succeeded when Germany agreed to submit its claims to the Hague Tribunal.

b. THE DRAGO DOCTRINE. The incident served as an excuse for Luis Drago, Argentina's minister of foreign affairs, to announce that no nation had the right to intervene in the affairs of another nation to collect debts due its citizens. The _Drago Doctrine_ was accepted by the American State department, and in modified form by the Second Hague Conference (1907).

3. The Roosevelt Corollary.

In his annual message of 1904, Roosevelt announced that chronic wrongdoing by any American republic might compel the United States to exercise an international police power to restore order. This meant that if any weak Caribbean or Central American nation was unable to meet its financial obligations, or to protect the lives and property of European nationals, the United States would intervene to forestall intervention by other powers. This was known as the _Roosevelt Corollary to the Monroe Doctrine._ It was applied in 1905 when Santo Domingo was unable to pay its European debts. Roosevelt placed an American financial expert in charge of the Dominican treasury until the debts were paid.

C. Roosevelt and World Politics.

The new international role of the United States became clear as Roosevelt led the country into world affairs, largely in the interest of global peace.

1. The Hague Conferences.

The world-wide democratic surge, of which American progressivism was a part, inspired an attack on the use of war as a means of settling international grievances. The _First Hague Conference_ (1899) was designed to set up machinery for the arbitration of conflicts among the twenty-six participating nations. The result was the establishment of the _Permanent Court of Arbitration_ to hear disputes and recommend settlements.

President Roosevelt was largely responsible for calling the *Second Hague Conference* (1907), where representatives from forty-four countries adopted additional rules governing arbitration as well as sanctioning the Drago Doctrine. Of the seventeen disputes settled by the Hague Tribunal between 1902 and 1917, four involved the United States. The most important concerned the rights of American fishermen in Canadian waters (1910) and was settled in America's favor.

2. Arbitration Treaties. In 1904 Roosevelt laid before the Senate treaties with twenty-two powers which bound the signers to submit all disputes to the Hague Tribunal save those involving vital interests, independence, or national honor. These were ratified in 1908-1909, extending the principle of arbitration.

3. Relations with Japan.

a. THE TREATY OF PORTSMOUTH. A *Russo-Japanese War* (1904-1905) threatened the *Open Door* in China by making Japan the dominant power in the Far East. Although sympathetic to Japan, Roosevelt persuaded both warring powers to recognize the neutrality of all Chinese territory outside of Manchuria. He also used the threat of American intervention on Japan's side to prevent France and Germany from aiding Russia. As the war drew to a close, he persuaded the belligerents to meet at Portsmouth, New Hampshire (September, 1905), to draft a peace treaty. His good offices brought the United States little advantage, for while Japan obtained many territorial concessions from beaten Russia, Roosevelt was blamed for blocking still more generous terms.

b. JAPAN AND THE OPEN DOOR. Japan's new strength continued to threaten the Open Door policy after 1905. To protect the American position, Roosevelt's Secretary of State, Elihu Root, negotiated the *Root-Takahira Agreement* (1908), in which the two nations agreed to respect each other's territorial possessions in the Pacific, and to support Chinese independence and the Open Door.

4. The Algeciras Conference. When war threatened between France and Germany over territorial claims in Morocco (1905-1906), Roosevelt urged France to agree to a conference on the question. The resulting Algeciras Conference (1906) temporarily settled the difference.

III. WOODROW WILSON'S FOREIGN POLICY, 1913-1917.

A. The Japanese Problem. Growing tension that resulted from American efforts to restrict Japanese expansion in the Far East was increased by a controversy over immigration. Since the 1890's, Californians had resented the influx of immigrants from Japan. They acted first in 1906 when San Francisco relegated Japanese children to separate schools. When Japan protested, President Roosevelt persuaded San Francisco to rescind its order, at the same time obtaining from the Emperor a *Gentleman's Agreement* (1907) to prevent the further immigration of coolie laborers. Although this was lived up to, continued nativistic sentiment in California led to the *Webb Act* (1913), which forbade Japanese to own land in the state. When this law was evaded by transferring land titles to American-born children (who were citizens under the Fourteenth Amendment), California adopted the *Asiatic Land Law* (1920) forbidding the practice. Each of these steps, which were taken over Wilson's protests, created friction between the two nations.

B. Panama Canal Controversy. As the Panama Canal neared completion, Congress passed the *Tolls Act* (1912) which provided that foreign vessels using the canal must pay larger fees than American vessels. *England* protested that this violated the "equality of treatment" guaranteed in the Hay-Pauncefote Treaty. Wilson supported England in this controversy, believing that friendship with that nation was essential in the troubled world situation. His pressure forced Congress to repeal the Tolls Act in 1914.

C. Wilson's Caribbean Policy.

1. "Dollar Diplomacy." As American investments in the Caribbean increased (see p. 136), a new element was introduced into American Caribbean diplomacy. Instead of directing its policy solely toward guarding approaches to the Panama Canal, the United States interested itself in protecting American investments which were threatened by internal revolutions. Although Wilson openly repudiated this "dollar diplomacy" he was responsible for repeated intervention in the Caribbean and Central American areas.

2. Intervention in Santo Domingo. When in 1916 a revolution threatened the local government, marines were sent to the island, where they remained for a decade. The occupation restored financial solvency and political tranquility to Santo Domingo, but was greatly resented by the natives. Troops were not withdrawn until 1924, and then American control of the customs service continued.

3. Intervention in Nicaragua. Marines who were landed in Nicaragua to prevent a revolution and protect American loans stayed on until 1925. The Republic's sovereignty was further invaded in 1914 when a treaty granted the United States the right to build a Nicaraguan canal and certain naval bases in return for a $3,000,000 payment. When the marines were withdrawn in 1925 such violent disorders broke out that they were returned in 1926. Nicaragua was actually an American protectorate, although the United States had no treaty rights to exercise such a power.

4. Intervention in Haiti. Financial anarchy in Haiti, with a threat of European intervention, led to the sending of troops to that Republic in 1915. A treaty that year also gave the United States control of the Haitian customs service, finances, and police force. Although the American administration was marked by efficiency, it was greatly resented.

D. Relations with Mexico.

1. Overthrow of Diaz. For thirty-five years Mexico was ruled by *Porfirio Diaz,* a dictator who ended popular government and awarded Mexico's lands to great estate holders. A revolution (1910-1911) that toppled Diaz from power was short-lived; a counterrevolution engineered by the landholders in 1913 restored a conservative government under General *Victoriano Huerta.* The internal situation in Mexico was now clear. On one side were the large landholders backed by foreign capital and with Huerta as their leader; on the other, the bulk of the middle class and peons who were led by *Venustiano Carranza.*

2. Wilson and Huerta. Most European powers recognized the Huerta regime but Wilson refused, despite pressure from American business interests whose $1,500,000,000 investment in Mexico gave them control of two-thirds of the nation's mines, oil fields, rubber plantations, and railroads. Wilson's refusal was based on the fact that Huerta's government rested on force. This represented a departure from traditional American policy, which had been to recognize any stable government, no matter how installed. The controversy over recognition was brought to a head in 1914 when Mexican police arrested several American sailors. When Huerta refused to apologize, the Mexican port of Vera Cruz was captured. War seemed certain until the *A.B.C. Powers* (Argentina, Brazil, and Chile) offered to mediate. When the United States accepted and Huerta refused, he lost support so rapidly that in July, 1914, he fled from Mexico.

3. Wilson and Carranza. The leader of the popular party, Carranza, became Mexican president in August, 1914. Two months later troops were withdrawn from Vera Cruz and the government given *de facto* recognition. Mexico remained chaotic for several years, however, largely because of the government's failure to satisfy the peasants' land hunger. In the resulting disorders 400 Americans were killed, while property losses reached $200,000,000. The principal troublemaker was *Francisco Villa,* a former bandit who led constant attacks on the Carranza government. To stop these, Wilson persuaded the A.B.C. powers to join the United States in affording full recognition to Carranza (1915). In retaliation Villa raided Columbus, New Mexico (March, 1916), killing seventeen Americans. With Carranza's permission the United States sent a military expedition under General *John J. Pershing* into Mexico on Villa's trail, but failed to capture the bandit. The troops were withdrawn in January, 1917, as America prepared to enter World War I.

4. The Mexican Constitution of 1917. A constitution adopted in 1917 not only contained provisions to aid workers and peasants but also proclaimed the national ownership of all oil and mineral resources. This threatened many American investors. In the resulting disorders Carranza was assassinated, and *Alvaro Obregon* became president (1920). He agreed (1923) that American mineral and oil rights obtained before 1917 would not be threatened, and that foreigners would be compensated for expropriated lands.

IV. AN APPRAISAL OF AMERICAN FOREIGN POLICY, 1900-1917.

A. World Role of the United States. During this period the United States had its first chance to practice the new role that it would play in the world. Its policy was directed to two ends: 1) *To maintain peace.* This was shown by its support of the Hague Conferences, international arbitration, the mediation of disputes, and other attempts to settle conflicts by means short of war. 2) *To protect downtrodden people.* This purpose underlay Wilson's Mexican policy with its refusal to recognize an unpopular government that had obtained power by force. In both of these objectives the United States assumed a positive world role to better the lot of men, just as its domestic legislation was directed to the same end.

B. The Role of the United States in Hemispheric Affairs. The high idealism displayed in world politics was in marked contrast to the imperialistic Caribbean policy of these years.

1. Reasons for Caribbean Policy. Three factors combined to force this policy on the United States: 1) *Dollar diplomacy* played a part as investments increased and investors brought pressure on the government to protect their loans. Yet they had little influence on Roosevelt or Wilson. 2) *Canal policy* was more important. Having based its whole defensive strategy on the Panama Canal, the United States could not afford to allow any European power to secure a foothold in the Caribbean. This explained intervention in many cases, as well as the Roosevelt Corollary to prevent European powers from using force to collect debts. 3) *Idealism* doubtless convinced Roosevelt and Wilson that they could better the lot of the common people by intervening. The health programs, educational innovations, and public works construction did benefit the areas materially.

2. Results of Caribbean Policy.

a. BENEFICIAL RESULTS. The United States did accomplish its purpose of protecting the entrance to the Panama Canal.

b. HARMFUL RESULTS. Latin Americans were left fearful and distrustful of the "Colossus of the North." This was especially the case with the A.B.C. powers, which felt that their stability and advanced civilization entitled them to be treated as equals. Not until the Good Neighbor policy of F. D. Roosevelt were more cordial relations restored.

ADDITIONAL READING

Thomas A. Bailey, *A Diplomatic History of the American People* (1940), surveys the entire subject. Roosevelt's canal policy is treated in Dwight C. Miner, *The Fight for the Panama Route* (1940), and in Mary W. Williams, *Anglo-American Isthmian Diplomacy* (1915). M. P. DuVal, Jr., *And the Mountains Will Move* (1947), tells the story of the building of the canal. Roosevelt's Caribbean policy is the theme of W. H. Callcott, *The Caribbean Policy of the United States, 1890-1920* (1942), while his Far Eastern policy is analyzed in Tyler Dennett, *John Hay* (1933), and in A. W. Griswold, *The Far Eastern Policy of the United States* (1938). Thomas A. Bailey, *Theodore Roosevelt and the Japanese-American Crisis* (1934), is an expert analysis of that subject. Wilson's controversy with Mexico is described in J. F. Rippy, *The United States and Mexico* (1931), and J. M. Callahan, *American Foreign Policy in Mexican Relations* (1932).

CHAPTER XI

The United States and World War I

1917-1920

⟮ PROGRESSIVISM AND WAR

Throughout American history each period of rapid progress toward economic, social, and political democracy has been brought to a close by a major war. This is because such periods infect the people with a crusading zeal that makes them willing to fight for their ideals. Thus the abolitionism that precipitated the Civil War was rooted in Jacksonian Democracy, while the idealism of the New Deal prepared the people to battle dictatorship in World War II. Similarly the progressive period inspired Americans to look upon World War I as a holy crusade in behalf of justice, democracy, and equality for all peoples.

I. THE ROAD TO WAR.

A. European Background. Between 1900 and 1914 Europe divided into two armed camps, with the _Central Powers_ (Germany and Austria-Hungary) on one side and the _Triple Entente_ (England, France, and Russia) on the other. The crisis that touched off the conflict between them came on June 28, 1914, when a Serbian patriot assassinated the heir to the Austro-Hungarian throne. When Austria declared war on Serbia, Russia came to the aid of her Slavic neighbor, and Germany joined the Austrians. One by one the other European nations were drawn into the conflict by the alliances that held them together, until the middle of 1915 when all the continent was at war.

B. The Problem of Neutrality. Although Wilson pleaded with the American people to remain neutral in thought and action (August 4, 1914), both their basic sympathies and the events of the war inclined them from the beginning to favor the Allies rather than the Central Powers.

1. Basic Factors Influencing Opinion.

a. CULTURAL TIES. Most Americans were conscious of their cultural affinity with England, based on a common background, language, and traditions. About one-half the people were of English or Canadian descent, and only one-fifth of German or Austrian background.

b. PSYCHOLOGICAL FACTORS. German militarism offended the sense of democracy engrained in the American people, while that country's ruthless invasion of Belgium aroused deep resentment. As the war progressed, an efficient British propaganda, which emphasized imaginary German atrocities, intensified the conviction that England was fighting for human decency. The Allies' cause was strengthened by the fact that they controlled most of the avenues of communication between Europe and the United States, excluding only the wireless and special correspondence.

c. ECONOMIC FACTORS. England's navy blockaded the Central Powers, confining all American trade to the Allied countries. This trade grew rapidly as American factories and farms assumed the task of sustaining the armies and civilian populations of the Allies. Munitions exports alone increased from $40,000,000 in 1914 to $1,300,000,000 in 1916. These purchases were financed by floating loans in the United States; by 1917 the Allied governments had borrowed $2,300,000,000 from Americans while loans to the Central Powers totaled only $27,000,000. This economic stake in an Allied victory probably influenced few people, for the businessmen who had purchased most of the bonds favored neutrality as the best means of obtaining additional profits.

2. The Conflict Over Neutral Rights. The efforts of

both warring groups to control the seas proved the decisive factor in forcing the United States into the conflict.

a. THE CASE AGAINST ENGLAND. Britain's attempt to starve the Central Powers into submission led her to violate all rules of international law as codified in the _Declaration of London_ (1909), which England had not signed. Among her questionable acts were: 1) extension of the _contraband_ list to include food and other items not previously considered articles of war; 2) expansion of the _doctrine of continuous voyage_ to allow the confiscation of goods in neutral vessels bound for neutral ports; 3) rationing goods sent to European neutrals by the United States to prevent them from sending their own produce to the Central Powers; and 4) blacklisting firms suspected of trading with Germany. Each of these steps was protested by the Wilson government, but England always replied that she had not signed the Declaration of London and was not bound to obey its provisions. Pro-Allied sentiment prevented Wilson from forcing Britain's hand with an arms embargo.

b. THE CASE AGAINST GERMANY. Faced with economic

THE ALLIES AND THE CENTRAL POWERS

ALLIES

ALLIES

CENTRAL

POWERS

ALLIES

ENGLAND   FRANCE   RUSSIA   GERMANY   TURKEY

ALSACE LORRAINE   BERLIN   BAGHDAD   CONSTANTINOPLE

Chart by *Graphics Institute*, N. Y. C.   From: Muzzey—*A History of Our Country*, New Edition, Ginn & Co.

strangulation unless the Allied blockade was broken, Germany resorted to the submarine warfare that finally brought the United States into the war.

I. *Beginning of Submarine Warfare.* In February, 1915, Germany announced that all enemy ships would be sunk on sight in the waters surrounding the British Isles, and that neutral ships should avoid the area to prevent "unfortunate mistakes." Wilson warned the Germans that they would be held "strictly accountable" for the loss of American lives or property. Despite this warning, a submarine on March 28, 1915, sank the British ship *Falaba,* and on May 1 the American tanker *Gulflight.* Germany apologized for the latter sinking, but refused to abandon submarine warfare.

II. *Sinking of the Lusitania.* On May 7, 1915, the crack Cunard liner, the *Lusitania,* was torpedoed off the Irish coast with a loss of 1200 lives including 128 Americans. Popular resentment in the United States was so great that war seemed certain. Wilson sent a series of notes demanding that Germany make reparation for damages and abandon her lawless practices; his second note was so warlike that his Secretary of State, *William Jennings Bryan,* resigned in protest, holding that Americans should not travel on belligerent ships. He was replaced by *Robert Lansing,* who was more sympathetic to England. Meanwhile a second British liner, the *Arabic,* was torpedoed on August 19, 1915. The protest was so violent that on September 1, 1915, Germany promised to sink no more passenger ships without provision for the safety of the passengers.

III. *The Sussex Pledge.* On March 24, 1916, the French liner, *Sussex,* was sunk, injuring several Americans. As this violated the *Arabic Pledge,* Wilson delivered an ultimatum in which he threatened to sever diplomatic relations unless unrestricted submarine warfare was abandoned. Convinced that war was certain unless she backed down, Germany issued the *Sussex Pledge* (May, 1916), agreeing not to sink merchant ships "without warning and without saving human lives." This ended the submarine controversy for nine months.

C. Preparedness for War. By 1916 the "rape of Belgium," the submarine warfare, and atrocity propaganda had convinced many Americans that only the defeat of the Central Powers would save the United States from eventual attack. As interventionist sentiment grew, Wilson made a vain effort to bring peace to Europe, at the same time preparing for war.

1. Wilson's Early Peace Efforts. The President was convinced that American participation could only be avoided by ending the war. In February, 1916, when the contestants were deadlocked on the western front, he sent his confidential agent, Colonel *Edward M. House,* to Europe with proposals for a peace conference. Both England and Germany rejected the proposal.

2. Military Preparedness. Pressure for an American armament program was exerted by the *National Security League,* which was financed by munitions and industrial interests, and by such influential spokesmen as *Theodore Roosevelt* and General Leonard Wood. Fearing that rearmament would increase the demand for war, Wilson resisted as long as possible, but backed down as the election of 1916 approached. Under his prodding Congress passed: 1) the *National Defense Act* (June, 1916) which increased the size of the army, placed the state militia under federal control, and inaugurated military training in schools and colleges; 2) the *Naval Appropriation Bill* (August, 1916) which authorized the construction of many new warships; and 3) the *United States Shipping Board Act* (September, 1916) which appropriated $50,000,000 to buy or build merchant vessels. At the same time Wilson created a *Council of National Defense* to mobilize industry if war came.

D. The Election of 1916.

1. The Nominating Conventions. The Democrats renominated Wilson on a platform boasting of his domestic reforms, tariff policy, and efforts to keep the peace. When the Republicans, refusing to heed the pleading of Progressives, chose as their candidate *Charles Evans Hughes,* the New York Supreme Court Justice, the Progressive Party retaliated by nominating Theodore Roosevelt once more. Roosevelt refused to run, asking Progressives to follow him back into the Republican camp. Most refused to do so, supporting Wilson instead.

2. The Election. Wilson's domestic program and the Democratic slogan *"He Kept Us Out Of War"* proved more effective than the Republican attacks on the President's diplomacy and pacifism. He was re-elected by a very close vote, having a popular majority of 600,000 and 277 electoral votes to 254 for Hughes. The South and Far West favored Wilson; the East and Middle West supported Hughes.

E. American Entry in World War I.

1. Wilson's Final Peace Efforts. Viewing the election as a mandate for his program, Wilson decided on a final attempt to end the European war by a negotiated peace. In December, 1916, he asked the belligerents to state the terms on which they would cease hostilities. He reported the results in a memorable address to Congress on January 22, 1917. The Central Powers, he said, demanded impossible territorial claims and reparations; the Allies also asked full reparations and guarantees for the future. As these terms were irreconcilable, Wilson laid down his own terms for a just peace: 1) it must be a "peace without victory"; 2) the right of self-determination and the equality of all nations must be recognized; 3) military and naval armaments must be limited; 4) the freedom of the seas must be guaranteed; 5) secret alliances must be abandoned; and 6) a league to enforce peace must be formed. These proposals aroused little enthusiasm in the United States and none at all among the belligerents.

2. Causes for American Entry.

a. RENEWAL OF SUBMARINE WARFARE. On January 31, 1917, Germany informed the United States that after February 1 all merchant ships bound for the British Isles or the Mediterranean, whether belligerent or neutral, would be sunk on sight. The Central Powers knew that this meant American entry, but believed their submarines could starve England into submission before aid became effective. Wilson severed diplomatic relations at once, then asked Congress for authority to arm merchant ships to run the submarine blockade. When a bill for this purpose was defeated by a filibuster of southern and western Progressives under *Robert LaFollette,* the President found authority for the step in an ancient statute. Between February 3 and April 1 eight American ships were sunk.

b. THE ZIMMERMANN NOTE. In February, 1917, the United States obtained a copy of a note from Germany to Mexico, promising that country Texas and the Southwest if it entered the war. When this was published on March 1 it aroused great resentment.

c. THE RUSSIAN REVOLUTION. In March, 1917, the Tsar of Russia was overthrown and a republican government established. Now all the Allies were democracies, all the Central Powers autocracies.

3. The United States Enters the War. On April 2, 1917, Wilson asked Congress for a declaration of war. On April 6 a war resolution was passed by overwhelming majorities that reflected the popular will.

II. THE UNITED STATES IN WORLD WAR I.

A. The Home Front. The Allies' supplies of food, munitions, and industrial goods were so nearly exhausted that November 1 had been set as the day they must sue for peace unless they received American aid. Hence the task of the United States was to mobilize not only manpower but factories and farms. This was entrusted to the *Council of National Defense,* which assumed dictatorial powers over the nation's economy.

1. Mobilizing Manpower. A *Selective Service Act* (May, 1917) required all men to register for a draft. Under this law 2,200,000 men were inducted into the army. With the regular army, national guard, and smaller branches of the service, this raised the armed force of the United States to 4,000,000. All were given six months' basic training in one of thirty-two camps, while officers were trained in other camps or in colleges. Eventually 2,000,000 men were sent overseas.

2. Mobilizing Industry. To consolidate factory production, the Council of National Defense in July, 1917, created a *War Industries Board* under *Bernard M. Baruch.* This was given dictatorial powers over manufacturing. It standardized products to cut costs, told factories what they could or could not manufacture, developed new industries, fixed prices, and in various ways increased the nation's production 20 per cent before the war's end.

3. Mobilizing Transportation.

a. OVERSEAS SHIPPING. An _Emergency Fleet Corporation_ (April, 1917) was authorized to purchase, build, or requisition enough ships to bridge the Atlantic despite submarine attacks. This organization, which worked under the direction of the _War Shipping Board,_ appropriated German ships that were in American ports, bought neutral ships, and built so many vessels that the tonnage of the merchant marine increased from one million to ten million. Within a year it was building two ships for every one sunk by submarines.

b. DOMESTIC TRANSPORTATION. The railroads soon bogged down under the heavy strain of moving goods to the east coast. In December, 1917, they were taken over by the government, which operated them henceforth as one system. This proved highly efficient, but the high rental costs and low rates charged shippers cost the government $700,000,000.

4. Mobilizing the Farmers.

To assure adequate food for the United States and its allies, a _Food Administration_ was created (August, 1917) with _Herbert Hoover_ in charge. This stimulated grain production by promising to buy all wheat at $2 a bushel, while the production of other crops was encouraged in the same way. At the same time consumption was curtailed by campaigns urging the people to "hooverize" or find substitutes for meat and cereals. Food exports in 1918 were twice those of any prewar year.

5. Mobilizing the Natural Resources.

A _Fuel Administration_ under Harry A. Garfield was created to stimulate production, and cut down consumption, of coal and oil. This not only spurred miners to greater efforts, but instituted "fuelless Mondays" and "gasless Sundays" as well as inaugurating daylight-saving time to conserve coal.

6. Mobilizing Finance.

The United States not only paid its own wartime expenses of $22,000,000,000 but loaned $9,000,000,000 to the Allies to purchase goods in this country. These sums were raised by: 1) taxes, which were increased in volume and variety; and 2) loans in the form of _"Liberty" bonds_ sold to the American people. In all, five issues were floated, of from $2,000,000,000 to $6,000,000,000, and all were oversubscribed.

7. *Mobilizing Public Opinion.*

a. DOMESTIC PROPAGANDA. Congress established the *Committee on Public Information* (April, 1917) under a liberal journalist, *George Creel,* to mobilize American thought. This committee inundated the nation with a flood of propaganda in newspaper advertisements, posters, motion pictures, books, pamphlets, and speeches. Every individual was made aware of the lofty war aims of the United States and its Allies.

b. FOREIGN PROPAGANDA. This was designed to break down the will to fight among enemy peoples. Wilson from the first held that the war was with the governments of the Central Powers, not with the people. This point he emphasized in a series of lofty messages, hoping to weaken enemy resistance and lay a moral basis for the peace negotiations. His program was climaxed on January 22, 1918, when he outlined to Congress the *Fourteen Points* that he deemed essential to a just peace. In addition to suggestions for territorial changes in Europe he proposed: 1) open diplomacy to replace secret treaties; 2) freedom of the seas; 3) removal of economic barriers between nations; 4) armament reduction; 5) readjustment of colonial claims with the people concerned having an equal voice in the settlement; 6) the redrawing of European boundaries along national lines; and 7) the formation of an association of nations.

c. TREATMENT OF DISLOYALTY. Although most Americans, including those of German descent, were completely loyal, a handful of Socialists branded the war as a capitalistic crime. Their utterances aroused a hysterical attack on disloyalty. Three measures were adopted: 1) an *Espionage Act* (June, 1917) provided heavy penalties for attempts to obstruct recruiting or spread treason among troops; 2) a *Sedition Act* (May, 1918) extended the penalties to those who obstructed the sale of bonds, discouraged recruiting, or uttered language abusive of the government, the Constitution, or the flag; 3) a statute of October, 1918, authorized the deportation without jury trial of aliens who advocated the overthrow of the government. Under these laws about 190 persons were tried (including Eugene V. Debs), almost half of whom were convicted. In addition, loyal German-

Americans were abused, the German language banned from schools, and persons with German names subjected to indignities.

B. The European Front.

1. Naval Operations. The navy's task was: 1) to sink submarines, and 2) to convoy troop ships. Under *Admiral William S. Sims* a mine barrage was laid along the coast of Europe to keep U-boats in port. In addition a device was perfected to detect submarines, thus making their destruction easier. About half the German undersea fleet was destroyed during the last year of the war. Ships were also convoyed successfully; only six transports were torpedoed and of these, two made port.

2. The Army in France.

a. TRANSPORTING THE ARMY. An *American Expeditionary Force* (A.E.F.) was sent abroad as soon as troops could be trained, although only 200,000 reached France during 1917. In 1918, however, nearly 2,000,000 reached the front. Secretary of War *Newton D. Baker* placed the A.E.F. under *General John J. Pershing,* while the task of shipping supplies was entrusted to the Services of Supply. This efficient organization built docks, erected warehouses, laid miles of railroad and telegraph lines, and distributed seven million tons of supplies.

b. THE MILITARY SITUATION. Germany's drive to end the war before American aid became effective almost succeeded. In October, 1917, Italy was demoralized by defeat at *Caporetto,* while in March, 1918, the Russian communists withdrew that country from the war with the *Treaty of Brest-Litovsk.* This allowed Germany to concentrate all her troops on the western front, where she enjoyed numerical superiority. Between March and June, 1918, she launched three offensives against the British and French troops who had held her at bay in northwestern France. By June 15 the Kaiser's armies reached the right bank of the Marne, threatening Paris. To check this drive, Marshall *Ferdinand Foch* of France was made supreme commander of all Allied forces, while American troops were rushed overseas so rapidly that between March and October, 1918, 1,750,000 reached France.

c. AMERICAN MILITARY OPERATIONS. American troops saw their first serious fighting after July 15, 1918, when the Germans began the *Second Battle of the Marne*. With the French they stemmed the advance on *Chateau-Thierry*, then led a counterattack on the German lines at Soissons. Again in September Americans won back the *St. Mihiel* salient, a triangle jutting into Allied territory. More important was the forty-seven-day battle, beginning in September, that captured the *Meuse-Argonne* area and cut a railroad that supplied much of the German front. More than 1,200,000 Americans fought in this battle. As similar defeats were suffered all along the Hindenburg Line, the Germans hastily installed a parliamentary government (October 3, 1918), and informed Wilson that they would consider peace on the basis of the Fourteen Points. After a month of negotiations General Foch was instructed to negotiate an armistice. This was signed on November 11, 1918, two days after the Kaiser fled to Holland. About 5000 American soldiers, however, co-operated with other Allied troops in fighting minor engagements against the Russian communists at Archangel and Murmansk (September, 1918-May, 1919). Another expeditionary force remained in eastern Siberia until January, 1920.

III. WILSON AND THE PEACE CONFERENCE.

A. Obstacles to a Just Peace.

1. The American Situation. Just before the armistice, sweeping victories in the *elections of 1918* gave the Republicans control of both houses of Congress. This repudiation of Wilson was due to dislike of his dictatorial methods and to normal dissatisfaction with wartime controls. The President was no longer able to speak for American opinion.

2. French and British Attitudes. Both were determined to punish Germany for causing the war. France especially wanted territorial concessions and reparations, as well as a permanently weakened Germany.

3. The Secret Treaties. Before and during the war the Allies negotiated numerous secret treaties providing for a division of spoils. Wilson knew of their existence but felt that his financial whip hand over the Allies would force them to abandon their selfish ambitions.

4. The Communist Menace. Communism threatened to spread over Europe amidst the chaos and poverty that followed the war. In the face of this danger Wilson was forced to accept any terms that would bring peace, rather than prolonging discussion while communism spread. All of these things doomed his hope for a just peace based on the Fourteen Points.

B. The Peace Negotiations.

1. The American Delegation. Breaking all precedent, Wilson led the American delegation to Paris. With him were Colonel House, Secretary of State Lansing, General Tasker H. Bliss, and Henry White, a career diplomat. Only White was a Republican, while no member of the House or Senate was included. Wilson deliberately chose a weak delegation as he expected to write the treaty himself.

2. The Negotiations. The Peace Conference opened at Versailles on January 18, 1919. All important decisions were made by the *Big Four: Wilson* for the United States, Georges *Clemenceau* for France, David *Lloyd George* for England, and Vittorio *Orlando* for Italy. Wilson was forced to back down repeatedly before these skilled diplomats, until little remained of the idealistic peace he had planned. Unsatisfactory as was the treaty, however, it was less selfish than if Wilson had not been there.

3. Terms of the Treaty of Versailles (June 28, 1919). The final treaty: 1) forced Germany to admit her guilt for the war; 2) stripped her of her colonies; 3) took from her Alsace-Lorraine, Posen, the Saar Basin, parts of Schleswig and Silesia, and other territories; 4) forced her to pay reparations (later fixed at $56,500,000,000) for the cost of the war; and 5) stripped away her entire military and naval establishment.

4. The League of Nations.

a. WILSON AND THE LEAGUE. On Wilson's insistence, the conference on January 25, 1919, authorized a special committee to draw up a constitution for a League of Nations. When adopted in February this was made an integral part of the treaty. Wilson later obtained amendments to the covenant (constitution) after consulting leaders at home, hoping to make the League acceptable to Americans.

b. Organization of the League. The Covenant of the League provided for: 1) an *Assembly* in which all member nations had an equal voice; 2) a *Council* made up of representatives from the United States, England, France, Italy, Japan, and four other nations elected by the Assembly; 3) a *Secretariat,* permanently located at Geneva, to handle routine work of the League.

c. Purposes of the League. Member nations pledged themselves in the Covenant to: 1) respect and preserve against external aggression the territorial integrity and political independence of all member nations *(Article X)*; 2) submit to the League all disputes threatening war; 3) employ military and economic sanctions against nations resorting to war; 4) reduce armaments; and 5) cooperate in setting up a *Permanent Court of International Justice* to settle disputes.

C. American Rejection of the Treaty.

1. Objections to the Treaty. Opposition to the Versailles Treaty was voiced as soon as it was submitted to the

THE LEAGUE of NATIONS

LEAGUE ASSEMBLY

PERMANENT COURT OF INTERNATIONAL JUSTICE

LEAGUE COUNCIL

Financial & Economic Section

Transit Section

Administrative Section

Mandates Section

SECRETARIAT

Disarmament Section

Health Section

INTERNATIONAL LABOR ORGANIZATION

Social Section

From: Muzzey—*A History of Our Country,* New Edition, Ginn & Co.
Chart by *Graphics Institute, N. Y. C.*

Senate for ratification on July 10, 1919. This was based on: 1) political jealousy aroused by Wilson's refusal to consult Republican senators in drafting the treaty; 2) liberals' dislike of the treaty's realistic features; 3) the opposition of such racial groups as German-Americans, Irish-Americans, and Italian-Americans, who resented the way their countries had been treated; 4) fear that participation in the League would involve the United States in European troubles. In addition, Republicans attacked the treaty as a means of discrediting the Democrats politically.

2. Division of the Senate. The Senate divided into three groups: 1) Democratic followers of Wilson who favored ratification at once; 2) *"Irreconcilables"* under *Hiram Johnson* of California, *William E. Borah* of Idaho, and *Robert LaFollette* of Wisconsin, who advocated isolation from Europe and the complete rejection of the League; 3) moderates who favored participation in the League only if certain *reservations* were added to the Covenant to protect American interests.

3. Action by the Senate. The leader of the *reservationists, Henry Cabot Lodge* of Massachusetts, proposed fourteen amendments to the League Covenant, the most important exempting the United States from sending troops under Article X without congressional approval. Wilson refused to accept this formula, carrying his case instead to the people with a speaking tour through the Middle West. There he suffered a paralytic stroke which permanently incapacitated him. On November 19, 1919, the League was defeated by the Senate, both with and without reservations. Again in March, 1920, it failed to receive the necessary two-thirds majority, although the vote was 49 to 35 in favor. When the Democrats were defeated in the election of 1920, the Republicans accepted the vote as a mandate against the League. On August 25, 1921, Congress adopted a *joint resolution* declaring the war at an end.

IV. MODERN IMPLICATIONS OF WORLD WAR I.

A. Why the United States Fought. World War I demonstrated that the United States could not stay isolated from any major European war. Historians have quarreled since 1917 as to the exact causes for American entry, but they agree that participation was inevitable. Their conclusions may be summarized in this way:

1. Cultural Ties. The American people were unneutral from the beginning, favoring an Allied victory. This was because: 1) a majority traced their ancestry to England or Canada; 2) they remembered French aid during the American Revolution and continued friendship with France since that time; 3) they were convinced that the struggle was between democratic and despotic nations. With the people unneutral, neutrality was impossible.

2. Influence of Allied Propaganda. The effectiveness of Allied propaganda was shown by the hysterical hatred of German-Americans and others suspected of disloyalty. Yet the propaganda was effective only because Americans wanted to believe. This was shown by the complete failure of German propaganda.

3. Economic Factors. During the 1930's many historians and politicians tried to prove that America's economic stake in an Allied victory forced American entry; participation, they said, resulted from pressure from munitions makers, international bankers, and other "merchants of death." Yet no shred of evidence can be found to show that bankers or munitions makers had any influence on the President or members of Congress who voted for war.

4. Idealistic Factors. More important than propaganda or economic factors were the ideals of the people and their President. The majority believed that the German "Rape of Belgium," Junker militarism, and the submarine campaign all showed that the Central Powers menaced civilization. President Wilson, moreover, felt that the United States would be in a stronger position to dictate a just peace as a participant than as a spectator.

5. National Interest. The principal cause for American participation was the same as in all wars: to protect the national interest. By the spring of 1917 Russia had withdrawn from the war and Italy was beaten. France was stalemated on the Hindenburg line while its resources dwindled; England was only months away from capitulating before the submarine blockade. American entry alone would prevent

Germany from reigning supreme over Europe. In such a situation the safety of the United States would have been threatened. The nation went to war to preserve its sovereignty and institutions.

B. Why the United States Rejected the League. Not one individual, but three groups, were to blame for the recurrence of isolationism that prevented the United States from joining the League of Nations:

1. The Democratic Irreconcilables. Wilson's failure to consult the opposition party in drafting the treaty, his unwillingness to take Senate leaders into his confidence, his dictatorial methods of dealing with Congress, and his refusal to compromise with the reservationists, all contributed to the rejection.

2. The Republican Irreconcilables. Equally to blame were the Republicans under Henry Cabot Lodge who used the treaty to discredit the Democrats. Lodge's reservations were actually designed to defeat the treaty, rather than make it acceptable. He hoped in his way to create an issue for the election of 1920.

3. The American People. At the beginning of the battle over ratification the majority of Americans favored the League. Yet they were so indifferent to world affairs that they allowed politicians of both parties to reject the instrument that might have prevented World War II. That second conflict was needed to teach them that the United States could only stay out of war by helping keep the world at peace.

ADDITIONAL READING

The European background is exhaustively studied in Sidney B. Fay, *The Origins of the World War* (1928), and B. E. Schmitt, *The Coming of the War* (1930). Works dealing with American participation are highly controversial. Walter Millis, *Road to War* (1935), and C. C. Tansill, *America Goes to War* (1938), reflect the isolationism of the 1930's in their overemphasis of economic forces and British propaganda. Newton D. Baker, *Why We Went to War* (1936), and Charles Seymour, *American Neutrality, 1914-1917* (1935), argue uncritically that the submarine campaign was principally responsible for American involvement. H. C. Peterson, *Propaganda for War* (1938), studies the influence of British propaganda, while Alice M. Morrissey, *The American Defense of Neutral Rights, 1914-1917* (1939), is a legalistic study. A readable account of the United States during the war is Frederic L. Paxson, *American Democracy and the World War: America at War* (1939). The fullest treatment of the fight for the League is D. L. Fleming, *The United States and the League of Nations* (1932). Two works on the same subject by Thomas A. Bailey, *Woodrow Wilson and the Lost Peace* (1944) and *Woodrow Wilson and the Great Betrayal* (1945), are marred by their hostile attitude toward Wilson.

Chapter XII

The Era of "Normalcy"

1920-1932

⟪ NATIONALISM AND CONSERVATISM

During the decade following World War I a war-weary people, disillusioned by the realities of the peace and rendered indifferent to society by prosperity, reverted to the conservatism and nationalism that was typical of all postwar eras. Yet the persuasive influences of progressivism and internationalism could not be completely rejected. On the domestic front the Republican presidents of the period praised laissez faire, yet adopted many of the regulatory measures that had proven efficient during wartime. In foreign policy they rejected the League and world cooperation, yet carried the nation into the world arena to a degree that would have scandalized isolationists a generation before.

I. READJUSTMENT TO A PEACETIME ECONOMY.

A. Economic Demobilization.

1. The Railroads. Wilson wished to return the railroads to private ownership but to retain the more desirable features of unified operation. The result was the *Esch-Cummins Transportation Act* (1920) which provided: 1) the Interstate Commerce Commission was authorized to evaluate railroad property and fix rates that would allow a fair return on the investment; 2) a *recapture clause* ruled that all returns over 6 per cent would be divided between the road and the government; 3) railroad combinations were encouraged in the interest of efficiency; and 4) a _Railway Labor Board_ was created to mediate labor disputes on interstate carriers. The act's failure to operate satisfactorily was due largely to a dispute between the I.C.C. and the roads on the means of evaluating railroad property for rate-fixing purposes. The I.C.C. wished evaluation to rest on reproduction cost in 1914; the roads, on reproduction cost in the 1920's, which would be far higher. The Supreme Court in _St. Louis and O'Fallon Railway Co. v. United States_ (1929) eventually accepted the railroads' contention, defeating the purposes of the act.

2. The Merchant Marine. The _Merchant Marine Act_ (1920) authorized the United States Shipping Board to dispose of the 1500 ships that it owned at the end of the war, and to loan the resulting proceeds to ship builders. When this failed to stimulate the construction of a sizeable merchant marine, the Jones-White Act (1928) increased the amount that could be loaned for ship construction and granted generous mail contracts to American vessels.

B. Veterans' Legislation.

1. Disability Compensation. A _Veterans' Bureau_ (1921) was authorized to administer pensions and hospitalization for the benefit of veterans disabled during the war.

2. Adjusted Compensation for War Service. A _Bonus_ for all soldiers, varying with the term of service, was advocated by the _American Legion_ (1919) and other veterans' organizations. An _Adjusted Compensation Act_ (1924) granted each veteran a twenty-year endowment policy based on the length of time he had served overseas. Owners could borrow against these from the government at 6 per cent interest. Pressure from a depression-ridden "Bonus Army" forced Congress in 1936 to authorize payment of the veterans' certificates in 3 per cent bonds that could be redeemed at once.

C. Social Readjustments.

1. Prohibition. The war allowed prohibitionists to argue that cereals should be used for food rather than for beer or whiskey. Their pressure led Congress to adopt the

Eighteenth Amendment (December, 1917), which was ratified by January, 1920. This forbade the manufacture and sale of all intoxicating beverages, which were defined by the *Volstead Act* (1919) as those containing more than one-half of 1 per cent of alcohol. Despite federal efforts to enforce the measure, drinking not only increased but became more fashionable during the next decade.

2. Women's Suffrage. The wartime efforts of women in jobs that ranged from Red Cross nursing to serving as "farmerettes" won support for women's suffrage. The *Nineteenth Amendment,* granting women the vote, was adopted by Congress in 1919 and ratified in 1920.

II. POLITICS OF THE 1920's.

A. The Harding Administration.

1. The Election of 1920. The Republicans nominated *Warren G. Harding,* a small-town Ohio politician whose party regularity and support of the Lodge reservationists appealed to standpatters. The platform attacked Wilson's "autocracy" and hedged on the League issue. *Calvin Coolidge,* governor of Massachusetts, was selected as Harding's running mate. The Democrats named *James M. Cox* of Ohio, a mild liberal, with *Franklin D. Roosevelt* as vice-presidential candidate. Their platform praised Wilson's record, and endorsed the League. The voters, reacting against wartime controls, gave Harding an overwhelming majority.

2. The Harding Scandals. Harding surrounded himself with mediocre politicians, many of whom were members of his "Ohio Gang." The result was a series of scandals that rivaled those of Grant's administration.

a. THE BUREAU SCANDALS. The director of the Veterans' Bureau, *Charles R. Forbes,* was found guilty of squandering $200,000,000 in his two years in office, much of it in fraudulent hospital contracts, and was sentenced to prison. The alien property custodian was disclosed to have fraudulently disposed of German chemical patents and other valuable property. Harding's Attorney General, *Harry M. Daugherty,* was dismissed from office as the result of the illegal sale of liquor permits.

b. THE TEAPOT DOME SCANDALS. In 1921 the administration of naval oil reserves was transferred from the Navy Department to Secretary of the Interior *Albert B. Fall*. Fall in 1922 secretly leased the *Teapot Dome Oil Reserve* in Wyoming to a prominent oil man, *Harry F. Sinclair*, and the *Elks Hills Reserve* in California to *Edward L. Doheny*. When a Senate investigating committee under *Thomas J. Walsh* of Montana disclosed that Sinclair had "lent" Fall $100,000, both Sinclair and Fall were imprisoned and the leases canceled.

3. Death of Harding. Although personally innocent, Harding was so demoralized by these revelations that he died on August 2, 1923.

B. The Coolidge Administration.

1. Coolidge as President. Coolidge became President on the death of Harding. A taciturn man with a reputation for honesty, he quickly won the confidence of his country. His well-publicized statement: "The business of America is business," summed up the laissez-faire philosophy that governed his administration.

2. The Election of 1924.

a. THE NOMINATING CONVENTIONS. Coolidge was nominated unanimously by the *Republicans.* The *Democrats,* on the other hand, were divided into an immigrant-labor-city faction led by Alfred E. Smith of New York, and a rural-southern-western faction under William G. McAdoo of California. When these two candidates remained deadlocked for ballot after ballot during the convention, the nomination was finally given to a conservative dark horse, *John W. Davis* of New York. Liberals, who could see no difference between Coolidge and Davis, joined with Socialists to form the *Progressive Party* which nominated *Robert M. LaFollette* of Wisconsin. Their platform called for tariff revision, public ownership of waterpower, farm relief, outlawing the labor injunction, and other progressive measures.

b. RESULTS OF THE ELECTION. Coolidge won a decisive victory, with an electoral vote of 328 to 136 for Davis and 13 for LaFollette. The Republicans also won control of both houses of Congress.

C. The Election of Herbert Hoover.

1. The Nominating Conventions. Coolidge declined to be a candidate in 1928, although his cryptic "I do not choose to run" allowed supporters to hope that he could be drafted. The *Republicans* nominated *Herbert Hoover,* an engineering-trained businessman whose administration of Belgian relief during the war pleased humanitarians and whose record as Secretary of Commerce under Coolidge won the confidence of businessmen. *Alfred E. Smith*'s popularity had grown so rapidly that he was nominated without difficulty by the *Democrats.*

2. The Campaign and Election. Although the platforms of the two parties were almost identical, the contest gained color through the personalities of the candidates. Smith departed from the Democratic platform to denounce prohibition and the partnership between Republican politicians and industrialists. Hoover retaliated by branding Smith's program as state socialism. Smith was handicapped, particularly in rural areas, by his Catholic religion, his opposition to prohibition, and his Tammany background. Hence he won only 87 electoral votes to 444 for Hoover. Even the Solid South went Republican, with the exception of the Gulf States, South Carolina, and Arkansas.

III. THE DOMESTIC SCENE UNDER REPUBLICAN CONTROL, 1920-1932.

A. Social Conflicts. The conservatism and nationalism of the era were shown in the wave of bigotry that swept the United States.

1. The Great Red Scare.

a. CAUSES FOR UNREST. The hysterical fear of anything that threatened the status quo was occasioned by: 1) The *spread of communism* in Europe after the Russian Revolution. 2) *Labor disputes* that multiplied when employers, freed of wartime controls, tried to offset gains made by organized labor during the war. Labor responded with strikes that involved 4,000,000 workers during 1919. Most famous were the *Boston Police Strike,* which was broken up by Governor Calvin Coolidge, and the coal strike of the United Mine Workers, which was defeated by the use of the federal injunction. 3) *The Recession of 1920.* Wartime

prosperity broke sharply in 1920 with the falling off of the
foreign demand for American goods. During 1921 business
failures left 5,000,000 men unemployed. Industry quickly
recovered, but agriculture remained depressed for a decade.

b. THE ATTACK ON MINORITY GROUPS.

i. *The Palmer Raids.* Sensing the popular hatred of
communism, Wilson's Attorney General, *A. Mitchell Palmer,*
during 1919-1920 deported suspected radicals, raided the
homes and offices of socialists and communists, and arrested
hundreds whose economic views were unorthodox. In the
end nearly all were released.

ii. *The Sacco-Vanzetti Case.* In 1920 two Italian immigrants, *Nicola Sacco* and *Bartolomeo Vanzetti,* were
arrested on a murder charge near Boston. Despite contra-
dictory evidence, they were sentenced to hang when the trial
revealed that they were atheists and anarchists. They were
executed in 1927 after a period of controversy that attracted
world attention.

iii. *Suppression of Socialists.* In 1920 the New York
legislature expelled five socialists for no other crime than
party membership. In twenty-four states criminal-syndical-
ism laws made membership in the Socialist or Communist
parties a criminal offense. This attack on civil liberties was
upheld by the Supreme Court in *Schenck v. United States*
(1919), which sanctioned the conviction of a man who had
criticized conscription, and *Abrams v. United States* (1919),
which imposed a twenty-year sentence on Jacob Abrams for
distributing a pamphlet asking workers to rise against American military intervention in Russia. Both cases were notable
for the ringing dissenting opinions of the great liberal justice, *Oliver Wendell Holmes.*

2. The Ku Klux Klan. The modern Klan originated in
Georgia in 1915 but gained strength only in the 1920's. Dedicated to an attack on Negroes, Jews, Catholics, aliens, religious modernists, pacifists, and internationalists, it grew so
rapidly that it boasted five million members by 1924, largely
in the West and South. Its program of terrorism not only
spread fear among minorities, but also allowed the Klan to
gain political control in several states, notably Indiana. This

eventually aroused resentment, but the Klan's decline after 1925 was due largely to internal corruption.

3. Immigration Restriction. Nativistic sentiment, together with fear of an alien flood from war-devastated Europe, was responsible for the _Immigration Act of 1921_ which limited immigration from any country to 3 per cent of that nation's nationals residing in the United States in 1910. This _Quota System_ not only reduced migration to a trickle, but also discriminated against aliens from southern and eastern Europe. The _Johnson Act_ (1924): 1) lowered the quota from each country to 2 per cent of that nation's nationals in the United States in 1890, further discriminating against the New Immigration; 2) allowed the unrestricted migration of native-born Canadians and Latin Americans; and 3) barred Oriental immigration entirely. This provision greatly offended Japan, which had already stopped migration to the United States under the Gentleman's Agreement (see p. 139).

4. Protests of the Intellectuals. The intolerance and nationalism of the 1920's aroused intellectuals not to protest but to ridicule. Some fled to Paris to escape a country so sunk in materialism that aesthetic values were forgotten. Others subjected their native land to tirades of abuse and criticism. Their leader was _Henry L. Mencken_, who turned his magazine, _The American Mercury_, into the bible of the intellectuals. Novelists reflected the same critical spirit, as attested by Sinclair Lewis' _Main Street_ (1920) and _Babbitt_ (1922), Sherwood Anderson's _Winesburg, Ohio_ (1919), and Theodore Dreiser's _An American Tragedy_ (1925).

B. Government and Industry, 1920-1932. The Republican legislative program was designed to aid business through budgetary reforms, tariff policy, and the sanction of industrial consolidation.

1. Budgetary Reforms. The Republican program of economy and tax reduction was aided by a congressional measure creating the _Budget Bureau_ (1921) to prepare estimates of federal revenue and recommend expenditures. Neither this nor the business-minded Secretary of the Treasury who served under Harding and Coolidge, _Andrew Mellon_, could affect many economies in government. Instead, tax reductions in the higher income brackets and on certain businesses were made possible only by the prosperity of the decade. This helped reduce the national debt from $24,000,-000,000 in 1920 to $16,000,000,000 in 1930.

2. Tariff Legislation.

a. THE FORDNEY-MCCUMBER TARIFF (1922). This raised tariffs to the highest level in American history. To temper criticism Congress authorized the Tariff Commission to recommend changes that would equalize production costs at home and abroad, and gave the President power to raise or lower duties as much as 50 per cent. This flexible clause was used thirty-seven times, thirty-two to raise duties.

b. THE HAWLEY-SMOOT TARIFF (1930). Hoover was apparently interested in genuine tariff reform, but lobbyist pressure on the Republican majority in Congress resulted instead in the _Hawley-Smoot Bill_, which raised duties another 20 per cent. Hoover signed the measure despite protests from many manufacturers and all economists. Within two years twenty-five nations passed retaliatory tariffs raising duties on American goods. This: 1) injured the foreign trade of the United States; 2) forced many manufacturers to move their plants abroad; and 3) fostered the spirit of economic nationalism that helped precipitate World War II.

3. Business Consolidation.

Holding companies and trade associations were used to create industrial monopolies with Republican approval.

a. HOLDING COMPANIES. These were corporations that owned the stock of several producing companies; in the field of hydroelectric power especially, holding companies were pyramided on holding companies for several layers above the actual producers of electricity. The resulting division of profits raised electrical rates. Nor did the _Federal Power Commission_ (1920) prevent this consolidation, as its sympathies were with the power interests. Liberal protests were led by Senator _George W. Norris_ of Nebraska, who campaigned for the government operation of a war-built power and fertilizer plant at _Muscle Shoals_ on the Tennessee River. This was branded as socialism by the Republican presidents, who twice vetoed Muscle Shoals bills.

b. TRADE ASSOCIATIONS. More than four hundred combinations of manufacturers were formed under Herbert Hoover as Secretary of Commerce. Through these, producers of particular commodities (hardware, textiles, etc.) united to pool information, fix prices, cooperate in advertising, standardize wages, share purchases, and in other ways eliminate competition.

c. RESULTS OF REPUBLICAN POLICY. By the end of the Hoover administration monopoly was more widespread than in 1900. Fifty-three per cent of the corporate wealth was owned by 594 corporations, while the largest twenty banks controlled 27 per cent of the nation's banking deposits. In the extractive industries one corporation owned all the aluminum deposits, another more than half the iron ore, and eight others three-fourths of the anthracite coal.

C. Government and Agriculture, 1920-1932.

1. Agricultural Depression. Agriculture never recovered from the Recession of 1920. As prices slid downward almost 75 per cent between 1920 and 1932, farm income declined from $15,000,000,000 to $5,000,000,000. This slump was caused by the contraction of European markets and world overproduction. At the same time higher taxes and mounting prices for manufactured goods further reduced the farmers' income, while the burden of debt contracted during the prosperous wartime period hung over their heads.

2. Republican Efforts at Reform.

a. EXPANDED CREDIT FACILITIES. In 1921 Congress revived the *War Finance Corporation* as a lending agency to finance the export of farm surpluses. The credit facilities of the *Farm Loan Banks* (see pp. 127-128) were also broadened, while the *Intermediate-Credits Act* (1923) authorized loans on livestock and crops bound for market.

3. Farmers' Demands. Acting through a bipartisan *Farm Bloc* in Congress, the farmers sought relief through two devices:

a. THE EQUALIZATION FEE. This was embodied in the *McNary-Haugen Act* which was debated in several congresses and passed in 1927 and 1928, only to be vetoed by President Coolidge. It provided that the government should purchase all surplus crops not needed to supply the domestic market. These would then be sold abroad at the world price. The loss suffered from any unfavorable difference between the world price and the tariff-protected domestic price would be met by an *Equalization Fee* collected from the growers.

b. THE EXPORT DEBENTURE PLAN. This proposed payment of government bounties for agricultural exports. These bounties would be paid in the form of *Debentures* which would be interchangeable with import duties. Such a bill was vetoed by President Hoover.

4. The Hoover Farm Program. To offset farmer agitation for the McNary-Haugen Act, Hoover urged on Congress the *Agricultural Marketing Act* (1929). This created a *Federal Farm Board* which was authorized to stimulate cooperatives, encourage crop limitation, and peg the price of crops by purchasing surpluses to withhold them from the market. The Board bought large quantities of wheat and cotton, only to see the price of those commodities decline still more, leaving the government with a heavy loss. The farm problem remained pressing at the close of the Hoover administration.

IV. FOREIGN POLICY OF THE REPUBLICANS, 1920-1932. The end of isolationism was shown by the way in which the Republican presidents, although professedly rejecting an international role for the United States, cooperated with other nations in seeking world collective security.

A. The Search for Collective Security.

1. Relations with the League and World Court.

a. PARTICIPATION IN THE LEAGUE OF NATIONS. The fifty-four nations that joined the League made it an instrument for world peace that the United States could not ignore. In 1922 Secretary of State *Charles Evans Hughes* began sending "unofficial observers" to sessions that involved American interests; after 1924 official delegates were sent. By 1932 the United States had adhered to thirteen international agreements arranged by the League.

b. STRUGGLE OVER THE WORLD COURT. The Permanent Court of International Justice was established at the Hague in 1922. Its organization was planned by an American jurist,

Elihu Root, and Americans were also included on its panel of eleven justices. President Harding in 1923 recommended adherence to the World Court, but the move was defeated by Senate isolationists. In 1926 the Senate finally voted to join if the Court would accept five reservations, the most important prohibiting the judges from handing down advisory opinions that involved American interest without American consent. Although these were accepted, the Senate took no further action. American adherence was finally rejected in 1935 by a Senate vote of 52 to 36—seven less than the needed two-thirds.

2. Naval Disarmament.

a. THE WASHINGTON CONFERENCE (1921). Nine nations, meeting at the invitation of the United States, heard Secretary of State Hughes propose a drastic cut in naval armament. The _Five-Power Treaty_ that resulted (1922) set the naval ratio in capital ships for the United States, Great Britain, and Japan at 5-5-3, with 1.75 for Italy and France.

b. THE GENEVA CONFERENCE (1927). The Five-Power Treaty did not outlaw competitive building of cruisers, destroyers, and submarines. To check this, President Coolidge called a five-power conference at Geneva in 1927. As France and Italy refused to attend, the conference accomplished nothing.

c. THE LONDON CONFERENCE (1930). A five-power conference called by President Hoover extended the capital-ship ratio to auxiliary ships, although allowing Japan somewhat greater strength. France and Italy refused to ratify the treaty, which was also abrogated by Japan in 1934.

3. Efforts to Outlaw War.

In 1927 the French Premier Aristide Briand suggested to Coolidge's Secretary of State. Frank B. Kellogg, a nonaggression treaty with the United States. Kellogg expanded this into an international document, known as the _Pact of Paris,_ or the _Kellogg-Briand Pact_ (1927), whose signers renounced war as an instrument of national policy. Although eventually agreed to by sixty-two nations, the Pact was ineffective as it lacked means of enforcement.

B. The Problem of War Debts. The United States loaned $10,000,000,000 to its Allies for war and reconstruction purposes. These were the _war debts._

1. Difficulty of Repayment. Repayment was difficult because: 1) High American tariffs prevented repayment in goods, while the United States already owned most of the world's gold supply; 2) The debtor nations had loaned money to other allied powers, and felt that these debts must be paid before they paid the United States; 3) The debtor nations hoped to make repayment by using German _reparations,_ but Germany had no means of paying the $33,000,-000,000 demanded of it, and defaulted within a year; 4) The Allies felt that their sacrifices in men and money during the early years of the war could only be compensated if the United States canceled the war debts. Americans, on the other hand, looked on the loans as investments that must be returned.

2. Financial Negotiations.

a. REFUNDING THE WAR DEBTS. Between 1923 and 1930 treaties were drafted with seventeen of the debtor nations to extend the period of payment and reduce the original 5 per cent interest charges by about one-half.

b. SCALING DOWN REPARATIONS. To facilitate German reparation payments that would allow the Allies to pay their war debts, the original excessive sum was gradually reduced. In 1924 the _Dawes Plan_ lowered the amounts due, worked out a schedule of payments, and arranged for loans from the United States to speed German economic recovery. By borrowing in the United States Germany met her payments under this plan until 1929, when she again defaulted. The _Young Plan_ (1929) further reduced the amount due to $27,000,000,000, spread payments over fifty-nine years, and provided for a further reduction should the United States consent to scaling down the war debts.

3. End of the Controversy. The great depression made payment of either reparations or war debts impossible. In 1931 President Hoover announced a one-year _moratorium_ on both. A year later the _Lausanne Conference_ (1932) reduced German reparations to $714,000,000 under the assumption that the United States would also cancel its war

debts. When Congress refused, all European nations save
Finland defaulted on their payments. By the end of 1933 the
controversy was over, leaving a residue of irritation behind.

C. Relations with the Far East.

1. The Rise of Japan. American interest in the Far
East declined as the Open Door policy and the acquisition of
the Philippines did not result in the expected economic benefits. Japan took advantage of this and of Europe's preoccupation in World War I to assert her own supremacy. In
1915 she forced China to accept her *Twenty-One Demands*
and thus become virtually a protectorate of Japan, which
also secured special concessions in Manchuria, Mongolia,
and the Shantung Peninsula. To placate the United States,
the *Lansing-Ishii Agreement* (1917) was negotiated, in
which both nations affirmed the Open Door and pledged
themselves to respect the territorial integrity of China.
Japan's propinquity, however, was recognized as giving her
a paramount interest in the Far East.

2. The Washington Conference (1921). This conference not only considered naval disarmament (see p. 171)
but the Far Eastern situation. Two treaties resulted:

a. THE FOUR-POWER TREATY (December, 1921). The
United States, England, France, and Japan pledged themselves to respect each other's rights in the Pacific area and
to settle all conflicts by joint conference.

b. THE NINE-POWER TREATY (February, 1922). The
signers bound themselves to safeguard China's rights and
interests, to respect its territorial integrity, to maintain the
Open Door, and to refrain from seeking special concessions
or spheres of influence. Although containing no provisions
for enforcement, these two treaties shifted the burden of
maintaining China's independence from the United States
and England to all the great powers.

3. Japanese Aggression. In 1931 Japan invaded Manchuria, violating the Washington treaties, the Kellogg-
Briand Pact, and the League Covenant. The United States
sent an official representative to sit with the League Council
in this emergency, but England's refusal to cooperate
doomed chances of positive action. Hoover's Secretary of
State, Henry L. Stimson, announced that his government

would refuse to recognise conquests made in violation of the Kellogg-Briand Pact—a declaration known as the _Stimson Doctrine_ (1932). Despite this rebuff, Japan set up in Manchuria the puppet state of _Manchukuo,_ then extended its military conquests into northern China. Continued protests led Japan to withdraw from the League in 1933. The chain of events leading to World War II had begun.

D. Relations with Latin America.

1. The Mexican Problem. The Mexican Constitution of 1917 gave the government ownership of all mineral and oil resources. If interpreted retroactively, this threatened to wipe out American investments of $300,000,000. The Harding government not only refused to recognize the Mexican government but threatened war until 1923, when the Mexican courts held that the provision was not retroactive. The controversy continued, however, as nationalization of resources went on. Not until 1927 was it brought to a close by a new ambassador, _Dwight L. Morrow,_ an able lawyer opposed to dollar diplomacy. His diplomacy persuaded Mexico to modify its oil and mineral laws, as well as to adopt a church policy less offensive to American Catholics.

2. The Caribbean Policy.

a. WITHDRAWAL FROM THE CARIBBEAN. Increasing governmental stability in the Caribbean and Central America, combined with growing public sentiment against dollar diplomacy, led to a gradual withdrawal of American marines from that area. They were removed from Santo Domingo in 1922 and from Nicaragua in 1925.

b. REDEFINING THE MONROE DOCTRINE. The Clark Memorandum, drafted by the State Department in 1928, stated that the Monroe Doctrine was directed toward Europe rather than Latin America, thus giving the United States no superior position over the other Republics in the hemisphere. This was a step toward interpreting the Doctrine as the joint concern of all the Americas rather than of the United States alone.

V. PANIC AND DEPRESSION, 1929-1932.

A. Prosperity in the 1920's.

1. Business Prosperity. After the recession of 1920

business enjoyed unparalleled prosperity, as the expansion of new industries (automobiles, radio, motion pictures, electrical appliances, and chemicals) lifted production to new heights. Prophets told the people that prosperity was a permanent feature of the "new economic era," and that both wages and output would spiral upward for all time.

2. The Speculative Boom. With security assured by the "new economy" Americans felt free to invest their savings in stocks. Speculative buying by all classes drove common stocks from 117 to 225 between December, 1928, and September, 1929. This rise encouraged people to buy widely on credit, confident that their investments would pay all debts. This, in turn, stimulated greater production. "Two cars in every garage" seemed within the reach of all.

3. Unsound Features of the Economy. Despite prosperity, the economy contained many weak spots: 1) Technological unemployment mounted steadily as machines took over the work of men. Between two and four million men were constantly out of work, decreasing buying power. 2) The agricultural depression after 1920 lowered the purchasing power of farmers. 3) Overseas trade steadily declined as a result of the Republican tariff policy and the disturbing influence of the war-debt and reparation controversies. 4) The new wealth was largely in the hands of the few, while the wages of the principal consumers—the workers—did not keep pace with prices. 5) Credit buying meant that many Americans were poor even though spending lavishly; once their confidence in the future was shaken, they would stop buying. 6) Production in basic industries began to slip in the late 1920's, as the demand declined for coal, textiles, new homes, steel, and automobiles.

B. The Crash of 1929.

1. The Collapse of the Stock Market. Stock prices began to decline on October 21, 1929. As panic selling spread, they plunged rapidly lower, losing 40 per cent in a month. For the next three years they slid downward at a slower rate; during the period the average of leading stocks fell from 252 to 61. Millions were ruined by the crash, while others who had thought themselves secure stopped buying luxuries in an effort to conserve their savings.

2. The Coming of the Great Depression. The collapse of public confidence slowed purchases of industrial and farm produce. Prices fell, business failures mounted, factories closed, the number of unemployed rose to 15,000,000 persons by 1932, and drastic wage cuts curtailed the purchasing power of those still working. Within three years 5000 banks closed their doors. Farmers were further hit by a severe drought in 1930 and subsequent years.

C. Hoover and the Depression. Hoover maintained that the panic was psychological, and that prosperity would return if manufacturers kept wages and prices up. When this plea failed he was forced to act.

1. The Unemployment Problem. Hoover insisted that the burden of relief should be borne by private philanthropy and local governments. He refused to sanction a dole or government-supported public works.

2. The Reconstruction Finance Corporation (1932). Democrats and progressive Republicans created the R.F.C. to loan money to banks and railroads on the theory that stability at the top of the business structure would eventually benefit all the people. In all the R.F.C. loaned $11,000,-000,000 without appreciably halting the depression. Its aid, however, doubtless saved many enterprises that would otherwise have failed.

3. The Norris-LaGuardia Act (1932). The product of efforts by Democrats and Republican insurgents, this measure outlawed the injunction in labor disputes.

VI. THE ERA OF "NORMALCY": AN APPRAISAL.

A. The Spirit of the 1920's. During the 1920's the American people were indifferent to domestic society and to the world. This was due to:

1. Disillusionment. Americans had sacrificed much during the progressive era and World War I to secure social justice for all, adjust economic inequalities, "make the world safe for democracy," end war, and check the persecution of minorities. Having pitched their hopes too high, they were utterly disillusioned by the realities of the postwar world. When autocracy, oppression, and war still continued, Americans came to the conclusion that the world was not worth saving.

2. Prosperity. With insecurity relegated to the past by technological changes, Americans could afford to think of themselves as independent of both society and government. Seldom have a people been so individualistic and materialistic as in the era of "normalcy."

B. Impact of American Disillusionment.

1. On Domestic Policy. Indifference to social problems was shown by the failure of Americans to punish the Republicans for the Harding scandals; almost half the voters stayed home at each election during the 1920's. Left free to follow their own policies without fear of public censure, politicians could openly support the upper class to which they belonged (by tariffs, tax reduction, aid to business consolidation, etc.) while ignoring the lower class (as indicated by their failure to enact farm or labor legislation). As a result, the economic order was thrown out of balance, with too large a share of the national wealth going to business leaders, too little to farmers and workers. The resulting decline in purchasing power was a fundamental cause of the great depression.

2. On Foreign Policy. Popular indifference to the actions of government officials was probably responsible for the enlightened American foreign policy of the era. These officials were less influenced by outworn traditions than the masses, and hence better able to see that the day of isolationism was gone. Their efforts toward world security, although fruitless, prepared the way for the important changes inaugurated by Franklin D. Roosevelt.

ADDITIONAL READING

Frederic L. Paxson, *Post-War Years: Normalcy* (1948), is a scholarly account of the period, while Karl Schriftgiesser, *This War Normalcy* (1948), stresses political events. Two collaborative books also present a well-rounded picture: Louis M. Hacker, ed., *American Problems of Today* (1938), and Isabel Leighton, ed., *The Aspirin Age, 1919-1941* (1949). Social developments are the theme of Preston Slosson, *The Great Crusade and After* (1930), and more popularly in Frederick L. Allen, *Only Yesterday* (1931). The economic scene is appraised in George Soule, *Prosperity Decade* (1947). Biographies include: Samuel H. Adams, *Incredible Era: The Life and Times of Warren Gamaliel·Harding* (1939), and William A. White, *A Puritan in Babylon: The Story of Calvin Coolidge* (1938). Aspects of intolerance are surveyed in J. M. Mecklin, *The Ku Klux Klan* (1924), and in G. L. Joughin and E. M. Morgan, *The Legacy of Sacco and Vanzatti* (1948). E. E. Schattschneider, *Politics, Pressures, and the Tariff* (1935), studies tariff making, while Charles Merz, *The Dry Decade* (1931), is an amusing account of the prohibition experiment. America's failure to enter the World Court is analyzed in D. F. Fleming, *The United States and the World Court* (1945). The story of the great depression is colorfully told in Gilbert V. Seldes, *The Years of the Locust: America, 1929-1932* (1933).

CHAPTER XIII

The New Deal

1933-1941

⟪THE PHILOSOPHY OF THE NEW DEAL
The domestic program of Franklin D. Roosevelt was not a
"revolution." Since the 1880's the American government
had assumed an increasingly positive role in safeguarding
human welfare; in both the states and nation an impressive
body of laws regulated business enterprise or sought to
guard the common man from the buffeting of economic
storms. This progressive tradition was forgotten during
World War I and the reactionary period that followed.
Hence Roosevelt's task was to bring government and the
economy abreast again after a twenty-year lag. This necessity, combined with the need for hurried action in the midst
of the great depression, created the impression that the New
Deal was revolutionary rather than evolutionary.

I. INAUGURATING THE NEW DEAL.

A. The Election of 1932.

1. The Republican Campaign. Recognizing the inev-
itability of their defeat as the depression party, the Republicans nominated _Hoover_ without enthusiasm. Their
platform praised his handling of the depression, which was
blamed on the European situation.

2. The Democratic Campaign. Roosevelt's popularity
as governor of New York (1928-1932) elevated him to the
leadership of his party, displacing Al Smith, who vainly led

179

a "stop Roosevelt" movement during the convention. When this failed, Roosevelt was nominated without serious opposition. The platform promised: 1) unemployment relief and social security; 2) legislation favorable to labor; 3) the "restoration of agriculture"; 4) federal regulation of security exchanges, utility rates, and holding companies; 5) the development of publicly owned electric power; 6) reciprocal trade agreements with other nations; 7) repeal of the Eighteenth Amendment; and 8) "a continuous responsibility of government for human welfare."

3. Results of the Election. Hoover campaigned on the theme: "It might have been worse." Roosevelt, on the other hand, stressed the plight of the "forgotten man" and promised a "new deal" for the people. This won him an unprecedented popular vote of 23,000,000 to 16,000,000 for Hoover, while the electoral vote was 472 to 59. Only two states outside of New England gave their votes to Hoover.

4. The Twentieth Amendment. This *Lame Duck Amendment,* which went into effect just as Roosevelt took office, provided that Congressmen should be seated on January 3 following each election, and the President inaugurated on January 20. It also gave Congress power to act should the President and Vice-President die in office.

B. The First Recovery Measures.

1. Inauguration of Roosevelt. By March 4, 1933, when Roosevelt was inaugurated, 15,000,000 people were out of work, while runs had closed virtually every bank in the country. Rather than minimizing the disaster as had Hoover, Roosevelt's inaugural address admitted the "dark realities of the moment" but called on the people not to lose hope. "The only thing we have to fear," he said, "is fear itself." Outlining a program for recovery, he warned that he would ask for broad executive powers to wage war on the depression if Congress did not act.

2. The Financial Crisis.

a. THE BANK HOLIDAY. With nearly all banks closed by runs and confidence at a low ebb, Roosevelt immediately declared an official *bank holiday* which closed all banks. At the same time he called Congress into special session to meet on March 9, 1933.

b. EARLY BANKING LEGISLATION. An *Emergency Banking Law* was passed only a few hours after Congress met. This provided for the early reopening of all sound banks, and named a Bank Conservator to aid those not in liquid condition. Most of the banks soon were functioning under this measure. An Economy Act (March 10, 1933) authorized the President to reduce government salaries, pensions, and veterans' benefits, affecting a saving of $500,000,-000 yearly. At the same time taxes were raised slightly in an effort to balance the budget.

II. THE NEW DEAL DOMESTIC PROGRAM, 1933-1936. The New Deal program aimed at three objectives: *relief* for workers, farmers, and the unemployed; *recovery* for the nation's economy; and *reform* to prevent economic maladjustments in the future.

A. Relief Measures, 1933-1936. Rejecting the dole as used in England, Roosevelt shaped a program of *work relief* that took many forms.

1. Emergency Relief Projects.

a. THE CIVILIAN CONSERVATION CORPS (April, 1933) was created to employ young men from destitute families. Scattered in 2600 camps, the 1,600,000 youths who received C.C.C. training performed an invaluable service in protecting natural resources, building parks, and the like.

b. THE FEDERAL EMERGENCY RELIEF ADMINISTRATION (May, 1933). The *F.E.R.A.* was designed to provide the states with relief funds until federal relief could begin functioning. Between 1933 and 1935 it distributed $3,000,-000,000 to the states for the unemployed.

c. THE CIVIL WORKS ADMINISTRATION (1933). The *C.W.A.* gave temporary work relief through the winter (November, 1933-May, 1934) to 4,000,000 jobless.

d. THE UNITED STATES EMPLOYMENT SERVICE (1933) was designed to link state and local employment exchanges into a nation-wide organization that would find jobs for the unemployed.

2. Long-Range Relief Projects.

a. THE PUBLIC WORKS ADMINISTRATION (June, 1933). Under Secretary of the Interior *Harold Ickes* the

_P.W.A._ was assigned numerous heavy construction projects —waterworks, schools, bridges, and the like. Operating through private construction firms, the P.W.A. eventually did much to relieve unemployment.

b. THE WORKS PROGRESS ADMINISTRATION (April, 1935). When early relief measures failed to ease pressure on the government, the President proposed that unemployables be returned to the states for direct relief, and that employables be assigned to socially valuable undertakings rather than trivial tasks. Congress responded by creating the _W.P.A._ under _Harry Hopkins_, with an initial appropriation of $5,000,000,000. By March, 1936, 4,000,000 persons were employed on the W.P.A., building schools, parks, roads, irrigation dams, and other civic improvements. Important branches of the bureau included the _Federal Arts Project_, which employed actors, painters, writers, and other white-collar workers in jobs suited to their skills, and the _National Youth Administration_ (N.Y.A.) which helped 400,000 youths continue their education.

B. Recovery Measures, 1933-1936.

1. Monetary Reform. The New Deal financial program was based on the theory that the dollar, deflated by the depression, must be inflated to raise prices.

a. REPUDIATION OF THE GOLD STANDARD. In April, 1933, the United States went off the gold standard, while a month later the President was authorized to inflate the currency by adding $3,000,000,000 in new treasury notes, or by reducing the gold content of the dollar up to 50 per cent. At the same time the government began purchasing gold at home and abroad at high prices, thus seeking to devaluate the dollar still further.

b. RETURN TO A PARTIAL GOLD STANDARD. Congressional and business criticism of "currency tinkering" forced Roosevelt to renew partial currency controls. In February, 1934, he reduced the gold content of the dollar to 59.06 cents, while Congress set up a $2,000,000,000 stabilization fund to regulate the devaluated dollar in relation to other forms of currency.

c. RESULTS OF MONETARY REFORM. The financial measures did not succeed in raising prices, while security holders lost heavily. On the other hand, foreign trade was stimulated by dollar devaluation, which lowered the price of American goods abroad.

2. Pump-Priming Measures. The New Deal attempted to stimulate industrial recovery by several measures designed to encourage private enterprise.

a. RECONSTRUCTION FINANCE CORPORATION. Although created by the Hoover administration, the R.F.C. was given new powers in 1934, when it was authorized to grant loans to industries as well as to railroads and banks. In all, $11,-000,000,000 was loaned before 1936, most of the money being returned shortly afterward.

b. RESIDENTIAL CONSTRUCTION. Home building had shrunk to a negligible point by 1933, while many home owners were unable to keep up their mortgage payments. To remedy this situation three measures were passed: 1) The _Home Owners Loan Corporation_ (1933) was authorized to loan money to mortgage holders faced with the loss of their property. The H.O.L.C. saved the homes of more than 1,000,000 persons. 2) _The Federal Housing Administration_ (1934) was empowered to insure mortgages issued by private concerns for construction purposes. 3) _The United States Housing Authority_ (1937) assisted local governments in slum-clearance projects and the building of low-cost housing.

3. Agricultural Recovery. Between 1920 and 1933 the value of farm holdings had declined $42,000,000,000, while by 1933 two of every five farms were mortgaged. The New Deal attempted to stimulate agriculture and thus restore farm purchasing power.

a. THE PROBLEM OF FARM DEBTS. Mortgage foreclosure proceedings threatened to reduce the nation to a system of tenant farming. To combat this several laws were passed:

I. _Federal Farm Loan Act_ (May, 1933). This created a Farm Credit Administration (F.C.A.) to refinance agricultural mortgages at 4 per cent (later 3 per cent), and to loan money to farmers who had already lost their lands by foreclosure.

II. _Frazier-Lemke Act_ (1934). This law, which post-poned mortgage foreclosure for six years if the farmer paid adequate rent during that period, was declared unconstitutional in the case of _Louisville Joint Stock Co. v. Radford_ (1935). A second Frazier-Lemke Act (1935) accomplished the same purpose for a three-year period.

III. _The Resettlement Administration_ (1935), which after 1937 was known as the _Farm Security Administration_ (F.S.A.) purchased 17,000 farms on submarginal lands, allowing their owners to move to better sites.

b. THE FARM CROP PROBLEM. Recognizing that foreign markets were closed to American agricultural produce, and that farmers produced more than the nation could consume, Roosevelt's agricultural program was designed to reduce the acreage devoted to basic crops, and eventually the number of farmers.

I. _Agricultural Adjustment Act_ (May, 1933). This created an _Agricultural Adjustment Administration_ (A.A.A.) authorized to enter into agreements with farmers willing to reduce the acreage of such basic crops as cotton, wheat, corn, and tobacco. Farmers accepting these agreements would be paid subsidies, the money to be raised by taxing processers of farm goods (flour millers, meat packers, etc.).

II. _Operation of Agricultural Adjustment Act._ During 1934 cotton growers withdrew 10,000,000 acres from production, wheat growers 8,000,000 acres, and other producers comparable amounts. The resulting increase in prices, combined with the shortages following a severe drought and the payment of government subsidies, raised farm income from $5,150,000,000 in 1932 to $8,700,000,000 in 1935.

III. _Overthrow of the A.A.A._ Opposition to the A.A.A. was voiced by consumers who resented increased prices, processers who objected to the tax on their services, and theorists who felt that an "economy of scarcity" was ill suited to a land where millions were underfed. An additional constitutional objection was raised by the Supreme Court in _United States v. Butler_ (1936). The Act was held unconstitutional as an invasion of the rights of the states, and an improper exercise of the congressional taxing power.

IV. *Soil Conservation and Domestic Allotment Act* (1936). This was the administration's attempt to salvage something from its farm program. Benefit payments were authorized for farmers who gave up the use of worn-out land or shifted crops in the interest of soil conservation. They were to be administered by the states under federal standards. The measure was largely ineffective.

4. Industrial Recovery Measures.

a. NATIONAL INDUSTRIAL RECOVERY ACT (1933). The *National Recovery Administration* (N.R.A.), under *Hugh S. Johnson,* was authorized to draw up a "code of fair competition" for each major industry. A "blanket code" promulgated by the President as a model for others prohibited child labor, set a thirty-six hour week for workers and a forty-hour week for clerks, and established a minimum wage of forty cents an hour. The act also included a section (*Section 7a*) requiring the codes to grant workers "the right to organize and bargain collectively through representatives of their own choosing." This was enforced by a *National Labor Board* (N.L.B.) under Senator *Robert F. Wagner* of New York.

b. OPERATION OF THE N.R.A. Within two years 750 codes were drawn up, largely by representatives of big business. These set minimum wages and maximum working hours, abolished child labor, established prices, limited production, and assigned quotas for particular plants. Small businessmen soon complained that the codes discriminated against them, while liberals charged that the N.R.A. was creating giant monopolies. Conservatives were equally exercised over the rights given labor in Section 7a, especially when workers staged a series of strikes during 1934 and 1935.

c. OVERTHROW OF THE N.R.A. The Supreme Court, in *Schechter Poultry Corp. v. United States* (1935), declared the National Industrial Recovery Act unconstitutional on three grounds: 1) the measure illegally delegated congressional power to the President; 2) it violated the commerce power by assuming that Congress had authority over production; and 3) it sanctioned the illegal invasion of state authority by the national government.

d. LATER INDUSTRIAL MEASURES. Two laws salvaged something from the wreckage of the N.R.A.: 1) The *Wagner-Connery Act* (1935) created a *National Labor Relations Board* (N.L.R.B.) to prevent unfair practices in labor relations affecting interstate commerce. These included the coercion of employees, company domination of unions, discrimination against union members in employment or tenure, and the refusal to bargain collectively with workers. 2) The Guffey Coal Act (1935) applied a form of code control to the coal industry. This measure was declared unconstitutional in *Carter v. Carter Coal Company* (1936).

C. Reform Measures, 1933-1936.

1. Reform in Banking and Finance.

a. GLASS-STEAGALL BANKING ACT (1933). Designed to prevent future collapses of the private banking system, this forbade banks to engage in the investment business, restricted the speculative use of bank credits, and expanded the Federal Reserve system to banks previously excluded. Its most popular provision created the *Federal Deposit Insurance Corporation* (F.D.I.C.) to insure all deposits up to $5000.

b. THE REGULATION OF SECURITIES.

I. *Truth in Securities Act* (1933). This required: 1) all securities offered for sale in interstate commerce to be registered with the Federal Trade Commission; 2) that each issue contain accurate information allowing the buyer to judge the soundness of the corporation; and 3) that the directors be held criminally liable for any false information.

II. *The Securities Exchange Act* (1934). All stock exchanges were required to obtain licenses from the *Securities and Exchange Commission* (S.E.C.) which was given broad powers to regulate their activities. The power of registering securities was also transferred from the Federal Trade Commission to the S.E.C.

2. Hydroelectric Power.

a. TENNESSEE VALLEY AUTHORITY (1933). The *T.V.A.* was created by the Muscle Shoals Act with power to build and operate power-producing dams in the Tennessee River Valley, to manufacture nitrates, to sell electric power, and to rehabilitate the seven-state area through which the river ran. This launched an important experiment in government ownership. By 1938 the T.V.A. was distributing electric power to 40,000 homes and farms; by 1941 it served 400,000 customers. Moreover, the lowered cost of electricity served as a "yardstick" for private companies in the area, forcing them to lower their rates enough to save $50,000,000 yearly for users. A similar program was begun in the _Columbia River Basin_ with the building of Grand Coulee Dam (1933) and Bonneville Dam (1937). These not only provided cheaper electricity for the Northwest but allowed a million acres of arid land to be reclaimed.

b. RURAL ELECTRIFICATION ADMINISTRATION (1935). The R.E.A. was authorized to build power plants and high tension lines in rural areas. Within five years it brought electricity to farmers in forty-three states.

c. WHEELER-RAYBURN ACT (1935). This authorized the S.E.C. to confine holding companies to natural regions, and to eliminate holding companies that had more than one intervening company between them and the operating company.

3. Social Security.

a. PRESSURE FOR SOCIAL SECURITY. In 1932 only twenty-eight states provided old-age assistance, and only two unemployment insurance, although both were common in European countries. Unemployment and the growing tendency of employers to hire only young workers created a popular demand for relief that took such dangerous forms as the _Townsend Plan._ This promised pensions of $200 monthly to all over the age of sixty, providing they spent all their money each month. To check the demand of millions for such unworkable schemes as this, a social security act was called for.

b. THE SOCIAL SECURITY ACT (1935). This provided: 1) old-age insurance, beginning at the age of sixty-five, and financed by an equal tax on the worker and employer; 2) unemployment compensation, administered by the states, but financed by a federal tax on payrolls; 3) federal aid to the states for destitute persons, child health, maternity care,

crippled children, the aged, and the blind; 4) administration
of the measure by a Social Security Board.

c. OPERATION OF THE SOCIAL SECURITY ACT. Within
two years old-age pensions and unemployment-insurance
schemes in all states insured 21,000,000 people against unemployment and 36,000,000 against a penniless old age.
Although attacked by conservatives as inflicting new burdens
on industry, and by liberals as providing insufficient benefits, the measure was welcomed by a majority of the people
and upheld as constitutional by the Supreme Court.

III. THE CLIMAX OF THE NEW DEAL, 1936-1941.

A. The Election of 1936.

1. Opposition to the New Deal. Although popular with
a majority of the people, the New Deal was attacked from
both right and left:

a. CONSERVATIVE OPPOSITION. Conservatives complained that the New Deal: 1) was fastening an unmanage-
able debt on the country ($34,000,000,000 by 1936) through
its deficit financing; 2) unreasonably interfered with business; 3) gave too much power to the President and thus
weakened democracy; 4) encouraged labor organization;
and 5) constantly violated the Constitution. These objections were voiced both by Republicans and by conservative
Democrats under Alfred E. Smith, who in 1934 formed the
Liberty League to combat Roosevelt.

b. RADICAL OPPOSITION. The masses were organized
by such rabble-rousers as Senator Huey P. Long of Louisiana, whose Share-Our-Wealth Society promised to divide
all wealth among the poor; Dr. Francis E. Townsend, who
promised pensions of $200 monthly to all over sixty; and
the Reverend Charles E. Coughlin, Detroit's radio priest,
who demanded a nationally controlled currency system. In
all, several millions followed these prophets, all of whom
were pledged to defeat Roosevelt in 1936.

2. The Candidates. The *Republicans* nominated *Alfred
M. Landon* of Kansas, who reminded his followers of a
middle-western Calvin Coolidge. The platform promised to
continue all New Deal measures, but without extra cost and

with no danger to the Constitution or the "American system of free enterprise." The _Democrats_ renominated _Roosevelt_ by acclamation and adopted a platform that eulogized the New Deal. Disgruntled supporters of Coughlin, Long, and Townsend banded together as the _Union Party_ to nominate Congressman _William Lemke_ of North Dakota. Their platform was a hodgepodge of promises to all groups represented in the party.

3. Results of the Election. Despite the almost solid opposition of the press, Roosevelt carried every state but Maine and Vermont ("As Maine goes so goes Vermont" became a popular Democratic jibe), with 523 electoral votes to 8 for Landon. Democrats also swept both houses of Congress. The Union Party polled only 900,000 votes, while the combined vote of Socialists and Communists was less than 300,000.

B. The Battle over Court Reorganization.

1. Origins of the Conflict. Between 1935 and 1937 the Supreme Court held seven basic New Deal laws unconstitutional, usually by a narrow majority. In all, the four conservative judges used such intemperate language that they were suspected of allowing prejudice rather than reason to dictate their decisions. Even Republicans were aroused when the majority held in _Morehead v. New York ex. rel. Tilaldo_ (1936) that state minimum-wage laws for women and children were unconstitutional. Democrats explained the Court's conservatism by pointing out that seven of the nine justices had been appointed by Republican presidents, while six were over seventy years of age.

2. The Court Reorganization Bill. In February, 1937, Roosevelt asked Congress to enlarge the Supreme Court from nine to fifteen members, if judges declined to retire at the age of seventy. The measure also proposed less controversial changes in the lower courts.

3. The Battle over Reorganization. The controversy over the court bill was occasioned by the fact that Congress was already beginning to strain against presidential control and welcomed a chance to assert itself. This was because: 1) the improved economic situation encouraged legislators to act on their own; 2) many Democrats viewed the President's dominance over Congress as an unwarranted extension of the executive power; 3) southern conservatives sought a chance to assert themselves without party censure; and 4) the overwhelming Democratic majorities in the 1936 election stimulated Democratic divisions by convincing many that the opposition was ineffective. Hence Republicans and Democrats alike denounced the "Court-packing" bill in a bitter debate that lasted through the spring and summer of 1937.

4. Reversal by the Supreme Court. While the debate raged, the Court suddenly reversed itself and handed down favorable decisions on several New Deal measures. The most important of these, _National Labor Relations Board v. Jones and Laughlin Steel Corporation_ (1937), upheld the National Labor Relations Act by ruling that labor relations in factories producing for interstate commerce were subject to congressional control. Other measures validated by the Court included the Social Securities Act, the second Frazier-Lemke Mortgage Law, a Railway Labor Act, and a Washington state minimum-wage law identical with the one held unconstitutional nine months before. A popular witticism of the day was "A switch in time saves nine."

5. Defeat of Court Reorganization. Congress defeated the Court Reorganization Bill in August, 1937. During the next few years Roosevelt achieved his end when the death or retirement of older justices allowed him to place younger and more liberal judges on the bench. The result was a series of progressive decisions for the first time since World War I.

C. Labor Legislation, 1936-1941.

1. Origin of the C.I.O. Economic recovery, and the growing strength of unions under the stimulus of New Deal laws, encouraged a division in the ranks of labor. This began when unskilled workers, long excluded from the American Federation of Labor, found a leader in _John L. Lewis,_ president of the A.F. of L. United Mine Workers, who maintained that unions should be organized along industrial rather than craft lines—that is, that all steel workers, or mine workers, or automobile workers, should be in one union regardless of crafts or skills. When the A.F. of L. refused to back him, Lewis formed the _Committee for Industrial Organization_ (C.I.O.) to organize the steel and automobile industries. His first victory was won when the _United Automobile Workers,_ a C.I.O. union, used the _sit-down_ strike to force recognition from General Motors Corporation (November, 1936). The _steel industry_ also came to terms in March, 1937, when the United States Steel Corporation accepted the C.I.O. as a bargaining agent for its employees. Violent strikes at plants of the Republic Steel Company and other smaller producers later won recognition there.

2. Division of the A.F. of L. By the fall of 1937 the C.I.O. had 3,700,000 members and the A.F. of L. 3,600,000. This led to such internal conflicts that in November, 1938, the two split, the Committee for Industrial Organization changing its name to the Congress for Industrial Organization.

3. Fair Labor Standards Act (1938). The C.I.O.-A.F. of L. conflict called attention to the need for additional labor legislation. The _Fair Labor Standards Act_ (1938) provided for an eventual forty-hour week and a forty-cent-an-hour minimum wage for all workers in firms producing for interstate commerce. This was to be approached gradually until the full objective was reached by 1945. The measure was popularly known as the _Wages and Hours Law._

D. Farm Legislation, 1936-1941.

1. Plight of the Farm Worker. The agricultural measures of Roosevelt's first term failed to solve the problem of _southern tenancy._ Almost half the southern farms were operated by _share croppers_ who benefited little from the crop-restriction program of the A.A.A. In desperation they formed the Southern Tenant Farmers' Union (1934) to press for relief. Equally alarming was the plight of those driven from their farms by the drought of 1934-1935 that turned much of the Southwest into a _dust bowl._ Many made their way into California, where they competed for the few jobs available. Their hardships were popularized by John Steinbeck's novel, _The Grapes of Wrath_ (1939).

2. Legislative Remedies.

a. THE BANKHEAD-JONES ACT (1937). The Farm Security Administration (F.S.A.) was authorized to make long-term, low-interest loans to share croppers who wished to purchase their lands. The F.S.A. also made subsistent grants to migratory workers in California.

b. The Agricultural Adjustment Act (1938). Replacing the law of 1933 that had been declared unconstitutional, this provided: 1) that the Secretary of Agriculture could fix the acreage for basic crops each year and establish "marketing quotas" to restrict the sale of surpluses; 2) that in bad crop years the A.A.A. would grant farmers "parity payments" sufficient to offset the difference between the low price and the price their produce would have commanded before World War I; 3) that farmers who adopted anti-erosion practices should be given conservation payments; and 4) that the government provide storage space and loans for surplus crops to assure an "ever normal granary." The measure failed to reduce the 1939 crop, while in subsequent years demands from war-torn Europe outbalanced supply.

E. Congressional Elections of 1938.

1. The Recession of 1937-1938. A sharp business recession, caused by the curtailment of government relief spending in 1936-1937, brought a return of hard times between August, 1937, and June, 1938. Revived federal spending restored comparative prosperity during the fall of 1938. The recession, however, was one factor influencing the election. The other was Roosevelt's attempt to *"purge"* anti-New Deal Democrats from Congress by appealing to the people for their defeat. This "interference" with legislative independence cost him some votes.

2. Outcome of the Elections. Although Democrats retained control of both houses of Congress, their majorities were so reduced that for the first time since 1933 the Republicans could operate as an effective minority.

3. Governmental Reorganization. Roosevelt seized the period of calm after the election to press for a reorganization of the executive departments of the federal government. This was designed to abolish overlapping bureaus, eliminate waste, and increase efficiency. Congressional authorization to carry out this reform (1939) resulted in elimination of twenty-three bureaus. Closely related was the *Hatch Act* (1939), which forbade employees below policy-making positions to engage in political activities.

IV. AN EVALUATION OF THE NEW DEAL.

A. End of the New Deal. For all effective purposes the New Deal came to an end after the Congressional elections of 1938. Roosevelt continued in office until his death in 1945, but during the remaining years, an effective Republican opposition and the preoccupation of the President with foreign affairs brought a virtual end to domestic reform.

B. Results of the New Deal.

1. Harmful Results. On the debit side, the New Deal: 1) vastly increased the federal debt; 2) stimulated the growth of class consciousness among farmers and workers; 3) fostered bureaucracy and administrative inefficiency; 4) slowed the growth of civil service reform by multiplying offices outside the merit system; 5) infringed upon free business enterprise; and 6) brought the nation face to face with its most serious future problem: How far could economic regulation be extended without sacrificing the liberties of the people? Although democracy was not threatened by any New Deal measures, the question remained one of the most troublesome confronting the United States during and after World War II.

2. Beneficial Results. On the credit side of the ledger, the New Deal: 1) allowed the nation to weather its most serious depression without upsetting the capitalistic economy; 2) brought labor and agriculture on the one hand, and industry on the other, into better balance; 3) fostered a more equitable distribution of the national wealth; 4) conserved many of the country's resources; and 6) established for all time the principle of positive government action to rehabilitate and preserve the human resources of the nation.

ADDITIONAL READING

Basil Rauch, *History of the New Deal* (1944), is a chronological account emphasizing political factors. Social and economic aspects are well treated in Dixon Wecter, *The Age of the Great Depression* (1948), while economic changes are analyzed in Broadus Mitchell, *Depression Decade* (1948). No satisfactory biography of Roosevelt has been written, although G. W. Johnson, *Roosevelt: Dictator or Democrat* (1940), contains much information, and Emil

Ludwig, *Roosevelt* (1938), is a penetrating analysis.
Frances Perkins, *The Roosevelt I Knew* (1946), is the best
of the personal reminiscences from the pens of those who
knew him. Another revealing portrait is Robert Sherwood,
Roosevelt and Hopkins (1948). David E. Lilienthal, *TVA:
Democracy on the March* (1944), describes the achievements
of the T.V.A. Herbert Harris, *Labor's Civil War* (1940)
tells of the origin of the C.I.O. The court reorganization
controversy is the theme of R. H. Jackson, *The Struggle
for Judicial Supremacy* (1941). A forthcoming book by
Arthur M. Schlesinger, Jr., *The Age of Roosevelt,* promises
to be the best general history of the period.

CHAPTER XIV

Foreign Policy
of the New Deal
1933-1941

((THE ROAD TO WORLD WAR II
World developments between World War I and World War
II were shaped largely by the breakdown of collective security. For this the United States was partially responsible.
Rejecting global responsibility, the American people revived
faith in isolationism, believing that they could stay aloof
from the troubles of Europe and Asia. By declining to join
the League of Nations and the World Court, by withdrawing from the Far East, and by erecting tariff barriers around
their country, they contributed to the rise of nationalism, at
the same time undermining the little faith left anywhere in
collective efforts to preserve the peace. Their selfishness left
the world prey to avaricious dictators whose totalitarian
states could only endure by expanding. This expansion
plunged the world—and the United States—into World
War II.

I. THE GOOD NEIGHBOR POLICY. In his inaugural address President Roosevelt dedicated the United
States "to the policy of the good neighbor—the neighbor
who resolutely respects himself and, because he does so,
respects the rights of others." This policy was effectively
applied toward certain Pacific areas and Latin America.

A. Philippine Independence.

1. Origins of Independence Movement. Although the United States promised the Filipinos their independence in 1916 (see p. 133), Republican presidents took no steps to carry out the pledge. The Democratic victory of 1932, and a depression-born desire to be rid of the "white man's burden," revived interest in separation. Four groups especially pressed for independence; 1) sugar growers who disliked competition from the islands; 2) organized labor resentful of Filipino immigration; 3) dairy interests seeking to exclude Philippine coconut oil; and 4) anti-imperialists who had long campaigned against domination of colonial peoples.

2. Achievement of Independence. The _Hawes-Cutting Act_ (1933), passed by a Democratic Congress in the last days of the Hoover administration, provided for freedom after ten years but gave the United States the right to retain military and naval bases on the islands. When this offer was rejected by the Filipinos, the _Tydings-McDuffie Act_ (1934) was passed. This gave up all claim to military bases, and left the problem of naval bases to future negotiations. Under this measure the _Philippine Commonwealth_ inaugurated its first president, Manuel _Quezon,_ in November, 1935. After the proscribed probationary period the Philippines attained their freedom on July 4, 1946.

B. Withdrawal from the Caribbean.

1. Change in American Policy.

a. DECLINE OF DOLLAR DIPLOMACY. Dollar diplomacy lost popularity during the great depression. This was because Americans believed: 1) that intervention in Latin America meant higher taxes for the benefit of a few business concerns; 2) that the ill will created by intervention handicapped trade relations; 3) that hemispheric solidarity was needed to combat European fascism; and 4) that they should set their own economic house in order before meddling with other nations.

b. STATEMENT OF AMERICAN POLICY. At a Pan-American Conference at _Montevideo_ (1933) Secretary of State _Cordell Hull_ joined with other American nations in accepting a pact that denied the right of any country to intervene in the affairs of other countries. Roosevelt also declared that the administration's policy was "opposed to armed intervention."

2. Application of the Policy.

a. ABROGATION OF THE PLATT AMENDMENT. When disorder broke out in depression-ridden Cuba, the United States not only refrained from sending troops but in May, 1934, signed a treaty abrogating the Platt Amendment (see p. 106).

b. WITHDRAWAL OF AMERICAN TROOPS. In 1930 President Hoover recalled marines from Haiti, and in 1933 from Nicaragua (see p. 174). Roosevelt continued this policy, withdrawing the last troops from Haiti in 1934, and in 1940 ending the American customs receivership over the Dominican Republic. In 1936 a treaty with Panama relinquished all rights to intervene in that country.

C. The Mexican Expropriation Controversy. Acting under the Constitution of 1917 (see p. 174) Mexico in 1938 expropriated foreign oil properties valued at $400,-000,000. Instead of intervening to protect American capital, the United States admitted Mexico's rights to take over these properties, but insisted that the owners be compensated. A joint commission agreed upon the sums due, and in 1939 the Mexican government began payment.

D. Reciprocal Trade Agreements. In June, 1934, Congress authorized the President to raise or lower tariff duties up to 50 per cent in return for reciprocal concessions from other nations. Within five years treaties were negotiated with twenty-one countries, including more than half the Latin-American republics. These treaties not only stimulated foreign trade, but helped undermine economic nationalism.

E. Achievement of Hemispheric Solidarity. The rise of dictators in Europe emphasized the need for unity in the Americas. This was achieved through a series of conferences: 1) The _Rio de Janeiro Conference_ (1933) condemned wars of aggression and bound the signers not to recognize territory acquired by force; 2) The _Buenos Aires Conference_ (1936), which was attended by Roosevelt, reaffirmed earlier pledges of collective security and pledged the American nations to consult together on peace measures whenever war threatened any one of them; 3) The _Lima Conference_ (1938) adopted resolutions condemning racial or religious persecution and declared against the activity of aliens who remained loyal to their native land—two measures aimed particularly at Nazi Germany.

F. Significance of the Good Neighbor Policy. In effect the United States used the good neighbor policy to declare that it was no longer the sole interpreter of the Monroe Doctrine. Instead, the nations of the western hemisphere would act together as equals in the quest for collective security.

II. THE PROBLEM OF NEUTRALITY, 1933-1939.

A. Rise of Totalitarianism. During the 1920's and 1930's four dictatorial powers rose to challenge the democratic nations:

1. The Union of Socialist Soviet Republics. Established by revolution in 1917, the U.S.S.R. based its economy on a Marxian system of government-owned land and industry. Power was centered in a restricted Communist Party, which after 1924 was dominated by _Josef Stalin_. He subordinated the plan for a world communist revolution that had been developed by Trotsky and earlier revolutionists, concentrating instead on the internal development of Russia through a succession of "five-year plans."

2. Italy. Following a march on Rome in 1922, _Benito Mussolini_ became dictator of Europe's first fascist nation. He preached the doctrine of state supremacy over the individual.

3. Germany. Within a few months after _Adolph Hitler_ was elevated to the chancellorship in 1933 he wiped out the last vestiges of democracy, substituting dictatorial rule through his _National Socialist,_ or _Nazi,_ Party. Like fascism, nazism elevated the state above the individual, as well as appealing to German racial prejudice by advocating the persecution of Jews and Catholics. Both systems were intensely nationalistic, advocating the right of expansion at the expense of weaker neighbors.

4. Japan. When the great depression played into the hands of its military leaders, Japan moved toward fascism in the 1930's. Advocating territorial expansion as the only cure for poverty, generals won control of the Cabinet and Emperor, then committed their nation to a program of aggression.

B. The End of Peace.

1. Warfare in China. Japan's expansion began in 1931 with the invasion of Manchuria and the creation of the puppet state of _Manchukuo._ This aggression united dissention-torn China under its leading generalissimo, _Chiang Kai-Shek_. Hence Japan, when she began an undeclared war on that nation in 1937, met strong resistance. For the next decade the two nations fought constantly, with the Nipponese steadily victorious. An incident of the war was the Japanese bombing of an American gunboat, the _Panay_ (1937), an act that aroused resentment but no demand for intervention.

2. Warfare in Africa. In 1935 Mussolini began a war of conquest against Ethiopia. When British opposition prevented the League of Nations from cutting off oil supplies to Italy—which probably would have ended the war—the Italians won an easy victory.

3. Warfare in Spain. A revolution against the Spanish Republican government (1936) was led by General _Francisco Franco_, whose fascist program soon attracted help from Germany and Italy. This foreign aid allowed Franco to win a complete victory.

4. Expansion of Germany. When a plebiscite showed that the people of the Saar Valley favored the move, Germany in 1935 annexed the region; a year later the Rhineland was occupied by force.

C. The American Reaction.

1. Rise of Isolationism. The events in Europe further convinced Americans that the rest of the world was not worth saving. Isolationist sentiment was also fostered by: 1) the great depression, which convinced many that the United States should concentrate on its own recovery; 2) the continued failure of the World War I allies to pay their war debts (see pp. 172-173) ; 3) the disclosure by a Senate committee under *Gerald P. Nye* of North Dakota (1934-1936) that during World War I bankers and munitions makers accumulated vast profits. This revelation proved to many people that the United States had been forced into the war by these "merchants of death." By 1937, about 70 per cent of the Americans believed that their country should not have entered World War I.

2. Neutrality Legislation. Isolationist sentiment was mirrored in a series of congressional acts designed to prevent American involvement in future wars :

a. THE JOHNSON ACT (1934) forbade debt-defaulting nations to market their securities in the United States.

b. THE NEUTRALITY ACTS (1935-1937). This group of laws : 1) laid an embargo on the shipment of all munitions, arms, and implements of war to belligerents ; 2) provided that all indirect war materials (steel, cotton, food, etc.) must be handled on a "cash and carry" basis—that is, they must be taken from the United States on the ships of a belligerent and paid for in cash ; 3) forbade American travel on belligerent ships ; and 4) denied belligerents the right to float loans in the United States.

c. MEANING OF NEUTRALITY LEGISLATION. Congress hoped that these acts would prevent the United States from becoming involved in future wars as it had in World War I. They were based on the assumption that *economic,* rather than idealistic, motives had been responsible for past participation. This represented a reversal of the traditional American stand for freedom of the seas.

3. Presidential Policy. Roosevelt had no sympathy for the neutrality acts, believing instead that the United States could remain at peace only by helping prevent the outbreak of a major war in Europe. As an advocate of *collective security,* he favored cooperation with the democracies to check and restrain the dictatorships before they became strong enough to bid for world power.

a. THE QUARANTINE SPEECH (1937). In an important address in Chicago, Roosevelt compared world lawlessness to a physical disease and urged the international quarantine of aggressors as the only means of preserving peace. The unfavorable reaction convinced the President that he could not muster support for such a program at that time.

b. NAVAL EXPANSION. Sure that the United States would eventually become involved in the war that was then starting, Roosevelt in 1934 asked Congress to enlarge the fleet to its full strength under the Washington and London treaties (see p. 171). After Japan and Italy refused to accept further naval limitations (1936), he requested a billion-dollar naval-building program (1938). The bill was passed after a long debate.

c. USE OF THE NEUTRALITY ACTS. Roosevelt used the acts whenever possible to punish attacking nations and aid attacked nations. In the Italian-Ethiopian War (1935) he applied the acts, knowing that Italy could purchase arms from the United States while Ethiopia could not. In the Sino-Japanese War (1937), on the other hand, he refused to invoke the laws, allowing the Chinese to continue arms purchases. The embargo was also applied during the Spanish Revolution (1937), despite objections from liberals who wished to aid the Loyalists as Germany and Italy were aiding Franco.

d. ACTION AGAINST JAPAN. The President showed his displeasure with Japan by announcing (July, 1939) that in six months the United States would abrogate a 1911 treaty between the two powers which guaranteed reciprocal trading rights. In effect this prevented Japan from buying gasoline, scrap iron, and other materials needed for her war on China.

III. THE APPROACH OF WAR, 1939-1940.

A. Outbreak of the War in Europe.

1. Expansion of Germany. In 1938 Hitler's troops added Austria to the Third Reich. Hitler then demanded the _Sudetenland_, an adjacent portion of Czechoslovakia inhabited largely by Germans. Although the Czechs were ready to fight, England and France accepted the _Munich Pact_ (1938) in which the Sudetenland was surrendered to Germany in return for a promise of no future aggression. The failure of appeasement was shown in March, 1939, when the Nazis conquered Czechoslovakia and Mussolini's troops overran Albania. The two dictators, in May, 1939, agreed on a ten-year military alliance known as the *Rome-Berlin Axis.*

2. End of Appeasement. Germany's annexation of Czechoslovakia showed England and France that the dictators could be stopped only by force. When Hitler was rumored to be planning a move against Poland, they promised that country all possible aid in case of attack. The one additional step necessary for war was taken in August, 1939, when Hitler negotiated a nonaggression pact with Russia, the *Moscow-Berlin Pact.* Thus assured of a peaceful western border, Germany was ready to plunge the world into World War II.

3. The War Begins. Immediately after the Moscow-Berlin Pact was signed, Hitler's troops invaded Poland. England and France declared war on Germany on September 3, 1939. Although both nations mobilized, little fighting took place for the six months that Nazis needed to overrun Poland. In the meantime, Russia annexed the Baltic countries and launched a war of aggression against Finland that lasted until March, 1940.

B. Impact of the War on the United States.

1. Division of American Opinion. With the outbreak of war Americans divided into two camps: 1) the *isolationists,* whose powerful America First Committee included such influential editors as William Randolph Hearst and Robert McCormick, and such politicians as Gerald P. Nye and Hamilton Fish; and 2) the *interventionists* whose program of all aid to the Allies "short of war" was sponsored by the Committee to Defend America by Aiding the Allies, which was headed by William Allen White, a Kansas newspaperman. President Roosevelt was an outspoken interventionist, while public opinion polls showed that 70 per cent of the people favored aid for the Allies.

2. Administration Policy.

a. CHANGES IN THE NEUTRALITY ACTS. Roosevelt was legally required to apply the arms embargo to all belligerents, thus cutting off munitions shipments to France and England. He therefore called Congress into special session to amend the laws (November, 1939). After repeated prodding, Congress: 1) repealed the arms embargo but applied the "cash-and-carry" requirement to all commerce with belligerents; 2) continued the prohibition on loans to belligerents; 3) stopped American ships from carrying passengers or materials to warring countries; and 4) banned American travel on belligerent ships.

b. EFFORTS TOWARD HEMISPHERIC SOLIDARITY. To unite the Americans and guard against the "fifth column" activity of German sympathizers, Roosevelt: 1) issued a call for a meeting of the foreign ministers of the American republics at Panama City (September, 1939). The resulting *Declaration of Panama* established a "safety belt" from 300 to 1000 miles wide around the Americas and warned belligerents against naval action in that area. 2) Called together a second conference of ministers at Havana (July, 1940). The *Act of Havana* forbade the transfer of any European colony in America to a non-American owner. Colonies in danger of falling into unfriendly hands were to be administered jointly by the American republics until final disposition was made. 3) Set up a Joint Board of Defense with *Canada* (August, 1940) to coordinate defense efforts.

C. The German Offensive in Europe. In the spring of 1940 Hitler launched a *"blitzkrieg"* similar to that used in the conquest of Poland. Using Fifth Columnists and paratroopers to soften resistance, he cut down opponents by giant air attacks, then drove his armies forward behind tanks and mechanized infantry. The Allies could not stem this well-geared assault. Denmark and Norway fell in April, 1940. A month later the Netherlands and Belgium succumbed. France capitulated in June, shortly after Italy entered the war. By summer, only England held out against the Nazi juggernaut.

IV. THE UNITED STATES ENTERS THE WAR, 1940-1941.

A. Preparation for War. The Nazi blitzkrieg convinced even isolationists that the United States must improve its defenses against an attack that now seemed probable.

1. Military Preparedness. During the summer of 1940 Congress appropriated $13,000,000,000 for the army, navy, and air force, levying new taxes to meet part of these expenditures. A *Selective Service Act* (September, 1940) required the registration of all men between twenty-one and thirty-five years of age. Of these, 800,000 were drafted for a year of training. Before they were released, the law was stiffened to require eighteen months of service and the registration of all between the ages of eighteen and forty-five.

2. Industrial Mobilization. The *Office of Production Management* (O.P.M.) was set up to put the nation's economy on a war footing. *William S. Knudsen,* a business executive, was placed in charge. At the same time the President sought to unite both parties behind the defense effort by adding two Republicans to his cabinet, *Henry L. Stimson* as Secretary of War, and *Frank Knox* as Secretary of the Navy.

3. Naval and Air Bases. In September, 1940, the President obtained from England ninety-nine-year leases on eight naval and air bases, scattered from Newfoundland to British Guiana, giving in return fifty over-age destroyers.

B. The Election of 1940.

1. The Candidates. The *Republicans* nominated *Wendell L. Willkie* of New York, a utility magnate and outspoken advocate of aid to England. The platform also favored support for Britain short of war, as well as national defense and most of the domestic reforms secured by the New Deal. The *Democrats* broke with precedent to nominate *Roosevelt* for a *third term.* The platform was almost identical with that of the Republican party, differing only in praising rather than condemning the past domestic achievements of the New Deal.

2. The Election. In a vigorous campaign Willkie praised most of the New Deal measures, but condemned the administration's waste, bureaucracy, dictatorial powers, and persecution of business. He also saw the *third term* as a step toward totalitarianism. Roosevelt refrained from campaigning until the last weeks of the election, allowing his record to speak for itself. This proved acceptable to the voters, who returned him to the White House with 449 electoral votes to 38 for Willkie. The Democrats also increased their majorities in both houses of Congress.

C. The End of Neutrality.

1. The Lend-Lease Act (March, 1941). Passed after a long debate, this allowed the United States to lend, lease, or otherwise transfer to nonaggressor nations any military equipment necessary for their preservation. Huge appropriations during the next months permitted mountains of goods to reach England. The United States was, in the President's phrase, the *"arsenal of democracy."*

2. The Greenland Base. In April, 1941, the anti-Nazi Danish minister to the United States granted American forces military bases on the Danish island of Greenland. This moved the American line of defense one step nearer the war zone.

3. The Atlantic Charter.

a. RUSSIA ENTERS THE WAR. After overrunning the Balkans during the spring of 1941, Hitler suddenly attacked Russia on June 22, 1941. This added another powerful nation to the anti-Nazi bloc, for while Stalin had shown no intention of attacking Germany during the period of the Moscow-Berlin Pact, he had been arming his country. Driven back during the summer and fall, the Russian armies stiffened during the winter of 1941-1942 and began to regain lost ground.

b. STATEMENT OF OBJECTIVES. To offset criticism of their partnership with totalitarian Russia, and to clarify their war aims, Roosevelt and Prime Minister *Winston Churchill* of England issued the *Atlantic Charter* (August 14, 1941). This stated that: 1) neither nation sought territorial gains; 2) both would respect the rights of all peoples to choose the form of government they wished; 3) both would cooperate in securing for all states access to the world's raw materials; 4) both would encourage international cooperation to secure just labor standards and social security; 5) both were committed to win for all people freedom from fear and want; 6) both favored the unrestricted freedom of the seas; and 7) both sought the disarmament of aggressor nations as a step toward permanent peace.

4. The Battle of the Atlantic. Heavy losses suffered by freighters carrying lend-lease supplies to England caused many Americans to demand that the United States provide convoys. The President, still reluctant to start a "shooting war," instead dispatched naval and air units to Iceland (July 7, 1941) to "patrol" the North Atlantic. They were ordered to report German submarines to the British, but not to fire themselves. When an American destroyer, the _Greer_, was attacked (September 4, 1941), Roosevelt ordered the navy to shoot on sight. In October another destroyer, the _Reuben James_, was torpedoed with a loss of seventy-six men. An outraged Congress on November 17, 1941, ordered the arming of merchant ships and the repeal of all neutrality legislation that required them to remain outside the war zone.

5. The Attack by Japan.

a. JAPANESE-AMERICAN RELATIONS, 1939-1941. Since September, 1939, when Japan formed a ten-year alliance with Germany and Italy, the three totalitarian powers had operated together. This _Rome-Berlin-Tokyo Axis_ endangered the United States after July, 1941, when the Japanese occupied French Indo-China, thus menacing the Philippines as well as British and Dutch possessions in southern Asia. In retaliation, all of Japan's assets in the United States were frozen. Prolonged discussions followed, as the American government sought to persuade the Japanese to evacuate Indo-China and Premier Tojo prepared for the attack that was already planned.

b. THE UNITED STATES ENTERS THE WAR. The attack came on _December 7, 1941_, when Japanese planes swooped down on the naval base at _Pearl Harbor_ in the Hawaiian Islands. Taken without warning, the Americans were unable to defend themselves; nineteen ships were sunk or put out of action. A day later Congress recognized the existence of a state of war between the United States and Japan. Germany and Italy declared war on America a few days later.

V. ISOLATIONISM vs. INTERVENTIONISM. Could the United States have avoided involvement in World War II? Was the course that it followed suitable for the nation in the case of future European wars? Those questions must be answered in appraising the New Deal's foreign policy.

A. The Isolationists' Argument. Isolationists believed that economic forces plunged the United States into World War I. Hence they reasoned that if no similar stake in an allied victory was developed during the European phase of World War II, participation could be avoided. This was the purpose of the neutrality acts. In passing them, isolationists failed to recognize that wars were fought for ideological as well as material motives. The American people were willing to enter World War II not to save their dollars, but to save democracy and to preserve their nation's sovereignty.

B. The Interventionists' Argument. Interventionists held that the United States could not stay out of any major European war. Peace, they said, could be preserved only if the nonaggressor nations banded together to suppress aggressor nations in their infancy, thus nipping any possible war in the bud. This required a degree of international cooperation that the Americans were not ready to accept in the 1930's. Their aloofness allowed Germany, Italy, and Japan to gain so much strength that a major conflict was needed to defeat them.

C. Conclusion. The history of the period demonstrated the correctness of those who argued for collective security. Even though protected from economic losses by the neutrality laws, the American people were wholeheartedly behind England from the beginning. So intense was their ideological conviction that they were ready for war before the President or Congress, should war prove necessary to save Britain. World War II taught the United States that it could never know peace in a war-torn world.

Additional Reading

Useful for early foreign policy of the period are *The Memoirs of Cordell Hull* (1948). H. J. Tasca, *Reciprocal Trade Policy of the United States* (1938), deals with that aspect of the New Deal policy, while developments in the Far East are summarized in T. A. Bisson, *American Policy in the Far East, 1931-1940* (1940). Forrest Davis and

E. K. Lindley, *How War Came* (1942), is an informal, semiofficial account of America's entry. The same story is presented in documentary form in *Peace and War. United States Foreign Policy, 1931-1941* (1943). Walter Millis, *This is Pearl!* (1947), is also a balanced and vivid account of the events leading to American participation. Equally useful is a collaborative history of the period: Allan Nevins and Louis Hacker, eds., *The United States and Its Place in World Affairs* (1943). Walter Johnson, *The Battle Against Isolation* (1944), describes the activities of William Allen White and other interventionists. Dexter Perkins, *America and Two Wars* (1944), deals with the diplomacy of American participation.

~~~~~~~~~~~~~~~~~~~~~

Chapter XV

World War II and Its Aftermath

1941-1957

~~~~~~~~~~~~~~~~~~~~~

❨ TOTAL WAR AND ITS RESULTS

World War II brought the realities of modern battle closer to the American people than any previous conflict in history. The gigantic number of men involved, the regulatory measures that governed the economy, and the terrifying implications of atomic warfare, all directly affected every man, woman, and child in the land. Thus enmeshed as parts of a gargantuan military machine, they were capable of such efforts that the dictators were first rolled back, then defeated. Nor did they retreat into the shell of isolationism once the war was won. Convinced at last that collective security alone could maintain peace, they helped form the United Nations, which promised a better world than the League of Nations that followed World War I. Yet even this peace agency was threatened when postwar nationalism divided the globe into two armed camps, one led by Russia, the other by the United States. At the half-century mark the world seemed about to return to a balance-of-power system that had been often tried and found wanting as a peace agency in Europe's past.

I. THE UNITED STATES IN WORLD WAR II.

A. The Period of Defeat, 1941-1942.

1. Japanese Victories in the Pacific Area. Japan won a series of spectacular victories during 1941 and 1942. The British naval base at Singapore, the Netherlands East Indies, Burma, Guam, Wake Island, and Hong Kong, all surrendered, allowing the Nipponese to concentrate their attack on the Philippines. There outnumbered Americans made a valiant stand on the _Bataan Peninsula_ and the island of _Corregidor_ before capitulating. Their commander, General _Douglas MacArthur,_ was ordered to Australia before the Philippines fell. Turning next to the _Aleutian Islands,_ the Japanese held Attu and Kiska by the end of the summer, 1942. By that time they had occupied a million square miles of territory.

2. German Victories in Europe. Hitler's troops pushed back the Russians during the summer of 1942, while his air force pounded England mercilessly and his submarines sank hundreds of American freighters. The Allied road back was a hard one, but their offensive began in the fall of 1942.

B. The War in Europe, 1942-1945.

1. The African Campaign. The Allied offensive in Europe began in November, 1942, when troops under General _Dwight D. Eisenhower_ overran French Morocco and Algeria, then turned against the large German force in _Tunisia._ This force surrendered in May, 1943, with a loss of 200,000 men killed or captured.

2. The Italian Campaign. With North Africa won, Eisenhower's forces invaded Sicily (July, 1943). Mussolini fell from power during the conquest of the island, allowing the Italian king to appoint a government that willingly surrendered to the Allies. German soldiers in Italy were not willing to capitulate, however, and some of the bitterest fighting of the war took place before June, 1944, when Rome fell. The nonfascist government that took control of Italy became a cobelligerent of the Allies.

3. The War Against Germany.

a. PREPARATIONS FOR A SECOND FRONT. After winning air supremacy by the beginning of 1943, the Allies were free to attack Germany with British bombers and American flying fortresses. From that time on, mass bombings of industrial centers softened Hitler's war machine. Germany was further weakened when its drive against Russia was stopped at _Stalingrad_ (1942). By 1944 the Russians had driven the Nazis from their soil and freed Finland, Rumania, Bulgaria, and large sections of Poland.

b. OPENING THE SECOND FRONT.

I. _The Battle of France._ On _June 6, 1944_, an Anglo-American force under General _Dwight D. Eisenhower_ and General Sir _Bernard Montgomery_ landed on the Normandy coast. Two million American troops who had been waiting in Great Britain were poured through this opening during the summer of 1944 to drive the Germans back across France. Paris was liberated on August 25, 1944, just after another landing was made on the Mediterranean coast. By November the last Nazi had been driven from French soil. A "Free French" committee under General _Charles de Gaulle_ took over the government of the liberated nation.

II. _The Battle of the Bulge._ A final German counter-offensive began in December, 1944, in the Belgium-Luxembourg sector. The Allied troops were thrown back almost to the sea, but rallied to regain lost ground by the end of January, 1945. Principally responsible for Allied success was the Third Army under General George S. Patton.

c. THE BATTLE OF GERMANY. The Russian winter offensive began in January, 1945, when five huge armies moved into Germany from the east. By March 1 they were thirty miles from Berlin. Anglo-American armies from the west crossed the Rhine on March 7, 1945, and six weeks later joined with the Russians at the Elbe. As Hitler and his top officials committed suicide or went into hiding, Germany surrendered unconditionally on _May 8, 1945._

C. The War in the Pacific, 1942-1945.

1. Beginning of the Pacific Offensive. Americans began the attack in the Pacific area during the summer of 1942 when the Japanese were checked, if not defeated, at the naval battles of _Coral Sea_ and _Midway._ In August, 1942, _Guadalcanal Island_ in the Solomon Islands was invaded; nine months later the _Aleutians_ were freed. Admiral _Chester W. Nimitz,_ commander of the Pacific fleet, was free to plan the offensive against Japan.

2. The Approach to Japan. American strategy called for a direct advance on Japan, with the more important Japanese-held islands captured and the others by-passed. _Saipan_ in the Marianas fell in June, 1944, and nearby Guam a month later. From airstrips on these islands superfortresses began bombing the Japanese mainland 1500 miles away. To shorten this distance the tiny volcanic island of _Iwo Jima,_ lying half-way between Guam and Tokyo, was captured after bitter fighting in March, 1945. The next jump was to _Okinawa,_ less than 400 miles from Japan; that island succumbed in June, 1945. After that bombers roared over the Japanese mainland almost constantly.

3. The Return to the Philippines. Following the same tactics of capturing some bases and by-passing others, General Douglas MacArthur's forces advanced northward from the south Pacific, landing on _Leyte Island_ in October, 1944. The landing was covered by naval forces under Admiral _William Halsey,_ who fought one of the war's decisive engagements in the _Battle of Leyte Gulf._ After conquering outlying islands, the Americans landed on the main island of _Luzon_ in January, 1945. Bitter fighting continued during the next months.

4. The War in China. The Chinese continued their heroic resistance, although they were crippled by lack of supplies after the closing of the _Burma Road_ by the Japanese in 1942. A token American air force under General _Joseph W. Stilwell_ gave some aid to Chiang Kai-shek, but not until January, 1945, was a new road, the _Ledo Road,_ opened between India and China. Properly supplied at last, the Chinese armies began driving back the Japanese invaders.

5. Final Conquest of Japan.

a. THE ATOM BOMB. The final blow necessary to force the Japanese to surrender was delivered in August, 1945, when atomic bombs were dropped on _Hiroshima_ and Nagasaki, two towns. The total destruction caused by America's terrifying new weapon not only hastened the end of the war but brought home to millions the realization that another world war would destroy civilization.

b. JAPANESE SURRENDER. Russia's declaration of war against Japan (August, 1945), coupled with fear of further atomic bombing, forced Japan to bid for peace. Delegations from the two nations signed the surrender terms on _September 1, 1945,_ Japan capitulating unconditionally.

D. The War on the Home Front.

1. Industrial Mobilization. The unity of opinion that followed the sneak attack on Pearl Harbor allowed the all-out war effort to surpass that of World War I. Industrial production was managed by a _War Production Board_ (W.P.B.) under _Donald M. Nelson_ which set prices, assigned quotas, converted factories to war tasks, and built $20,000,000,000 worth of new plants. The result was a staggering increase in the volume of production, which was valued at nearly $200,000,000,000 by 1944. To ration scarce peacetime goods and keep prices down, an _Office of Price Administration_ (O.P.A.) was given authority to fix prices and allot civilian supplies (1941). Similarly a _War Labor Board_ (W.L.B.) pegged wages, while unions enforced a no-strike pledge so successfully that industrial disputes all but disappeared. This remarkable teamwork won the _"battle of production"_ and allowed the United States to support an armed force of 12,000,000 men and women.

2. Financing the War. The United States spent $300,-000,000,000 during the war. Most of this sum was raised by borrowing; bonds of every size were sold so successfully that by 1945 the national debt reached $252,000,000,000. Taxes were also increased to unprecedented levels, particularly income taxes, which after 1943 were collected at the source rather than at the end of the year. These, together with corporation taxes, excess-profits taxes, and luxury taxes, allowed the United States to pay 40 per cent of its war costs from taxation, a higher figure than ever before.

3. Civilian Liberties in Wartime. The government imposed fewer restrictions on personal rights than in World War I. Only the Japanese-Americans were treated badly. Thousands of Nisei who lived near the Pacific coast were moved inland to relocation camps where they could be watched, even though they showed every evidence of loyalty.

II. EVOLUTION OF THE UNITED NATIONS.

A. Allied Cooperation in Wartime.

1. Military Conferences. The leaders of the three Allied powers, Franklin D. Roosevelt, Winston Churchill, and Josef Stalin, met regularly to work out military strategy and plan the peace. At the _Moscow Conference_ (October, 1943), they agreed on plans for a second front and pledged themselves to establish an international organization of peace-loving nations when the war was over. At the _Cairo Conference_ (November, 1943), they agreed to continue fighting until Japan was expelled from China. At the _Teheran Conference_ (November, 1943), they settled details of the second front, while Stalin accepted the principle of continued Russian collaboration with the two western powers after the war.

2. Conferences on Postwar Problems. Delegates from the Allied nations met in May, 1943, to create the United Nations Relief and Rehabilitation Administration (*U.N.R.R.A.*) to speed economic reconstruction when the war was over. In July, 1944, the _Bretton Woods Conference_ drew up plans for an International Bank for Reconstruction and Development to help stabilize the world's currencies with the return of peace. The _Dumbarton Oaks Conference_ (October, 1944) drafted tentative proposals for a United Nations charter.

B. The Election of 1944.

1. The Candidates. The _Democrats,_ recognizing the popular demand for Roosevelt's continued leadership during the closing years of the war, renominated the President for a fourth term. _Harry S. Truman_ of Missouri, a party regular, was named vice-presidential candidate. The _Republicans,_ rejecting Wendell Willkie for his liberal views, nominated _Thomas Dewey_ of New York.

2. Results of the Election. The two candidates agreed in their support of the New Deal domestic program and foreign policy. Dewey based his campaign on the need for a change, while Roosevelt capitalized on his success in the war and the fact that his experienced leadership was essential for an enduring peace. The voters returned the President with an electoral vote of 432 to 99.

C. The Yalta Conference (January, 1945). This was the most important of the wartime conferences of the three Allied leaders. Roosevelt felt that his task was to win Stalin to the principle of a United Nations, thus preventing a return to the "world communist revolution" program of the past. To achieve this he made certain concessions:

1. Concessions to Russia. These included: 1) three Russian votes in the Assembly of the United Nations; 2) the veto power over acts of the United Nations for members of its Security Council; 3) territorial concessions in eastern Poland; and 4) dominance over Manchuria.

2. Concessions from Russia. Russia promised in return: 1) democratic governments for Poland and Yugoslavia; 2) support for the United Nations; 3) to enter the war against Japan after the close of the war in Europe. Military leaders at the time agreed that this last concession was worth any sacrifice.

3. Postwar Plans. The Yalta delegates also agreed: 1) that Germany should be divided into four military zones under England, France, Russia, and the United States, with Berlin an international area; 2) to call a conference of delegates to meet at San Francisco in April, 1945, to draft a charter for the United Nations.

D. The San Francisco Conference (April, 1945). Despite the tragic *death of Roosevelt* on April 12, 1945, delegates drafted the charter of the United Nations.

1. Organization of the United Nations.

a. GOVERNMENTAL ORGANIZATION. The United Nations was composed of: 1) an *Assembly* of from one to five delegates from each member nation who would vote as a unit; 2) a *Security Council* of five permanent members (England, France, China, Russia, and the United States) and six members chosen by the Assembly for two-year terms. No decision of the Security Council became binding without the concurrence of the five major powers; 3) a *Secretary-General* chosen by the Assembly to coordinate the branches of the United Nations; and 4) an *International Court of Justice* of fifteen justices meeting at the Hague to settle disputes between nations.

THE STRUCTURE OF THE UNITED NATIONS

GENERAL ASSEMBLY

Up to five delegates from each of fifty-five member nations, but only one vote for each nation. Its duties are to discuss any questions within the scope of the Charter, and submit recommendations to members or to the Security Council.

SECRETARIAT

Secretary General at head, includes research, administrative staffs, reports to Assembly, Security Council.

SECURITY COUNCIL

Eleven members—the Big Five permanent, other six elected for two-year terms by Assembly. It investigates international disputes, takes action against aggressors if necessary.

ECONOMIC & SOCIAL COUNCIL

18 members elected by Assembly. Studies economic, political problems through commissions, and special agencies below.

INTERNATIONAL COURT

Fifteen members chosen by the Assembly. They meet in permanent session to decide legal disputes which arise between nations.

EDUCATIONAL SCIENTIFIC AND CULTURAL ORGANIZATION

Organized to foster world intellectual cooperation through education, science and culture.

INTERNATIONAL MONETARY FUND

Also part of Bretton Woods plan; to be used by members to help stabilize currencies.

WORLD HEALTH ORGANIZATION

Will serve as research organ and as an information center on world medical developments.

TRUSTEESHIP COUNCIL

Includes Big Five and all nations that administer trust territories, some others elected by Assembly.

ATOMIC ENERGY COMMISSION

Includes eleven members of Security Council plus Canada. Considers problems relating to atomic energy.

MILITARY STAFF COMMITTEE

Composed of Chiefs of Staff of the Big Five. Under Council, advises on armed forces placed at disposal of U.N.

CONVENTIONAL ARMAMENTS COMMISSION

Explores the possibilities for general disarmament and suggests stages by which it can be accomplished.

FOOD AND AGRICULTURAL ORGANIZATION

Research and study organization; endeavors to raise world food and nutrition standards.

INTERNATIONAL LABOR ORGANIZATION

Includes labor-management delegates; to raise world employment, welfare standards.

INTERNATIONAL CIVIL AVIATION ORGANIZATION

Deals with the complex economic and legal problems in commercial air transportation.

INTERNATIONAL BANK

Established by the Bretton Woods agreement. Provides loans for reconstruction and development.

INTERNATIONAL REFUGEE ORGANIZATION

Being established. Successor to UNRRA. Will care for refugees; resettle displaced persons.

INTERNATIONAL TRADE ORGANIZATION

Set up to promote world trade, reduce tariffs, eliminate restrictions.

UNIVERSAL POSTAL UNION

Established in 1874 to reduce costs; increase efficiency of international mail service.

INTERNATIONAL TELECOMMUNICATIONS UNION

Established in 1932 to reduce costs; increase efficiency of international telephone, telegraph, radio services.

Graphics Institute for The New York Times

b. Minor Agencies. Subsidiary agencies created by the Charter included: 1) an *Economic and Social Council* of eighteen members to deal with a variety of international problems such as the narcotics trade and postwar reconstruction: 2) a *Trusteeship Council* to supervise colonial possessions taken from Germany and Japan; 3) the United Nations Educational, Scientific, and Cultural Organization (*U.N.E.S.C.O.*) to stimulate international educational and cultural progress.

E. Achievements of the United Nations.

1. The East-West Division. The Assembly and Security Council met first at London in 1946, and subsequently in New York, which was selected as the permanent headquarters. The early meetings showed a division into two blocs, one dominated by Russia, the other by the United States. This was so complete that few decisions could be reached in the Security Council; Russia, which was outvoted by the western bloc, used the veto power thirty times in the first three years. To save the situation, a *Little Assembly* was formed of one delegate from each nation. Its decisions, reached by a two-thirds vote, did not have the force of law but registered world opinion.

2. Settlement of Disputes.

a. Palestine. A special committee of the United Nations recommended (August, 1947) that Palestine be divided into three states, one Arab, one Jewish, and one the independent city of Palestine. Although this pleased neither Jews nor Arabs, England announced that it would give up its mandate over the area in May, 1948. Hence the Jews proclaimed the independent state of *Israel.* A war with the Arabs that followed was settled by a United Nations mediator, Dr. Ralph Bunche of the United States.

b. Atomic Energy Control. The United Nations in January, 1946, created an *Atomic Energy Commission* to recommend means of international control of this weapon. It soon found itself deadlocked between plans already devised by the United States and Russia; the former wanted an international commission to control atomic energy, with the unrestricted right to inspect all nations; the latter desired an international agreement to abandon atomic warfare, an agreement enforceable only by each nation. When these two points of view proved irreconcilable, nothing was accomplished. Again in 1949, when scientists reported the explosion of an atomic bomb in Russia, the United States offered its plan, but with no results.

III. THE FIRST TRUMAN ADMINISTRATION, 1945-1948. Truman was elevated to the presidency by the death of Roosevelt on April 12, 1945.

A. Domestic Problems.

1. Military Demobilization. After the defeat of Japan, pressure for the return of all overseas troops was so great that the United States was faced with the danger of having insufficient soldiers to occupy the defeated countries. Hence the first *peacetime draft* (May, 1946), allowed the conscription of men over eighteen for one year. The returning soldiers were aided by a *G. I. Bill of Rights* (June, 1944) which provided veterans with: 1) unemployment insurance of $20 weekly for fifty-two weeks; 2) government-guaranteed loans for business or home-building purposes; and 3) free education in colleges or vocational schools.

2. Economic Demobilization. The industrial transition to a peacetime economy was planned by the *Office of War Mobilization and Reconversion* (O.W.M.R.) which had been set up in 1944.

a. INFLATION. Price controls maintained by the O.P.A. grew unpopular with peace, especially as many Americans believed with the National Association of Manufacturers that inflation could best be combatted by allowing free competition to force prices to their natural levels. Congress reflected this view when it extended the life of the O.P.A. (1946) but with such limited powers that Truman vetoed the bill. Actually the end of price control sent prices skyrocketing; by December, 1946, the consumers' index was 31.7 per cent higher than a year before. Prices continued to rise for two more years before production caught up with demand.

b. THE LABOR PROBLEM. Strikes multiplied after the war as workers sought to retain the high wages obtained by overtime work. As a result, new wage schedules calling for increases of about eighteen cents an hour were adopted by most major industries. During the next two years _second round_ and _third round_ increases were also obtained. A fourth round wage boost was denied in 1949 when a Presidential Fact Finding Board headed by Dr. Carroll R. Daugherty recommended a company-supported pension plan rather than an increased salary for steel workers. When management rejected this proposal, steel and coal strikes followed. Before the end of 1949, however, major companies had capitulated and granted modified pension plans. The new pattern for labor stressed eventual _security_ rather than immediate higher wages.

c. THE RACIAL PROBLEM. During the war a _Fair Employment Practices Committee_ (F.E.P.C.) protected workers from discrimination because of race, color, or creed. A bill to make the _F.E.P.C._ permanent was advocated by both parties in 1944, but when such a measure was introduced in Congress during 1945 it was talked to death by a filibuster of southern congressmen.

3. The Eightieth Congress.

a. THE ELECTION OF 1946. The congressional elections of 1946 gave Republicans a majority in both houses as voters, rebelling against wartime controls and taxes, turned out the party in power. This gave the Republicans their chance to develop a reconversion program.

b. ECONOMY MEASURES. A _tax bill_ (1947) substantially reduced taxes, especially in the upper income brackets. This was vetoed by Truman, who held that an unbalanced budget would result. Congress sustained the veto by a narrow majority.

c. THE TAFT-HARTLEY ACT (1947). This Republican attempt to deprive labor of some of the power gained during the New Deal: 1) banned the closed shop, which forbade the hiring of nonunion men; 2) permitted employers to sue unions for broken contracts or damages inflicted during strikes; 3) forced unions to abide by a sixty-day "cooling-off period" before striking; 4) required unions to make public their financial statements; 5) forbade them to contribute to political campaigns; 6) ended the "check-off system" in which the employer collected union dues; and 7) required union leaders to swear they were not communists. Denounced by labor as a "slave bill," the measure was passed over Truman's veto.

B. Foreign Problems.

1. Underlying Factors. Foreign policy after 1945 was shaped by the conflict with Russia. Convinced that the Soviets had returned to their prewar policy of fomenting world communist revolution, the western powers adopted a *"get tough" policy* designed to restrict communism to the U.S.S.R. and its satelite states: Poland, Bulgaria, Rumania, Yugoslavia, and Czechoslovakia. In turn Russia withdrew behind an *Iron Curtain* that hid her actions and motives from the western world. The resulting war of nerves—the *cold war*—affected every phase of foreign policy.

2. Drafting the Peace Treaties.

a. THE POTSDAM CONFERENCE (July, 1945). Stalin, Truman, and Clement L. Attlee, representing the newly elected Labour government of England, agreed on the administration of defeated Germany. They decided that policy would be determined by an *Allied Control Council* of American, English, French, and Russian generals who would administer the four military zones into which the country had been divided at the Yalta Conference. They further agreed that peace treaties should be drafted with the minor enemy powers before those with Germany and Japan.

b. TREATIES WITH MINOR POWERS. The task of drafting treaties with Finland, Hungary, Bulgaria, Rumania, and Italy was entrusted to a *Council of Foreign Ministers* representing England, Russia, and the United States, with France participating in the Italian settlement. This Council called together delegates of all twenty-one Allied nations for a peace conference at Paris in May, 1946. The resulting treaties, which were signed in February, 1947, deprived all five defeated countries of territory, assessed heavy indemnities, and stripped away their military power.

c. TREATIES WITH GERMANY AND JAPAN. By the time the minor treaties were completed, the breach between the United States and Russia was so wide that no effort was made to draft treaties with Japan and Germany.

3. Occupation of Enemy Territory.

a. TRIAL OF THE WAR CRIMINALS. In 1945 the leading Nazis still alive were brought before an international military tribunal at _Nuremberg_ to stand trial for beginning the war and employing inhuman tactics during the fighting. So effective was the prosecutor, Justice _Robert H. Jackson_ of the United States Supreme Court, that eleven were executed and eight imprisoned. Similar trials in Japan resulted in the execution of Premier Hideki Tojo and six others, with prison sentences for a large number. Minor war criminals were tried during the next years.

b. MILITARY OCCUPATION OF GERMANY. Members of the Allied Control Council failed to cooperate in administering Germany. After repeated bickering, the United States, England, and France united their three zones into a unit popularly known as _Trizonia_ (1946), while Russia continued to administer its zone independently. This division led to an open break (1948) when the Russian representative withdrew from the Allied Control Council in a dispute over currency problems, then ordered a blockade of Berlin. As 2,000,000 Germans in the western zone of Berlin were threatened by starvation, the Allies developed the _air lift,_ shuttling in food and supplies by cargo plane. Not until May, 1949, was the blockade lifted on the promise of a complete discussion of the whole problem by the Council of Foreign Ministers. With this tense situation resolved, the people of western Germany drafted plans for a federal republic, based on democratic principles and with provisions for the admission of new states from the Russian zone whenever they wished to join. Thus the framework was laid for a German republic.

c. MILITARY OCCUPATION OF JAPAN. Although an _Allied Council_ was set up in Tokyo with delegates from the United States, Russia, China, and England, the actual administration of Japan was entrusted to the country's conqueror, General _Douglas MacArthur._ Under his direction a democratic diet was elected (April, 1946) to draw up a constitution similar to that of the United States. This document called for the dissolution of large landed estates, as well as of industrial and banking monopolies. Although the new constitution pointed the way toward eventual reform, it failed to improve Japan's acute economic crisis, or to resolve the conflict between Russia and the United States which prevented the drafting of a permanent peace treaty. In 1950 American troops still occupied Japan, and American supplies were still essential to its economy.

4. Relations with Former Allies in the Orient.

a. RELATIONS WITH CHINA. A strong communist movement that had been suppressed during the war challenged the Nationalist government of Chiang Kai-shek as soon as Japan was defeated. The United States sent General _George C. Marshall_ to China (December, 1945) in a futile effort to secure peace, but he returned after a year with little good to say for either the Nationalists or the Communists. From that time on the United States followed a hands-off policy. By 1950 the Communists had conquered most of China and established a communist state in close cooperation with Russia. On January 5, 1950, the President announced that the United States would not aid the Chinese Nationalists in their last stronghold on Formosa.

b. RELATIONS WITH KOREA. An independent Korea was agreed upon at the Cairo Conference (1943). At the end of the war Russia and the United States divided the country into two halves for military occupation. By 1948 two governments had formed, a Korean People's Republic in the Russian zone, and a Republic of Korea in the American zone. Tension between the two reflected the tension between eastern and western worlds.

5. Relations with Europe.

a. EXPANSION OF RUSSIAN INFLUENCE. Communist minorities in France, Italy, Turkey, and elsewhere gained strength amidst the economic chaos following the war, creating the impression that Russian influence would soon extend over all Europe. President Truman decided on a showdown in Greece, where a conservative government installed by England was being resisted by liberals and communists. When England withdrew its garrisons in 1947 the United States made Greece its frontier against Russia.

b. THE TRUMAN DOCTRINE (March, 1947). In asking

Congress for American aid for Greece and Turkey, Truman
laid down the doctrine that "it must be the policy of the
United States to support free peoples who are resisting attempted subjugation by armed minorities or by outside pressure." He stated that this "should be primarily through
economic and financial aid which is essential to economic
stability and orderly political processes." The support given
the _Truman Doctrine_ by both parties originated the _bipar-
tisan foreign policy_ that prevailed through 1950.

c. THE MARSHALL PLAN (June 5, 1947). Secretary of
State _George C. Marshall,_ in a commencement address at
Harvard, stated that as a stable European economy was
needed to maintain democratic institutions, the United States
was willing to aid any country that was willing to cooperate
for its own recovery. The result was the _European Recovery
Plan_ (E.R.P.) for the rehabilitation of Europe, displacing
the U.N.R.R.A. (see p. 214).

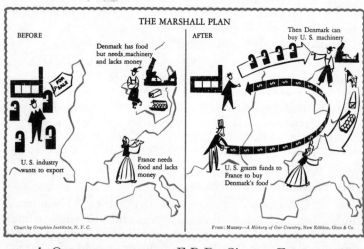

THE MARSHALL PLAN

BEFORE

Denmark has food
but needs machinery
and lacks money

U. S. industry
wants to export

France needs
food and lacks
money

AFTER

Then Denmark can
buy U. S. machinery

U. S. grants funds to
France to buy
Denmark's food

Chart by Graphics Institute, N. Y. C.   From: Muzzey—A History of Our Country, New Edition, Ginn & Co.

d. OPERATION OF THE E.R.P. Sixteen European nations drew up plans for economic recovery (July, 1947) that
called for nearly $20,000,000,000 in American aid. In April,
1948, an initial grant of $5,000,000,000 was voted by Con-
gress, which also established the _Economic Cooperation
Administration_ (E.C.A.) under _Paul G. Hoffman_ to administer the program. In their eagerness to obtain E.R.P. funds

the European nations rejected communist bids for power in elections. Thus the Marshall Plan proved effective in confining communism behind the Iron Curtain. Recovery was slow, however, with the prospect that E.R.P. aid would be needed well into the 1950's before Europe's economy was stabilized.

IV. THE SECOND TRUMAN ADMINISTRATION, 1949-1953.

A. The Election of 1948.

1. Party Divisions. The *Democratic Party,* almost certain of defeat after the reversals suffered in 1946, renominated *Truman* without enthusiasm and pledged both repeal of the Taft-Hartley Act and adoption of a civil rights program (see below). *Thomas E. Dewey* of New York was named the *Republican* candidate on a platform favoring a "minimum" amount of governmental control over business. Two splinter groups showed their dissatisfaction with the major parties by nominating candidates. Conservative Southerners, resentful of the Democrats' civil rights stand, formed the *Dixiecrat Party* with Governor J. Strom Thurmond of South Carolina as its nominee. Liberals fearful that Truman's "get-tough-with-Russia" policy would lead to World War III banded together as the *Progressive Party* under Henry A. Wallace.

2. Results of the Election. The Republicans, convinced that Truman's unpopularity assured his defeat, campaigned half-heartedly and at an emotional level holding little appeal. Truman, on the other hand, staged a vigorous battle which so captured the popular imagination that he snatched victory from defeat. In a major political upset, he was elected with 304 electoral votes to 189 for Dewey. The Dixiecrats won 39 electoral votes in the deep South, while the Progressive Party, which was discredited by communist support, polled only a million popular votes and no electoral votes.

B. The Truman Domestic Program.

1. Governmental Reorganization. From the time he entered the White House, Truman worked effectively to streamline the government's administrative machinery. In 1947 he consolidated the offices of Secretary of Navy and Secretary of War into a *Secretary of Defense;* at the same time he named a bi-partisan commission under ex-president Herbert Hoover to suggest other changes. When the _Hoover Commission_ reported in 1949 a Congressional Reorganization Plan was adopted which authorized the President to carry out its recommendations. During the next months numerous bureaus and agencies were consolidated, and the post office reformed. The people also ratified the _Twenty-second Amendment_ to the Constitution (February, 1951), limiting presidents to two terms.

2. The Fair Deal Program. Truman's progressive program made little headway in the Eighty-first Congress (1949-1951) where it met consistent opposition from Republicans and conservative Southern Democrats. His efforts to repeal the Taft-Hartley Act (see p. 220) and to secure enactment of a national health insurance program both failed. Congress, however, did amend the _Fair Labor Standards Act_ (see p. 191) to raise minimum wages from forty to seventy-five cents an hour, alter the _Social Security_ Act to increase by 10,000,000 the number of workers eligible for benefits (August, 1950), and adopt a National Housing Act (July, 1949), alloting federal funds to assist cities in slum clearance and the erection of low-cost housing. An _Agricultural Act_ of 1949 promised continued government support for commodity prices up to 90 per cent of parity, with parity based on prices between 1939 and 1949.

3. Civil Rights Program. A distinguished Commission on Civil Rights appointed by Truman recommended: 1) a federal anti-lynching law; 2) the abolition of poll-tax requirements for voting; 3) the federal enforcement of laws forbidding discrimination in hiring or segregation of races on busses and trains; and 4) a law requiring nondiscrimination as a condition for all federal grants-in-aid for housing or education. When this forward-looking program was laid before Congress, southern legislators threatened a filibuster. An administrative bill to allow a majority (rather than two-thirds) of the Senate to limit debate was defeated by an alliance of Republicans and Southern Democrats, ending hopes that the civil rights program could be adopted.

4. End of Fair Deal Program. Republican gains in the 1950 elections reduced Democratic majorities in the Eighty-second Congress (1951-1953) to the point that Truman abandoned all efforts to carry out his Fair Deal program during his last two years in office.

C. The Truman Foreign Program.

1. The Cold War in Europe.

a. CREATION OF THE GERMAN REPUBLIC. With hopes of a united Germany dissipated by the continued "cold war" between Russia and the United States (see pp. 221-225), a *Federal Republic of Germany* was created in May, 1949, under the supervision of the Allied High Commission. Russia answered by setting up the German Democratic Republic of East Germany under its control.

b. THE NORTH ATLANTIC TREATY. Fearful lest these frictions lead to war despite the efforts of the United Nations, the Senate in June, 1948, authorized the President to develop collective defense arrangments with friendly powers. The result was the *North Atlantic Treaty* (April, 1949), in which twelve western nations: 1) agreed that an attack on one would be considered an attack on all; and (2) bound themselves to use force to maintain the security of the North Atlantic area. A year later the *North Atlantic Treaty Organization* (NATO) was created to integrate western Europe's military forces under one commander, *General Dwight D. Eisenhower*.

c. THE POINT FOUR PROGRAM. Acting upon a recommendation in Truman's 1949 inaugural address, Congress in 1950 made the first of several appropriations designed to make technological and scientific information available to underdeveloped nations. This aid was designed to strengthen such areas economically and make them less susceptible to communist infiltration.

2. The War in Asia.

a. AMERICAN INTERVENTION IN KOREA. In June, 1950, open warfare in Korea began between the Russian-dominated Korean People's Republic (north of the 38th parallel) and the American-backed Republic of Korea (see p. 223). As the North Korean troops, apparently well supplied from Russia, advanced rapidly southward, fear mounted that docile acceptance of the situation would encourage communist aggression in Berlin, the Philippines, and the area south of Communist China. Hence the United Nations Security Council adopted a resolution urging member nations to furnish South Korea with assistance. Two days later (June 27, 1950), Truman ordered air and sea forces into action, at the same time instructing the American fleet to repel any attack on Formosa by Communist China. These forceful moves were almost universally praised by Congress and the people as necessary to halt the advance of world communism.

b. COURSE OF THE KOREAN WAR. When token aid proved ineffective in stopping the North Korean armies, a United Nations army was created under the American, General Douglas MacArthur. As this gained strength, largely in the form of troops sent by the United States, the tide was turned in September, 1950. By the end of November, MacArthur's forces had driven northward across the 38th parallel, only to be turned back there by an army of Communist Chinese troops that had been concealed in the mountains. A brief retreat was followed by a long stalemate. Impatient with inaction, General MacArthur issued a series of belligerent statements demanding the right to reinvade North Korea. Truman, fearful lest these demands precipitate a full-scale war with Communist China, removed MacArthur from his command (April, 1951), at the same time opening truce talks with the North Koreans.

c. THE TRUCE NEGOTIATIONS. Truce negotiations dragged on through the summer and autumn of 1951 with little progress reported on the two areas of disagreement: location of the truce line and procedure for the exchange of prisoners. The continued fighting to little apparent purpose turned American opinion against the war and against the Truman administration which was blamed for failure to settle the conflict.

D. Impact of the Korean War on the United States.

1. The Loyalty Program. The Korean War, following on the "cold war," made Americans increasingly aware of threats to their national security, and particularly from native communists. These fears were seemingly given tangible basis when *Alger Hiss,* a former state department employee, was convicted of giving a self-confessed ex-communist "courier" several top-secret documents (January, 1950). Congress reflected public alarm when it passed the *McCarran Internal Security Act* (September, 1950), requiring the registration of all communist-front organizations with the Attorney-General and forbidding aliens who had been communists to enter the United

States. At the same time the older Smith Alien Registration Act (1940) which forbade any person to teach the desirability of overthrowing the government by force, was used to convict eleven members of the Communist Party. When the Supreme Court upheld their conviction (June, 1951), they began serving terms up to five years. This encouraged an outburst of state laws inflicting "loyalty oaths" on workers or providing for the investigation of "subversives." The leader of this "red hunt" was _Senator Joseph R. McCarthy_ of Wisconsin whose indiscriminate and reckless accusations popularized the term "McCarthyism" as a synonym for the repression of civil liberties.

2. Mobilzation of the Nation.

a. INDUSTRIAL MOBILIZATION. Economic policy during the Korean War was based on the assumption that World War III could be prevented by strengthening the United States and its allies to the degree that the Soviet Union would not dare risk aggression. Congress implemented this policy by appropriating $24,937,000,000 for defense and $10,065,000,000 for foreign aid (September, 1950). To turn this money into armaments, an Office of Defense Mobilization was created under Charles E. Wilson of the General Motors Company.

b. THE THREAT OF INFLATION. With increased employment and a decline in the production of civilian goods, prices started upward. To check this trend, Truman created the Office of Price Stabilization (OPS) and the Wage Stabilization Board. Opposition to wage and price controls was so strong that both measures proved ineffective. Instead the inflationary spiral was to curve upward for at least a decade.

E. The Election of 1952.

1. Decline in Democratic Popularity.

Despite the nation's prosperity, the Democrats lost favor as the election of 1952 approached. This was due to: 1) the unpopularity of the Korean War; 2) the revelation of certain "Truman Scandals" involving bribery and "fixers" in the Reconstruction Finance Corporation, the Internal Revenue Bureau, and the Department of Justice; 3) the disclosure by the Senate _Kefauver Committee_ of a link between criminal elements and the Democratic machine in several large cities; and 4) the government's seizure of the steel mills to insure continued military production during the 1952 strike, giving rise to the charge of dictatorship against the President.

2. The Party Conventions.

a. THE REPUBLICAN CONVENTION. Factions representing the conservative neo-isolationism of *Senator Robert A. Taft* and the liberal internationalism of *General Dwight D. Eisenhower* struggled to control the Republican convention when it met at Chicago in July, 1952. The latter triumphed when Eisenhower was nominated on the first ballot, with Richard M. Nixon of California as his running-mate. The platform pledged continued support to the policy of collective security, but promised to end the "negative" policy of containment for communism. Its domestic planks approved most Fair Deal measures, but favored tax reduction, removal of economic controls from business, and the substitution of state for federal management of health insurance and civil rights.

b. THE DEMOCRATIC CONVENTION. With Truman not a candidate, a battle for the nomination was waged by Senator Estes Kefauver of Tennessee and *Governor Adlai E. Stevenson* of Illinois, with the latter victorious on the third ballot. The platform defended the Roosevelt-Truman record, promised repeal of the Taft-Hartley Act, and pledged aid to farmers and small business men.

3. Outcome of the Election.

a. THE EISENHOWER VICTORY. Although Stevenson conducted a vigorous campaign marked by speeches clothed in faultless prose and sparkling with wit, he had little chance against Eisenhower's popularity. The latter devoted his relatively few speeches to attacking the "corruption and inefficiency" of Truman, and pledged himself if elected to visit Korea to bring a speedy end to the war. He won 55.1 per cent of the popular vote, and 442 electoral votes to only 89 for Stevenson. The Republicans also won control of the House by a margin of 221 to 212, and of the Senate by a one-vote majority.

b. REASONS FOR REPUBLICAN VICTORY. The voters' decision to overthrow the party that had been in power since 1933 was based on: 1) a desire to repudiate "Trumanism" which had become associated with corruption and inefficiency; 2) dislike of the Korean War which was costing the nation heavily in lives and money; 3) a popular suspicion that Democrats were "coddling" communists in government posts; 4) the feeling that it was "time for a change"; and 5) Eisenhower's tremendous personal popularity.

V. THE EISENHOWER ADMINISTRATIONS, 1953—

A. Inaugurating the Republican Program.

1. Nature of the Program. In a dramatic gesture, Eisenhower devoted his entire inaugural address to foreign policy. Holding firmly to the internationalist program followed by Roosevelt and Truman, he pledged American cooperation with other powers "to remove the causes of mutual fear and distrust among nations," at the same time denouncing appeasement. In later messages to Congress he outlined a *foreign policy* that: 1) promised continued aid to American allies; 2) pledged continuation of the Reciprocal Trade program and other measures designed to stimulate international exchange; and 3) repudiated past agreements with governments that permitted the "enslavement" of peoples. His *domestic program* promised: 1) tax reduction only after the budget was balanced; 2) a revision of taxes to favor small business; 3) the extension of social security to additional millions; 4) changes in the controversial Taft-Hartley and McCarran acts; and 5) the abolition of all control over wages and prices by April 30, 1953. Although the program was designed "to follow a middle way between the untrammeled freedom of the individual and demands for the welfare of the whole nation," it more closly paralleled those of the New and Fair deals than it did the demands of conservatives within the President's own party.

2. The Eisenhower Cabinet. The cabinet appointments announced by Eisenhower revealed that large-scale industry would be better represented in the government than in the past. *John Foster Dulles,* an internationalist with diplomatic experience, was named Secretary of State. Other important appointments included Charles E. Wilson, former president of General Motors, as Secretary of Defense, and George M. Humphrey, a Cleveland industrialist, as Secretary of the Treasury. When Congress established a new *Department of Health, Education and Welfare* Eisenhower named as its head the second woman cabinet member in history, Mrs. Oveta Culp Hobby.

3. Fulfilling Campaign Pledges. During the first months of the new administration Eisenhower's popularity was great enough to win from Congress several measures to which he was committed: 1) 183,000 officeholders were dropped from the federal payroll; 2) the Truman budget was reduced; 3) wage and price controls were abolished; 4) the Reconstruction Finance Corporation was allowed to expire; 5) taxes were reduced slightly for those in the upper-income brackets; and 6) a Tideland Oil Bill passed (May, 1953) which handed over to the coastal states all rights to offshore oil for exploitation by private interests rather than the federal government.

4. End of the Korean War. True to his campaign promises, Eisenhower made a three-day inspection of the Korean battlefields shortly after his election (December, 1952), but this gesture failed to break the deadlock in truce negotiations. This was not broken until the death of _Joseph Stalin_ (March 5, 1953) forced Soviet officials to relax world tensions until they had recast the power structure within the USSR. Their unusually peaceful attitude was reflected by the communist negotiators in Korea who finally backed down on their demand that all prisoners be returned by both sides, whether willing or not. On July 27, 1953, a truce was signed which allowed prisoners unwilling to return to their native country to be handled by representatives of neutral nations.

B. The Eisenhower Domestic Program.

1. The "New Republicanism." The President's "honeymoon" with his party ended with the death of Senator Robert A. Taft on July 31, 1953. Although more conservative than Eisenhower, Taft had held Republican Congressmen in line to support administration measures. With his death opposition to the presidential program mounted in the ranks of conservative Republicans and Southern Democrats; most support for the Eisenhower measures was provided by Northern Democrats and a smaller number of liberal Republicans. The _Congressional elections of 1954_ actually strengthened Eisenhower's hand by returning Democratic majorities in both houses of Congress, 48 to 47 in the Senate, and 232 to 203 in the House.

2. Public versus Private Power. Although Eisenhower publicly supported a "partnership" between government and industry in the production of electrical power, his administration alarmed conservationists and public power interests by turning over a number of power sites in the West to private corporations. He also supported the _Dixon-Yates Contract_

(June, 1954), which authorized private companies to build a generating plant at West Memphis, Arkansas, to supply additional power to the Tennessee Valley Authority for use in producing atomic materials. Opposition to this contract was so vehement that the President backed down in July, 1955, when the city of Memphis decided to build its own municipally controlled plant. The Dixon-Yates contract was then cancelled. On the other hand, the President approved a congressional measure authorizing construction of the long-awaited *St. Lawrence Seaway* to allow ocean transportation between the Atlantic and the Great Lakes (May, 1954), although public power would be generated at several of the dams. He also vetoed a bill that would have exempted natural gas producers from direct federal regulation (February, 1956).

3. Farm and Labor Legislation. Declining farm income after the Korean War posed a major political problem. The Eisenhower administration held that this was caused by the agricultural surpluses in storage, and that these could be reduced by lowering parity payments to farmers below 90 per cent of parity, thus discouraging large plantings. Democrats, on the other hand, maintained that farm income must be maintained by payments of 90 per cent of parity on all base crops. When the Democratic measure failed to pass Congress, the administration-backed Agricultural Act of 1956 (May, 1956), introduced the principle of the *"soil bank."* Under this, farmers were paid to withdraw marginal lands from cultivation. Organized labor fared better, largely by capitalizing on its own unity. Demands for wage increases were negotiated yearly; in June, 1955, the United Auto Workers won an additional victory when the Ford Motor Company accepted the principle of a "guaranteed annual wage." Similar contracts were later negotiated with other firms geared to seasonal production. The most significant step on the labor front was the merging of the two largest unions as the *American Federation of Labor and Congress of Industrial Organizations,* with a membership of 15,000,000 (December, 1955).

4. The Eisenhower Legislative Record. Among other significant measures secured by the President were: 1) a three-year extension of the *Reciprocal Trade Agreements Act* (May, 1955); 2) a measure providing for federally supported public housing (August, 1955); 3) a revision of the *Fair Labor Standards Act* to raise minimum wages from seventy-five cents to one dollar an hour (August, 1955) ; and 4) a multi-million dollar *highway construction program* supported by both federal and state funds and financed by an increase in gasoline and trucking taxes (June, 1956). He failed to win approval for: 1) statehood for Hawaii and Alaska; 2) an expanded public housing program; 3) federal aid for school construction; 4) a federally supported public health plan; and 5) a civil rights law that would guarantee political and social equality for all citizens.

5. The Desegregation Issue. The most controversial issue of the Eisenhower era was provided by the Supreme Court when it held that *segregation of white and Negro children in state schools was in violation of the 14th Amendment* (May, 1954). In a subsequent decision (May, 1955), the Court refused to set a date when segregation must end, stating instead that when a "reasonable start" toward integration had been made by school officials, "additional time" would be allowed as required in the "public interest." Under these mandates, integration proceded steadily in the border states despite occasional flareups of violence engineered by racists. In the Deep South opposition to the Court ruling increased, with some states such as Virginia, Alabama, and Georgia moving to abolish public schools rather than allow a mingling of the races. In March, 1956, nineteen southern Senators and eighty-one Representatives issued a manifesto pledging the use of "all lawful means" to reverse the "unwarranted" court decision.

C. The Eisenhower Foreign Program.

1. The Cold War in Europe. Despite the calmer international atmosphere after the death of Stalin, the administration continued its efforts to strengthen defensive alliances with European nations. In October, 1954, the Paris Agreement gave West Germany its sovereignty and admitted the new nation to NATO with a contribution of 500,000 troops. This agreement was ratified by all NATO powers by April, 1955; a month later Russia suddenly agreed to a peace treaty for Austria (signed May, 1955). These indications of allied solidarity and USSR reasonableness encouraged Eisenhower to call a "summit meeting" of the heads of state of Russia, England, France, and the United States for Geneva in July, 1955. The high point of the *Geneva Conference* came when the President proposed a general disarmament plan that included the

international exchange of armament blueprints and aerial inspection. While later discussions showed that the United States
and Russia were still poles apart, Americans were further encouraged by a growing restiveness among peoples behind the
Iron Curtain. In October, 1956, demonstrations in Poland
resulted in lessened USSR controls there, although a more
violent rebellion in Hungary (October 23-November 4, 1956)
was answered by a massive Russian invasion that turned world
sentiment against the Soviets to a degree unknown since World
War II.

2. *The Cold War in Asia.* The American program in the
Far East suffered a major set-back when a nineteen-nation
Geneva Conference (April-July, 1954) ended the seven-year
war in Indochina by granting the northern half of that country
to a communist government. To prevent further deflections of
this nature, the Eisenhower government organized the *Southeast Asia Treaty Organization* (SEATO) as a counterpart of
the NATO (September, 1954). Communist China answered
by announcing (November, 1954) that eleven American airmen who had been forced down within that country had been
sentenced to long prison terms as spies. At the same time the
Chinese prepared for an all-out attack on the Nationalist
Chinese stronghold of Formosa. Eisenhower answered this
step by securing from Congress authority to use armed forces
to defend Formosa and neighboring islands (January, 1955).
In the face of this firm stand, the Communist China government backed down, announcing in April, 1955, that it was
willing to discuss the whole status of the Formosa Straits. The
eleven American airmen were released in August, 1955. Negotiations between the two powers begun shortly afterward held
hope that eventually Formosa would be neutralized under the
United Nations, thus removing one trouble spot.

3. *The Cold War in the Middle East.*

a. BACKGROUND OF THE PROBLEM. In seeking to build up
an anti-Russian bloc among Arab nations, the United States
and Britain in December, 1955, promised Egypt funds needed
to build the *Aswam Dam* on the upper Nile. When Egypt's
president, *Gamal Abdel Nasser,* continued to import arms from
Russian satellite nations, the offer was withdrawn (July, 1956).
Nasser retaliated by seizing the Suez Canal and announcing
that the dam would be built from its revenues. On September
14, 1956, Egypt began operating the canal.

b. Outbreak of Egyptian War. Complicating the Egyptian problem was the prolonged skirmishing between the Jewish state of Israel and the Arab states of Egypt, Jordan, Lebanon, and Syria. Israel, capitalizing on the Western World's dislike of Egypt after the Suez seizure, on October 29, 1956, invaded the Egyptian Sinai Peninsula. Britain and France immediately issued an ultimatum calling on both nations to cease fighting and withdraw troops to a point ten miles from the canal. Israel accepted this demand unconditionally, but Egypt refused. Hence Britain and France attacked Egypt on October 31, 1956. All three invading forces won easy victories, the Israelis overrunning the Sinai Peninsula and the Gaza Strip, and the British-French forces captured Port Said, Port Fuad, and portions of the canal.

c. End of the Egyptian War. As soon as war broke out, the United States acted through the United Nations to stop hostilities. A Security Council resolution (November 2, 1956) called for an immediate cease-fire and withdrawal of invading forces. Four days later a similar resolution was adopted by the General Assembly, at the same time as a UN police force was created to occupy disputed areas as withdrawal went on. Britain and France agreed on November 7 to the cease-fire order and to withdraw, while Israel also promised to give up the Sinai Peninsula but made no commitment concerning the Gaza Strip. The invading forces of the three powers began withdrawing on November 30, 1956, as UN police forces arrived to take their places.

d. The Peace in the Middle East. In an effort to prevent Russian from capitalizing on the Near East situation, the President in January, 1957, asked Congress for authority to: 1) use United States forces to protect any middle eastern nation that desired help against aggression from "any nation controlled by international Communism"; and 2) send upward of $400,000,000 to the Middle East to strengthen the economy of governments there. Although the debate on this *"Eisenhower Doctrine"* allowed Democrats to criticize the administration's foreign policy, the authority was granted early in 1957. At the same time the President worked through the United Nations to secure a permanent settlement. When Israel refused to back down in its decision to occupy the Gaza Strip, Eisenhower supported the Asian-Arab bloc within the UN in a resolution demanding the application of sanctions against that country (February-March, 1957). Although the troubled Near East situation seemed far from a settlement, statesmen were confident that the issue was too localized to expand into World War III.

D. The 1956 Election.

1. *The Rival Candidates.* A heart attack suffered by President Eisenhower on September 24, 1955, threatened to prevent him from standing for reelection. He recovered rapidly, however, and on February 29, 1956, announced his candidacy. On August 22, 1956, he was renominated by the Republicans at a San Francisco convention, with Richard Nixon again his running-mate. The Democrats, meeting in Chicago, once more chose Adlai Stevenson to head their ticket, with his principal rival for the nomination, Estes Kefauver of Tennessee, as his vice-presidential candidate. The platforms of the two parties varied little, for both promised a progressive domestic program and a continued international approach to world problems.

2. *Outcome of the Election.* The threat of a Middle Eastern war increased Eisenhower's great popularity on the eve of the election. Hence he received 457 electoral votes to only 74 for Stevenson. Again the Democrats captured control of both houses of Congress, with a majority of 49 to 47 in the Senate and 233 to 200 in the House.

3. *Launching the Second Administration.* Eisenhower's policies inspired a more general attack during the first months of his second administration than in all of his first. Liberals attacked the President for: 1) his Middle Eastern policies which were held partially responsible for the outbreak of warfare; 2) the "Eisenhower Doctrine" with its "blank-check" authority to use armed forces in a manner likely to precipitate war; and 3) his alliance with the Asian-Arab nations in demanding sanctions against Israel unless that nation withdrew from the Gaza Strip. Conservatives voiced opposition to the President for his: 1) request for a $71.8 billion budget, the largest in peacetime history; 2) demand that Congress appropriate $1,300,000,000 for school construction; 3) proposal to change the Walter-McCarran Immigration Act to admit more refugees and to base quotas on the 1950 census rather than earlier enumerations (January, 1957). While neither foreign nor domestic policy was likely to be changed by these criticisms, they indicated that Eisenhower's last three years in office would be less harmonious than those of his first administration.

VI. AMERICA FACES THE FUTURE. As the American people moved into the second half of the twentieth century they were faced with a number of serious questions:

A. Were They Committed to Their New World Role? The conduct of both parties indicated that isolationism was forever discredited in the United States. Instead the Americans were convinced that they could know neither peace nor prosperity unless the rest of the world was peaceful and prosperous. This was possible only through continued positive action on a world-wide scale. The new internationalist spirit was shown as clearly by the Republicans' decision to by-pass Senator Taft in the 1952 convention as it was by the support given President Truman's decision to intervene in Korea in 1950 or President Eisenhower's determination to use force in the Middle East in 1957 if that became necessary to hold back communism.

B. Would the United Nations Guarantee Future Peace? Only time would answer, but hope that a major war could be averted was growing with each passing year. The United Nations operated amidst the worst possible conditions, for the world was dominated by two giant power blocs under the United States and Russia, and in periods of crisis each would be inclined to by-pass international machinery rather than risk its own national status. Despite these handicaps, world diplomats had repeatedly shown their ability to localize potentially dangerous conflicts, as they had in Korea in 1950-51 and in Egypt in 1956-57. Internationalists hoped that this step-by-step procedure could hold off a major war until an effective world government was created with sovereignty of its own.

C. Was World War III Inevitable? Again only the future could reveal the answer. Advocates of the Truman and Eisenhower doctrines insisted that heavily armed and prosperous democratic nations could confine communism until it withered and died. Opponents of this "containment" policy argued that the emergence of eastern and western power blocs had returned the world to a balance-of-power system that must inevitably lead to war.

D. Would the United States Return to an Era of "Normalcy"? The postwar trend indicated that this was unlikely. Memories of the great depression and the terrors of nuclear fission were so close to the people that their quest was for security, both for the individual and the nation. Never again would they favor the complete freedom that had, in the 1920's, led inevitably to panic and war; better, they reasoned, that man's economic liberties be somewhat confined than destroyed altogether through communism or dictatorship. This was shown by the willingness with which they accepted Eisenhower's "New Republicanism," in the same spirit that they had Roosevelt's "New Deal" and Truman's "Fair Deal." In each instance they expressed the belief that a partially controlled economy was essential to maintain the national prosperity that would allow the United States to play a vigorous international role as leader of the free nations. This, in turn, would keep the world at peace until the gulf separating the democratic and communistic powers could be bridged by the United Nations.

ADDITIONAL READING

Three important series now in preparation will tell the story of American military participation in World War II: Kent R. Greenfield, ed., *United States Army in World War II* (1947–in progress); W. F. Craven and J. T. Cate, eds., *The Army Air Forces in World War II* (1948–in progress); and Samuel E. Morison, *History of the United States Naval Operations in World War II* (1947–in progress). Donald M. Nelson, *Arsenal of Democracy* (1946) describes industrial production, while Edward R. Stettinius, Jr., *Lend-Lease. Weapon for Victory* (1944) deals with aid to the Allies. J. P. Baxter, *Scientists Against Time* (1946), tells the story of the atomic bomb. A convenient summary of American-European relationships is in Vera M. Dean, *Europe and the United States* (1950), while conflicts in the Far East are the theme of Harold M. Vinacke, *United States and the Far East, 1945-1951* (1952). Thomas A. Bailey, *America Faces Russia* (1950), and Vera M. Dean, *United States and Russia* (1947) deal with Russian-American controversies. A brilliant and readable summary of the entire 1945-1955 decade is Eric F. Goldman, *The Crucial Decade* (1956).

Examination Questions

Three types of questions are employed in most American history courses: 1) objective questions, 2) identification questions, and 3) essay questions. These are used by instructors in a variety of combinations. Thus one examination may consist entirely of objective questions; another may combine objective questions and essay questions; still another may employ identification questions and essay questions. Usually students are told in advance the kind of questions that will be asked. If not, they should be prepared to deal with all three types. The examples given below will make this preparation easier.

I. OBJECTIVE QUESTIONS. Objective questions are so named because they can be graded objectively—that is, without resort to any subjective judgment on the part of the reader—and rapidly. Hence they are usually employed in large courses. Four types of objective questions are commonly used: 1) true and false, 2) multiple choice, 3) association, and 4) completion.

A. True or False Questions. As with all objective questions, the true or false questions are distributed to students in mimeographed or printed form. Answers are marked directly on the printed pages, which are then returned to the instructor. In this type the student is required to designate whether a large number of brief statements are true or false. Typical questions of this sort follow:

1. Andrew Johnson broke sharply with Lincoln and worked with radical Republicans in formulating reconstruction policy. **F**

2. The Greenback Party was against inflation and in favor of sound money and the gold standard. F

3. The Pendleton Act re-established the free coinage of silver. F

4. Josiah Strong's philosophy was based on a strong belief in the destiny of the "Anglo-Saxon race" and the "mission" of America to "civilize" the lesser peoples of the world. T

5. The Haymarket riot brought about the downfall of the Greenback Party. F

6. The federal government's policy toward the railroads was one of strict control before 1887. F

7. The case of *Munn v. Illinois* held a federal income tax unconstitutional. F

8. The "long and short haul" referred to the long drive of cattle from Texas to the railroads. F

9. The Populist revolt during the 1890's was in reality the forerunner of the progressive movement of the early 1900's. T

10. The trend toward the consolidation of industry accelerated during the early years of the twentieth century. T

11. The Republican Party became the center of agrarian resistance to the growth of big business following the Civil War. F

12. The isolationist Hearst press attacked the McKinley Republicans for playing up Cuban incidents and precipitating a war with Spain. F

13. Before becoming President, Woodrow Wilson had served as governor of New York. F

14. The progressive measures of the Taft administration outnumbered those of Theodore Roosevelt's administration. T

15. W. J. Bryan resigned as Wilson's Secretary of State because he thought the President a pacifist. F

16. The Zimmermann note proposed an alliance between the United States and Germany in case of a war with England. F

17. The Progressive Party nominated Robert LaFollette of Wisconsin for the presidency in 1912. F

18. The Pure Food and Drug Act was passed largely as a result of such books as Upton Sinclair's *The Jungle*. T

19. The government's victory in the Northern Securities case was the first of importance under the Sherman Antitrust Act. T

20. The Hepburn Act extended the power of the Interstate Commerce Commission over express companies, pipe lines, etc. T

21. The Congressional insurgents of 1910-1912 were made up of progressive Republicans who attacked the Old Guard and its point of view. T

22. The first successful reduction of the tariff since the Civil War was accomplished during Wilson's first administration. T

23. The muckrakers were writers who urged the United States to enter World War I two years before it did so. F

24. The chief purpose of the Federal Reserve Act was to provide a flexible banking system to meet the needs of industrialized America. T

25. The Clayton Antitrust Act of 1914 was designed to modify the too stringent regulatory features of the Sherman Antitrust Act. F

26. The "Roosevelt Corollary" to the Monroe Doctrine stated that the United States should cooperate with Latin America in the interests of hemispheric peace. F

27. The Sherman Antitrust Act was designed to break up large combinations in restraint of trade and split them into units that would compete with each other. T

28. Successful German propaganda almost led the United States into war with England in 1916. F

29. Woodrow Wilson inaugurated a preparedness program to stave off infringement of American neutral rights. T

30. The revolution in Russia in 1917 made it easier for the United States to join the Allies. T

31. German opposition to Wilson's fourteen points led to their failure as a basis for an armistice. F

32. Wilson championed the principle of national self-determination, but exceptions to the principle were made at Versailles. T

33. World War I stimulated a vast increase in progressive legislation. F

34. The Fordney-McCumber Tariff of 1922 promoted the recovery of world trade following World War I. F

35. Our immigration laws passed during the 1920's opened the country's gates still wider to Europe's oppressed. F

36. Though the United States did not join the League of Nations, it did participate in many of the League's programs. T

37. The chief object of New Deal legislation was to provide relief for the unemployed. F

38. New Deal domestic monetary policies were designed to further deflation. F

39. The Supreme Court upheld the constitutionality of the National Industrial Recovery Act on the basis of the commerce clause of the Constitution. F

40. Wendell Willkie and F. D. Roosevelt differed radically in their attitudes toward international affairs. F

B. Multiple Choice Questions. In this type of examination the student is confronted with a series of statements, only one of which is correct. He must designate which one. Typical multiple-choice questions follow:

1. The "grandfather clause" (1) determined whether or not you were a Democrat (2) gave the Negro protection at the polls (3) was part of the reform legislation of the Reconstruction period (4) <u>denied Negroes the franchise in the South</u> (5) helped the Republican Party.

2. Immigration to the United States in the 1880's and 1890's originated largely in (1) England (2) Ireland (3) northern Europe (4) southern Europe.

3. The Interstate Commerce Act (1) <u>forbade rate discrimination</u> (2) allocated lands to the railroads (3) provided free passes for Civil War veterans (4) gave the President power to fix railroad rates.

4. The Granger cases (1) authorized Congress to regulate railroads (2) <u>allowed the states to regulate business clothed in a public interest</u> (3) banned the coinage of silver dollars (4) forbade the Grange to set up cooperatives.

5. Granger laws were upheld by the Supreme Court in (1) the Wabash case (2) <u>Munn v. Illinois</u> (3) Minnesota rate case (4) Brief case.

6. The Panic of 1873 was caused by (1) <u>a postwar deflation</u> (2) the financial manipulations of Jay Gould (3) the draining away of the gold reserve.

7. The problem of the surplus revenue became acute in (1) the 1870's (2) <u>the 1880's</u> (3) the 1890's.

8. The Insular cases held that (1) <u>the Constitution does not follow the flag</u> (2) the United States must follow a policy of isolation (3) all islands adjacent to the United States belong to the United States (4) the Bering Sea is a closed sea.

9. The Open Door Policy involved (1) the observance of Chinese laws by foreigners (2) trade opportunities in Latin America (3) free immigration to the United States (4) <u>equal trading opportunities in China for all nations.</u>

10. The American shift toward internationalism in the late nineteenth century was (1) gradual and unconscious (2) rapid and deliberate (3) <u>the result of the Spanish-American War</u> (4) the result of new imperialistic policies (5) due to the writings of Schurz and Mahan.

11. Which of the following was not in the Omaha platform (1) <u>unimetalism</u> (2) control of railroads (3) direct election of Senators (4) postal savings legislation.

12. The progressive movement was basically (1) revolutionary (2) radical (3) <u>an expression of liberal democracy</u> (4) a partisan approach to social problems.

13. Woodrow Wilson's philosophy was expressed in the term (1) the New Nationalism (2) <u>the New Freedom</u> (3) the New Deal.

14. American intervention in Cuban affairs was based on (1) the Teller Amendment (2) <u>the Platt Amendment</u> (3) the Hay-Herran Treaty (4) the peace treaty with Spain.

15. Theodore Roosevelt made one of his great contributions to the United States in (1) his policy of conservation (2) mediation in the Russo-Japanese War (3) trust busting.

16. Robert LaFollette was (1) a Populist leader (2) a progressive Republican (3) Secretary of the Interior under Taft (4) a Democratic congressman.

17. Muckraker was a term used to designate (1) miners working under ground (2) writers exposing evil conditions (3) isolationists (4) interventionists.

18. Acceptance of the Drago Doctrine by the United States would have led to (1) better relations with Italy (2) the application of the Roosevelt Corollary to the Monroe Doctrine (3) better relations with Latin America.

19. The British black list referred to (1) German leaders (2) German spies (3) members of the German bund (4) firms suspected of trading with the enemy.

20. The Sussex Pledge was made by (1) England (2) Germany (3) Ireland (4) the United States.

21. American soldiers in World War I fought in the battles of (1) Ypres (2) Argonne (3) Caporetto (4) Archangel.

22. The final cause for American entry into World War I was (1) insults to our ambassador in Germany (2) the invasion of Belgium (3) the sinking of American naval vessels (4) the resumption of unrestricted submarine warfare.

23. The Teapot Dome scandal referred to (1) the breakdown of the railroads in 1918 (2) corrupt naval oil leases (3) bribery in connection with the veterans bureau (4) corruption in building the Pacific railroads.

24. The Washington Conference of 1921 (1) established reciprocal trade agreements (2) set up the Pan-American Union (3) gave Korea to Japan (4) limited naval armament (5) proposed a soldiers' bonus.

25. The Dawes Plan (1) scaled down German reparations payments (2) proposed priming the pump for recovery (3) favored reducing tariffs to increase trade (4) reduced the German war debt.

26. The Immigration Act of 1924 established (1) a quota of 3 per cent of each nationality here in 1910 (2) a quota of 2 per cent of each nationality here in 1890 (3) a quota of those who had jobs contracted for in this country.

27. Harding's opponent in the campaign of 1920 was (1) Lansing (2) McAdoo (3) Cox (4) Garner.

28. In respect to political corruption, the Harding administration has often been compared to that of (1) Grant (2) Johnson (3) Arthur (4) Cleveland.

29. The government under Coolidge succeeded in (1) taking the United States into the World Court (2) reducing the national debt (3) passing the McNary-Haugen Act (4) repealing the Eighteenth Amendment.

30. The Good Neighbor Policy had especially to do with American relations with (1) Canada (2) The Philippines (3) Mexico (4) Latin America (5) Russia.

31. The Neutrality Acts of 1935-1937 were designed to (1) defend freedom of the seas in wartime (2) keep the United States out of European wars (3) define the rights of neutral nations (4) form a union of neutral nations in defense of neutral rights.

32. F. D. Roosevelt proposed to reorganize the Supreme Court because in his opinion (1) it exceeded its rights under the Constitution (2) its Republican members were active in politics (3) it neglected its duties (4) its conservative bias prevented social progress.

33. The Stimson Doctrine proposed (1) nonrecognition of Japanese conquests in Manchuria (2) better relations with Latin America (3) payment of the European war debts (4) naval expansion.

34. The economic collapse that led to a Democratic victory in 1932 occurred (1) 1928 (2) 1929 (3) 1930 (4) 1931.

35. The New Deal tapered off after (1) the first three months (2) 1938 (3) the Supreme Court intervened (4) the Republicans gained control of Congress in 1936.

36. The destroyer deal with England gave the United States (1) airplanes (2) naval and air bases (3) control of Iceland (4) safe passage across the Atlantic.

37. The Atlantic Charter resembled (1) the Monroe Doctrine (2) <u>Wilson's Fourteen Points</u> (3) the Neutrality Acts (4) the Good Neighbor Policy.

38. Isolationists in the United States prior to Pearl Harbor belonged to (1) the Republican Party (2) <u>the America First Committee</u> (3) the Fight for Freedom Committee (4) the Ku Klux Klan.

39. American isolationist sentiment favored (1) repeal of the Neutrality Acts (2) lend-lease aid to China (3) <u>the Johnson Act</u> (4) arming of American merchant ships.

40. The Marshall Plan proposed (1) miltiary intervention against the Chinese communists (2) <u>the economic rehabilitation of Europe</u> (3) confining communism to eastern Europe (4) military aid for Greece.

C. Association Questions. A student is confronted with the lists of names, dates, and events, then asked to associate those that are connected or arrange them in proper sequences. The following two examples illustrate this type of question:

1. One term in Group II and one term in Group III are closely associated with a term in Group I. Letter the appropriate terms in Group II and Group III with the letter (a). Proceed through the rest of the question in the same way:

Group I	Group II	Group III
a) Platt Amendment	b Rebates	e Populists
b) Hepburn Act	f Northern Securities case	i W. G. Harding
c) Hay-Herran Treaty	a Cuban independence	j War debts
d) Upton Sinclair	h Civil rights	a Admiral Dewey
e) Crime of 1873	n Jones Act, 1916	c Colombia
f) T. Roosevelt	e Free silver	g Treaty of Versailles
g) H. C. Lodge	i Oil lands	f Interstate commerce
h) 14th Amendment	c Panama	h Due process of law
i) Teapot Dome	k Labor rights	d Muckrakers

j) Dawes Plan	_l_ Caribbean	_b_ Great Northern Railroad
k) N.I.R.A.	_d_ Meat inspection	_l_ Clark Memorandum
l) Roosevelt Corollary	_m_ Japan	_m_ Manchuria
m) Stimson Doctrine	_g_ League of Nations	_n_ Tyding-McDuffie Act
n) Philippines	_j_ Reparations	_k_ Wagner Act

2. Rearrange each of the following in the order of occurrence. Place the proper number in the space at left:

Group I

1. (2)   1. Pendleton Act
2. (1)   2. Homestead Act
3. (3)   3. Dawes Act
4. (4)   4. Hepburn Act
5. (5)   5. Norris-LaGuardia Act

Group II

1. (3)   1. Briand-Kellogg Pact
2. (5)   2. Atlantic Charter
3. (1)   3. First Hague conference
4. (4)   4. London disarmament conference
5. (2)   5. Wilson's Fourteen Points announced

Group III

1. (2)   1. Pearl Harbor attack
2. (4)   2. Stimson Doctrine
3. (1)   3. Yalta conference
4. (5)   4. Roosevelt's quarantine speech
5. (3)   5. Opening of second front

D. Completion Questions. The student is presented with a number of statements which must be filled in with the proper date, name, or event. The following examples will illustrate this type of question:

1. Lincoln's successor __ANDREW JOHNSON__ although he attempted to carry out the basic __RECONSTRUCTION__ policies of the wartime President, lacked the __POLITICAL__ acumen to win Congress to his point of view.

2. Cleveland devoted his entire congressional message in __1887__ to the subject of the __TARIFF__.

3. The __ROOSEVELT__ Corollary to the Monroe Doctrine denied to European nations the right to use force in collecting __DEBTS__ in __THE AMERICAN HEMISPHERE__.

4. Henry George's important book, __PROGRESS OR POVERTY__, argued in favor of a __SINGLE__ tax on land.

5. Theodore Roosevelt became President on the death of __McKINLEY__ in __1901__.

6. The principal financial measure of Wilson's administration was the __FEDERAL RESERVE ACT__.

7. The leader of the reservationists, __HENRY CABOT LODGE__, was not so much interested in making the __LEAGUE OF NATIONS__ acceptable to the United States but in defeating it entirely for __POLITICAL__ reasons.

8. The __FORDNEY McCUMBER__ Tariff of 1922 and the __SMOOT-HAWLEY__ Tariff of 1930 __RAISED__ levels to the __HIGHEST__ point in history.

9. Relief, __RECOVERY__, and __REFORM__ were the triple purposes of the New Deal.

10. F. D. Roosevelt's Secretary of State, __CORDELL HULL__, worked with the President in carrying out the __GOOD NEIGHBOR__ Policy.

II. IDENTIFICATION QUESTIONS.

The student is given a list of names or events, and asked to write a brief note about each. Occasionally a list of well-known quotations is substituted for the names or events. As identification questions are frequently employed to test the student's knowledge of the text or other assigned reading, he should take pains to include in his answer material that could be drawn from those sources only. The answers should be brief and compact, but crammed with information. Typical questions follow:

1. Write brief notes to explain the significance of the following: Henry George, John Fiske, Joseph Pulitzer, Henry H. Richardson, Eugene Debs, Washington Gladden, Edward Bellamy, O. H. Kelley, Lincoln Steffens, John Steinbeck.

2. Write brief notes on : the Hay-Herran Treaty, Crime of 1873, *Ex Parte Milligan,* Mugwumps, Alabama claims, Greenback Party, Dawes Act, *Looking Backward,* Chautauquas, Venezuela boundary dispute, McNary-Haugen Bill, Wagner Act, Stimson Doctrine.

3. Identify as closely as possible and discuss as fully as you can the significance of the following quotations :

(a) "Rum, Romanism, and Rebellion."

(b) "Raise less corn and more hell."

(c) "Liners will not be sunk without warning and without saving human lives, unless these ships attempt to escape or offer resistance."

(d) "It is a condition which confronts us, not a theory."

(e) "Nor shall any state deprive any person of life, liberty, or property without due process of law."

(f) "We are opposed to the free coinage of silver except by international agreement . . . which we pledge ourselves to promote, and until such agreement can be obtained the existing gold standard must be preserved."

(g) "The Gilded Age."

(h) "Property becomes clothed in a public interest when used in a manner to make it of public consequence and affect the community at large."

III. ESSAY QUESTIONS.

Essay questions are used more widely than any other type, either by themselves or in connection with objective questions or identification questions. As they are the most difficult kind to answer properly, adequate time should be spent in preparation for them. This time can be used intelligently only when the student realizes the *purpose* of an essay question.

An instructor who gives properly prepared essay questions is testing his students' ability to 1) *understand* the material of the course, 2) *organize* that material intelligently, 3) *select* the most important events for discussion, and 4) demonstrate *factual knowledge.* If the student will always remember that his grade will depend on all four of those attributes, he should be able to handle the essay question satisfactorily. They should be kept constantly in mind both when studying for an examination or when writing one.

Understanding of the material is the first requisite of a good answer. A penetrating essay on a phase of history cannot be written from memory alone; the student must immerse himself in the material so thoroughly that he completely masters the subject. This is necessary as the essay question usually does not test knowledge already familiar to the student (a chapter of the text or a classroom lecture, for example). Instead it forces him to combine information drawn from several sources, arrange that information in an unfamiliar pattern, and draw conclusions that may be new to him. This requires a thorough understanding of the material.

Organization is equally important. Any intelligent essay must be built upon a carefully planned framework; only then will the events unfold in the logical sequence that gives meaning to the past. No instructor is satisfied with a jumbled mass of information, no matter how exact that information may be. Before starting to write an essay question the student should work out an outline in his mind, or perhaps even jot one down on a blank page of his examination book.

Selection of the material to be included in an essay question tests both the student's intelligence and his familiarity with the subject matter. Any well-prepared person would be able to write for an hour or more on most essay questions. To answer them in the limited time available he must choose only the most essential material, eliminating that which is less important. This requires both a thorough knowledge of the subject and a common-sense ability to distinguish between the essential and the nonessential.

Factual knowledge is also needed for a proper answer to an essay question. Many students on an examination may understand, organize, and select their material well. In that case the instructor is certain to give the highest mark to the one whose essay contains the largest amount of exact information.

With these four points in mind, the student should read carefully the following essay questions, selecting those that fall within the field covered in the portion of the course on which he is to be examined. He will note that some are _general essay questions_ covering a wide range of time; these are likely to appear on final examinations. Others are *specific essay questions* dealing with briefer episodes of history. These are used on both final examinations and on the shorter examinations that occur periodically in every course. They have been grouped below to conform to the chapters in this outline.

A. General Essay Questions.

1. Describe the changing relations between business and government, 1865-1916, or 1917-1950.

2. Discuss the decline of laissez faire in America since the Civil War.

3. Consider the history of the tariff, 1865-1900, or 1900-1950, in the light of various factors that have influenced legislation.

4. Describe the changing interpretation of the commerce clause (or the Fourteenth Amendment) in the light of the various factors influencing each change.

5. Discuss the attempts of the federal government to regulate banking (or railroads) from the Civil War to the present.

6. "The almost continuous demand for inflation, growing stronger during the periods of economic depression, has been an outstanding characteristic of American economic history." Discuss fully.

7. Discuss the history of American agriculture from the Civil War to the present in the light of the various factors which influenced it.

8. "Since the Civil War there has never been any real difference between the major parties." Do you agree? Discuss.

9. Account for the rise of minor parties, describe the various types, and show the influence, if any, they have had on American political development.

10. Compare Harding and Grant, and their administrations.

11. As a well-informed citizen, how would you have cast your ballots in 1896, 1916, 1924, and 1932? In each case name the principal candidates and issues involved.

12. How far does American history demonstrate the truth of Madison's dictum that war is the mother of executive aggrandizement?

13. Discuss the meaning of the first section of the Fourteenth Amendment in the light of the leading Supreme Court decisions interpreting it.

14. Account for the changing attitude toward immigration, 1865-1950, and describe the measures adopted by the government as a result.

15. Describe the growth and decline of the American colonial empire, 1865-1950, indicating the factors that have led to each increase or decrease.

16. Trace the history of our relations with Japan since 1900.

17. Account as fully as you can for the shifts in the attitude of the American public toward participation in world affairs since the Civil War.

18. Describe the changes in religious thought and institutions since the Civil War, and account for them.

19. Prepare an outline for a history of literature (or religion, or education) from the Civil War to the present, indicating the social and economic forces responsible for each important development.

20. What concept do you find most useful in interpreting American history since the Civil War: the concept of the frontier, the concept of the section, or the concept of the class struggle?

B. Specific Essay Questions.

I. *Reconstruction, 1865-1877.*

1. "The period of Reconstruction was not a 'tragic era' but a blessing in disguise for the South." Do you agree? Justify your answer.

2. "No president has been so thoroughly misunderstood by his contemporaries as Andrew Johnson." Do you agree? Explain fully.

3. Distinguish between the Lincoln Reconstruction Plan, the Johnson Reconstruction Plan, and the Congres-

sional Reconstruction Plan. Which do you think should have been applied?

4. "The story of the Negro in Reconstruction is not so much a story of the Negro himself as it is the record of the competition of the Southern and Northern whites for the control of a docile race." Discuss fully.

5. Why should the radical Republicans have objected as violently as they did to Johnson's Reconstruction Policy?

6. "The Congressional Policy of Reconstruction was tantamount to a declaration that a successful war, waged for the preservation of the Union, had the legal effect of dissolving it." Explain and discuss.

II. *The Revolution in Economics, 1865-1890.*

1. Discuss the bases for the economic revolution in the United States that followed the Civil War.

2. Why were no transcontinental railroads built before the Civil War, and why did construction proceed so rapidly from that time on?

3. Account as fully as you can for the consolidation of industry in the period after the Civil War and appraise the benefits and evils that resulted.

4. Explain the speed with which the industrial revolution transformed the economy of the United States.

5. How do you account for the close cooperation between government and business in the period between 1865 and 1900?

6. Describe immigration to America, 1865-1900, accounting for each change, and discussing the impact on the United States.

III. *Closing the Frontier, 1865-1890.*

1. "The rapid settlement of the West in the period after the Civil War was a calamity, not a benefit, to the nation." Discuss.

2. "The mining frontier differed from other frontiers in two ways: it moved from west to east, and it engulfed the least attractive areas first." Explain.

3. Had you been in control of the national government, how would you have modified or changed the Indian policy of the period 1865-1890?

4. Discuss the rise and decline of the range cattle industry, accounting for each phenomenon.

5. Was the land system employed in settling the Great Plains satisfactory? If not, how could it have been improved?

6. Account as fully as you can for the late settlement of the Great Plains, and the rapidity of settlement once the process was begun.

IV. *Business and Politics, 1868-1890.*

1. Discuss the influences that made possible the re-establishment of the two-party system in the years 1865-1900.

2. "It is in vain to search the Republican and Democratic national platforms between 1868 and 1896 for any clear-cut antithesis on any real issue." Discuss.

3. Explain the fact that both major parties avoided dealing with the major problems stemming from the industrial revolution.

4. Discuss the sources, growth, and achievements of the movement for civil service reform in the period before 1900.

5. "Cleveland was not a man of great courage or independence of mind; he merely asserted the philosophy of the group which had captured control of the government during the Civil War." Do you agree? Discuss.

6. Name the outstanding events of Cleveland's first administration, and discuss fully any one of them.

V. *The Assault on Laissez Faire, 1868-1890.*

1. Describe the organization, methods, and objectives of the Knights of Labor and the American Federation of Labor, accounting as fully as you can for any differences.

2. "The American Federation of Labor succeeded, if you call it success, only because it was willing to sacrifice the interests of the great mass of American workers." Do you agree? Discuss.

3. Account as fully as you can for the failure of farmers and workers to cooperate in forming a new political party during this period.

4. "The attempt of the federal government to regulate the railroads simply resulted in the substitution of new evils for old ones." Do you agree? Explain.

5. Describe and account for the transition from state to federal control of interstate carriers.

6. Why did the Interstate Commerce Act and the Sherman Antitrust Act fail to accomplish the purposes for which they were designed?

VI. *The Urban Impact, 1868-1890.*

1. Trace the connection between humanitarian striving and the revolution in economics of the post-Civil War era.

2. Describe the effects of the impact of urbanization and new scientific concepts on religion, 1865-1890.

3. How generally was the Gospel of Wealth accepted in the period following the Civil War, and how influential were the writings of those who proposed reform?

4. "Throughout the history of civilization the city, rather than the country, has been the cradle of cultural progress." Explain.

5. Analyze in detail the impact of the machine age on one of the following: literature, religion, or the status of women.

6. Does the term "the Gilded Age" properly characterize the intellectual and cultural progress in the period 1865-1900?

VII. *The Populist Era, 1890-1900.*

1. Discuss the causes and nature of the agricultural depression, 1870-1896, and describe its economic and political results.

2. In what way did the gold standard figure as an important political question between 1865 and 1900? How, in each case, was the problem solved?

3. Does the record of the Republican Party from 1865-1900 justify its claim to being the sound-money party?

4. Discuss the antecedents and subsequent history of the Omaha platform of 1892.

5. "The capture of the Democracy by the forces of free silver gave the death blow to Populism." Do you agree? Discuss.

6. "It is a mistake to speak of the last decade of the nineteenth century as the 'Gay Nineties.' On the contrary it was a time of sober thought and grim endeavor, filled with the dread menace of class conflict and social upheaval." Discuss.

VIII. *America and the World, 1877-1900.*

1. "Between Fish and Hay a procession of politicians sat at the right hand of American presidents and directed foreign affairs of the nation without plan or purpose." Do you agree? Discuss.

2. How do you account for the growing interest of the United States in the Pacific after the Civil War?

3. Assess James G. Blaine as a diplomat. Do you feel that he deserves to rank among the outstanding secretaries of state?

4. "The Spanish-American War is usually taken as the date for the emergence of the United States as a world power." Amplify or comment on this quotation.

5. Account as fully as you can for the growth of American imperialism before 1900.

6. "The great danger of the Open Door doctrine lies in the inference that it is something for which the United States would or should go to war." Explain and discuss.

IX. *The Progressive Period, 1900-1917.*

1. Assess the factors responsible for the rise of progressivism. Which do you consider most important?

2. Describe the attempts of progressives to democratize, in state and union, the government of the United States. To what extent were they successful?

3. "Theodore Roosevelt was the direct heir and beneficiary of the Populism he had once so bitterly assailed." Discuss.

4. "Despite Roosevelt's skill at grabbing the spotlight, progressivism made greater strides under Taft." Do you agree? Discuss.

5. "Conservatives who thought Roosevelt too radical, and radicals who thought him too conservative, failed to perceive that he sought to hold an even balance between the contending elements in modern society." Explain.

6. Describe and contrast the New Nationalism of Roosevelt and the New Freedom of Wilson, accounting for any differences.

X. *Foreign Policy of the Progressive Period, 1900-1917.*

1. Trace and explain the development of American Caribbean policy, 1898-1917.

2. Do you agree that Roosevelt's action in regard to Panama was "indecent, not to say unwise"?

3. Was "dollar diplomacy" or "canal diplomacy" most influential in turning American interest toward the Caribbean and Central America?

4. Was Wilson's recognition policy toward Mexico justified?

5. Discuss Theodore Roosevelt's relations with Japan and the "Japanese menace," 1900-1908.

6. Were the anti-imperialists justified in maintaining that America's new imperialism reversed the trend toward democracy that had gone on since 1776?

XI. *The United States and World War I, 1917-1920.*

1. Was Wilson's administration neutral?

2. Why did the United States declare war on Germany rather than England?

3. Describe Wilson's efforts as a peacemaker, 1914-1917, and account for America's entry in the war.

4. "Upon Wilson's narrow partisanship may be placed the blame for America's failure to join the League of Nations." Do you agree? Explain.

5. How do you explain the rejection of the Versailles Treaty and the League of Nations by the United States?

6. Was the United States right in refusing to join the League of Nations?

XII. *The Era of "Normalcy," 1920-1932.*

1. How was the postwar spirit of nationalism reflected in the United States?

2. "In both domestic and foreign policy the period from 1920 to 1932 witnessed an almost continuous reaction from the idealism of Wilson." Explain.

3. What did President Harding mean by "normalcy"? To what extent did the Harding-Coolidge era approximate his ideal?

4. "In the quarter-century following American entry into World War I, the quest for security against both outer and inner threats to the country's well-being became, for the first time, a national purpose." Explain.

5. "Under Coolidge and Hoover the United States followed a pseudo-internationalism marred by two principal defects: unwillingness to recognize that disarmament was dependent on political security, and refusal to admit that a country could not profitably export goods without importing them." Explain and discuss.

6. "To all intents and purposes the United States by 1932 had become a member of the League of Nations, the Republican Party to the contrary notwithstanding." How far does the evidence support these assertions?

XIII. *The New Deal, 1933-1941.*

1. "The so-called 'Roosevelt revolution' was not a revolution at all, but rather the culmination of forces at work since 1898." Explain.

2. Do you agree with the statement: "Always, F. D. Roosevelt labored in the spirit of Macaulay's dictum: 'Reform in order to Preserve.'" Discuss.

3. "From the conservatives' point of view, F. D. Roosevelt's greatest sin was the deliberate abandonment of economic individualism." Do you agree? Discuss.

4. Trace the major proposals directed toward farm relief from the era of the Populists to the present.

5. Trace the changing relations between government and business during the administrations of F. D. Roosevelt.

6. Should Congress have accepted Roosevelt's proposal to reorganize the Supreme Court? Why?

XIV. *Foreign Policy of the New Deal, 1933-1941.*

1. Discuss the shift in American public opinion from isolationism to internationalism, 1920-1941, in the light of the various factors that influenced the change.

2. Explain the failure of the "Neutrality Acts" to keep the United States out of World War II.

3. Describe and evaluate the changes in American policy toward Latin America from 1898 to 1941.

4. Describe and contrast American policy toward Europe in the two periods, 1914-1917 and 1939-1941, accounting for any differences.

5. As an informed member of Congress, how would you have voted on the following questions: reciprocal trade agreements, conscription, and repeal of the arms embargo? In each case explain your reasons fully.

6. As an informed voter in 1940, would the "third-term tradition" have influenced you for or against Roosevelt? Why?

XV. *World War II and its Aftermath, 1941-1950.*

1. Would you agree with military strategists that the United States was wise in concentrating its war efforts first in Europe and then in the Pacific, rather than the reverse?

2. Describe and contrast federal attempts to control civilian life in World Wars I and II, accounting for any differences.

3. Contrast the League of Nations and the United Nations as instruments for world peace.

4. Do you believe that the United Nations has been, and will be, an effective device to keep the peace? If not, what changes would you propose?

Index

Greenbacks, use of, 42; as device for inflation, 87-88; in Panic of 1893, 91-92

Guam, annexed by United States, 109

Hague Conference, 137-138

Haiti, expansion into, 140; withdrawal from, 197

Halfbreeds, 48-49

Halsey, William, 212

Hammer v. Dagenhart, 128

Hancock, Winfield S., 48

Hanna, Marcus A., in election of 1896, 94; blocks progressive reform, 119

Harding, Warren G., as President, 163-164; and League of Nations, 170-171

Harris, Joel Chandler, 83

Harrison, Benjamin, as President, 53-54; in election of 1892, 90; Hawaiian policy of, 102; foreign policy of, 104

Harte, Bret, 82-83

Hatch Act, 35

Hawaii, American expansion into, 101-102; annexation of, 109; government established for, 132

Hawley-Smoot Tariff, 168

Hayes, Rutherford B., Reconstruction policy of, 10; as President, 45-47

Hay, John, as Secretary of State, 110; relations with Panama, 134-135

Haymarket Riot, 63-64

Hay-Pauncefote Treaty, 134

Haywood, "Big Bill," 116

Hearst, William Randolph, as editor, 82; agitates for Spanish American War, 106; opposes World War II, 202

Hepburn Act, 121

Hepburn v. Griswold, 42

Higher Criticism, 76

Hill, James D., 24

Hitler, Adolph, rise of in Germany, 198-199

Hoar, George F., as anti-imperialist, 109

Hoffman, Paul G., 224

Holding companies, growth of, 68; during 1920's, 168; regulation of, 187

Holladay, Ben, 31

Holliday, Cyrus K., 24

Holmes, Oliver Wendell, 166

Home Owners Loan Corporation, 183

Homestead Act,,defects of, 36

Homestead Strike, 65

Hoover, Herbert, in World War I, 151; in election of 1928, 165; as Secretary of Commerce, 169; farm program of, 170; handling of Great Depression, 176; in election of 1932, 179-180

Hopkins, Harry, 182

House, Edward M., 148

Howells, William Dean, 83

Huerta, Victoriano, 140-141

Hughes, Charles Evans, in election of 1916, 148-149; as Secretary of State, 170-171

Hull, Cordell, as Secretary of State, 196-198

Hull House, 73

Idaho, mining frontier in, 30

Immigration, as source of labor supply, 17-18; opposition to, 79-80; restriction of in 1920's, 167

Imperialism, origins of, 99-101; during Progressive Period, 131-137, 139-140

Income Tax, declared unconstitutional, 90-91; authorized by amendment, 124; adopted, 126

Indian Wars, 31-33

Industrialization, following Civil War, 15-25; results of, 25-27

Industrial Workers of the World, 116

Injunction, use of in labor disputes, 66; outlawed in Clayton Act, 128; outlawed in Norris-La Guardia Act, 176

In Re Debs, 65